KAIGHLA UM DAYO

Things That Shatter

A Memoir

This book was professionally typeset on Reedsy.
Find out more at reedsy.com

For my babies:

This is my story to tell, my loves, and though it involves you, it's not your story. Your stories are your own to tell or conceal, and they are sacred. Honor them.

"That's what she was—broken pottery, patched up with gold, the gold shimmering through the places where she had been cracked open, and left bleeding."

—Kiran Manral,
Missing, Presumed Dead

Contents

Preface

Let's cut to the chase, shall we, and open with a spoiler: I am a Muslim.

If you saw the cover and were hoping for a bitter account, written by a former Muslim, claiming to have the "inside look" of just how bad things really are—a sort of shocking word-porn to justify the prejudice you may have—you've picked up the wrong book.

First and foremost, this book is my re-declaration of faith: "There is no God but God." It's my re-affirmation that I, like all women, have intrinsic worth in God's eyes; there is no middle-man between God and His creatures, and our value as women is entirely independent of our relationships with the men in our lives.

I know there will be people who will read this book and believe that the sheikh's actions and teachings are acceptable by Islamic standards. Such readers, if they are Muslim, are in desperate need of a renewed study of Islamic ethics. Others—white supremacists and Islamophobes, for example—will perhaps read this book and feel vindicated in their ignorant, blanket presumptions that Muslim men are wholesale evil, that Arab culture, as a monolith, is depraved, that they were right all along in thinking that Islam oppresses women, and more.

It is not my intention to validate any of the sheikh's heinous teachings or the things he did to me and the other women in his care. On the contrary, my ex-husband, the sheikh, is a textbook narcissist who behaved in ways not befitting a Muslim, and certainly not a Muslim leader. Like so many men in a position of religious authority, he used traditionally-misogynistic interpretations of our religious texts to justify his beliefs and actions, and he was blinded by his arrogance. But I didn't know that then, naïve new Muslim that I was, and I am still coming to terms with the extent of the damage he inflicted on my psyche and on my relationship with God.

While I was married to the sheikh (and for quite a long time afterward), I believed everything he taught me, but everything he taught me was a lie meant to control and break me to his will—lies many Muslims have come to believe are true, while many others reject them. Muslims are people, and people are flawed—full stop.

In telling my story, I am doing just that: telling *my story*. I do not claim to represent other Muslims, or Islam as a religion. I reject any such representation claim. I absolve myself of any association readers may generate in their minds between my experience and the broader Muslim experience.

That being said, I'd love to say that my ordeal with the sheikh was unique—that he is one particularly bad apple in an otherwise good orchard—but my larger experience as a western, female convert to Islam is *not* rare by any means, and in some ways, it's relatively mild. There is a complex web of cultural mores and taboos keeping men like the sheikh in power, and keeping women who question them subjugated—especially women without a support system.

The truth is that it's quite easy to create an entire worldview that is centered on a misogynistic reading of many religious texts, justifying the sometimes-rampant abuse we find in our communities. It can be hard sometimes to maintain a different, more balanced worldview, but that's because of faulty customs originating in various cultures, not values rooted in these religions themselves.

The version of Islam I embraced as a young woman is extremely narrow-minded, artificially exclusive, and excessively cruel—something I didn't see until many years later because of the candy-coating it was covered in when presented to me, as it so often is presented to potential converts.

By contrast, the *real* Islam—the gift of beauty, justice, and mercy, given to humanity by our beautiful, just, and merciful Creator—is much broader, deeper, more inclusive, and harder to find in the muck of what so many people call "Islam" today, and it's mine as much as it's anyone else's.

1

The Departure

Kolkata, India

November 5th, 2007

Good morning, Kolkata. This is the last morning I will greet you, at least for now.

You gave me your people—the sick, dying, destitute, poverty-stricken. You gave me your cities—full of pollution, rank with the smell of urine, feces, fried everything, and death, but alive, busy, and thriving, causing me to step back and take it all in.

My eyes have seen your Mother Ganges with her worshipers and candles floating, and her children gathering to bathe in her. They have been irritated by the smoke of hundreds of bodies being purified with fire to cleanse their souls of sin.

I have watched helplessly as people died, watched as the very life ran out of their veins, as their heart and lungs gave way. I have seen the sick and dying care for the sicker and those closer to death.

I have seen the majestic Himalayas covered in snow and the fog of 100,000 years of mystery. I have seen the Sun rise over them and set among them.

I have seen half-naked babies running through the streets, playing hide-and-seek together. I have watched lovers caress in secret nooks and crannies of the city, trying to reconcile their human desire with their traditions and the restrictions of an ancient faith.

I have seen both rich and poor alike bow down to a dead piece of wood and pour water into its mouth, wrap garlands of flowers around its neck, and throw their money at its feet, all in the hope of becoming wealthier, or giving birth to a son rather than a daughter, or delaying death—that inevitable visitor to us all.

I have tasted the rarest, choice spices, and indulged my mouth with flavors that shock the senses. I have smelled the wafting fragrance of tea leaves being dried to perfection in Darjeeling.

I have gasped for air simply walking down the road as Kolkata's million cars raced past me, emitting their poisonous gases into the precious little oxygen. I have held my breath as the smell of garbage and human and animal waste filled the air around me and refused to be shaken.

I've been mesmerized by the cries of Muslim prayer callers, calling God's people to stop whatever they're doing and bow down.

I have heard the laughter of mothers and children in the slums as they braid one another's hair and gossip, and I've heard the wailing of parents and grandparents as their children were taken from them too soon.

I have met some of the wisest people I've ever known here, all of us trying to learn the meaning of life and our place in the scheme of things. I have abandoned some of my beliefs and accepted other ones. I have broken a heart and repaired another, cast off a burden and picked up another. I have opened my eyes and also have closed them. I have given my heart, my strength, my voice, my hands, my life to you, India, and I shall never, ever, ever be the same.

* * *

In the summer of 2007, I was in the middle of my Bachelor's program at a small Bible college in central Illinois, working to become a missionary. I needed to save money to purchase my ticket to and from India that fall, and working at a camp that provided food and lodging so I could save all my money seemed like the smartest choice. Thankfully, I was hired on as a cook at a Christian camp in central Colorado.

One afternoon, I came into the kitchen and found our resident baker, Marie, immersed in her work. She glanced up at me when I walked in the room, then snickered to herself and got back to work.

"What?" I whined. "Don't tell me you've seen another fire truck on campus?!"

"Oh yes. A pretty large one, actually," she said, smiling at me playfully.

"Dammit!" I whisper-yelled. "What have I done this time?"

Marie was the owner's best friend, so she had an in with the boss and her husband. Every week, it seemed, I was getting in trouble for something or other, and most times I had no idea what I'd done wrong.

We—adults ranging in age from eighteen- to twenty-five-years old—had signed a pretty extensive contract when we were hired, agreeing we would not drink alcohol (unless of age, and then not "excessively"), use drugs, engage in extramarital relations, or watch R-rated movies.

I had no problem abstaining from drugs or alcohol or sex—good Christian girl that I was at that point—but I got in trouble so often for so many strange reasons that Marie and I had taken to developing a code-word system so she could alert me when she knew I was soon to be on the chopping block, yet again: a small fire truck meant a minor infraction, while a large one was serious, and multiple was bad, *bad* news.

A few hours later, just as Marie warned me, I was summoned to the boss' husband's office. As I walked in, Walt invited me to sit down. "Do you know why you're here today?" he asked, seeming annoyed already. "I think you do, Kaighla."

I sat for a moment trying to recall anything I may have done wrong in the previous week but drew a blank.

"Isn't it true that you watched a prohibited movie on Tuesday night?" he asked. "In your bunk with your headset on? Does that ring a bell?"

Of course. I had indulged myself by watching Russell Crowe utilize his amazing calves in "Gladiator" on Tuesday night, and right in the middle, one of the two conservative homeschooled sisters from Texas had hopped up on my bunk at just the wrong moment.

Freaking snitch, I thought to myself.

"I think you don't understand how things work around here. My wife may be your manager, but I am the boss, and I have authority over you, Kaighla," he said smugly.

I sat staring at him for a moment, wondering how on earth a man becomes so power-obsessed that running a tiny, irrelevant camp in central Colorado gets him off.

"Yes, Walt. You are the boss. You're right. I'm sorry I watched the movie," I said.

"Good," he replied smugly. "But this is the fourth time this month you've been in my office, and the fourth time you've sat here and feigned repentance. I am not buying it as easily this time."

Now I was irritated. "I know you're mad at me, Walt. But seriously… it wasn't like a porno or something. I am twenty years old, not a young kid, and it was rated R for violence. Can you calm down?" I pleaded.

He stood then and actually began to shout at me. "No, you listen to me! Paul advised women to remain silent in church. Why? Because it's a man speaking to them—a man speaking for God. I am a man and I speak for God in your life, period, so you'd better do as I say," he said, calming down then and sitting in his squeaky wooden chair.

It's astonishing to me that this wasn't the first or last time a man used such arguments to silence me—in fact, over the course of my life, men from all walks of life have used such arguments when trying to control my naturally inquisitive, rebellious spirit.

I should have quit that day, but I didn't. I needed that money for my trip to India in the fall, so I stuck things out for another six weeks. Somehow, I managed, again and again, to avoid getting fired or throwing in the towel.

To distract myself from the rigors of my situation that summer, I threw myself into books, and predominantly books about Christian spirituality. I enjoyed reading *Blue Like Jazz* and *Searching for God Knows What* by Donald Miller, as well as *Messy Spirituality* by Mike and Karla Yaconelli, *Emotionally Healthy Spirituality* by Peter Scazzero, and *Dark Night of the Soul* by Christian mystic, St. John of the Cross.

In all these books, I was searching for something missing from my spiritual life—a true, deep connection to God that extended beyond the happy, comfortable, prosperity-Gospel message I had been given. I wanted something more solid than "feeling" God's spirit moving. I wanted to *know* God, even in the dark nights of my soul, even when life was messy, even when I was questioning, and especially when I felt emotionally unwell.

A few weeks later, we finished our jobs at the camp, and I embarked on what would be the most transformative trip of my young life up to that point.

* * *

I originally went to Kolkata, India to serve at a fellow seminary student's preschool on the outskirts of the city. I was there as a missionary, and yet by the time I arrived in India I was on the brink of losing what little faith in Christianity I still had. My time spent at the camp that summer was the last in a long string of such experiences wherein my faith in Jesus was challenged by a man telling me I was wrong about what God expected of me, and claiming authority in my life based solely on his genitals.

When I stepped off the plane in India, my heart was ripe for a revolution.

I imagined a very different, and decidedly more exotic, life than the one I faced when I arrived in India. Rather than getting to truly experience India, I was placed under house arrest by my hosts "for my protection," they said. I was literally locked into their small, squat house with the maid and the children of my hosts, expected to babysit for free when I wasn't working at their school teaching English to four-year-olds, also for free.

There was a pond right outside my room that served as a local bath, a laundromat and dish-washing site, and a place to catch up on the latest gossip. Just two weeks into my stay, a man tried to hang himself from one of the tall palm trees that dotted the perimeter of the pond, and no one batted an eye. This was a place of poverty and of hardship, colored by the constant struggle to eke out a meager existence.

I wasn't allowed to go anywhere but to and from school, or to the market with David. No matter how much I protested, they wouldn't even allow me to walk the half mile that separated our house from the preschool, insisting instead that I take a bicycle-rickshaw back and forth to the school. Bapul—a close friend of the family and the principal of the preschool—doubled as my bodyguard, and he rode his own bicycle alongside me.

Each day, David—my host and friend from Bible college—would sit with me at the dining room table and regale me with stories of the foreigners he'd heard about being kidnapped, harassed, raped, and murdered that week.

"You should be very wary of speaking to anyone in a friendly tone," he'd say. "These people are bad, and they will hurt you, just because you're white and they think you're rich. Just stay here with us and everything will be ok."

David had been raised in a Muslim family in a village near Kolkata, and he had chosen to embrace Christianity as a young man—something only the bravest people did in his corner of India. Religion is not a personal choice in much of the world; it is and always has been a social marker for people in India, and to convert is to make an open declaration that you are leaving

7

your social community, your *people*, to join the opposing team.

David was vague in the details of his conversion, only telling me that converting had nearly cost him his life, and that Islam was evil, through-and-through.

"You should not have come here unmarried," David said one afternoon. We were sitting in the only air-conditioned room in the house. He sat in his casual evening-wear, which consisted of a thin, long cotton sarong he'd tied around his waist, coupled with a white, tight-fighting tank-top.

"This life is hard for anyone," he said, "but it's especially wearing on single people. It would have been better for you if you'd married before coming here. Your husband could protect you."

I was only twenty years old and marriage seemed a far-off gambit. My on-again/off-again boyfriend, Jin, was definitely not interested in marrying me anytime soon. A first-generation Korean-American man seven years my senior, Jin struggled with his feelings for me and his parents' distaste for my racial and cultural heritage. But he was my first true love, and our relationship was full of all the requisite drama and passion of young love. The idea that I could spend my life with anyone but him seemed impossible.

It was an emotional outburst on my part that had sparked the conversation with David that evening. We'd been out and about in the city all day, looking for a tailor to make custom clothes to fit my tall, thick body. Within the span of four hours, we'd ridden in a taxi, two rickshaws, and one auto-rickshaw, and faced death, head-on, countless times. Traffic in India is panic-inducing, to say the least, for even the most stable person, and I was far from that.

When we finally arrived home that evening, I'd collapsed

in bed and begun crying, quietly at first, and then louder, totally unable to control myself. The death-threat traffic, the noise, the smells—it was all too much. I thought I'd locked my bedroom door, but apparently not, because a few minutes into my interlude, David's ten-year-old son had pushed the door open and saw me crying, then ran to alert his parents.

"I think you should go home," David said, "and come back after you've married your boyfriend, or someone else. Just come back with a husband."

I'd worked all summer at that camp, I'd allowed myself to be talked-down-to, and I'd saved every dime I could—all so that I could come there, to Kolkata, to serve Jesus by helping David's pupils to learn English so they could have a better chance at escaping their otherwise grim futures in the slums.

"No, I don't want to go home yet," I replied, gaining some semblance of dignity. "I will try harder to manage things."

"Okay, good," he said. "Let's all do our best for the Lord."

That arrangement lasted exactly three weeks before I refused to stay a moment longer and embarked on my own into the wild unknown.

* * *

In mid-September, I found out about an organization in Kolkata, called Sari Bari, that worked to save women and children from human trafficking in the Red Light District. I reached out to one of the directors, an American woman a few years older than me, and told her of my plight. Within a matter of days, she'd convinced my hosts to allow me to go have lunch with her in a big mall quite a distance from their home.

"You don't have to stay there," she said. "You could stay on

Sudder Street and volunteer around the city. That's what I did when I first came to India."

The possibility of leaving David's house but staying in India had never crossed my mind. "But he says it's very dangerous for foreigners," I replied.

"Okay, I hear all the same news stories he does. I know it happens. But honestly, I've been living here for five years now, and I feel safer jogging in the Red Light District than I did back home in Seattle. It's worth a try before you give up and head home, don't you think?"

I went back to David's house that day, with my new friend by my side, and declared I was leaving his house. He looked at me with scared, watery eyes, and begged me to reconsider, but I would not be moved.

My erstwhile rescuer went with me to Sudder Street and helped me book a room at The Salvation Army hostel. It was one of many in the neighborhood, and was at least a hundred years old and crumbling.

Sudder Street and the surrounding area seemed perfectly designed to cater to tourists. It was chock-full of street-food vendors, international and domestic calling booths, stores selling baggy Ali Baba-style pants, and restaurants with a mix of beloved Indian favorites and vaguely European fare.

Most of the tourists in the area were working for various charities around the city, and a good portion of us made our way every morning via subway and rickshaw to one of the dozen homes and hospitals founded by Mother Theresa through her non-profit organization, The Missionaries of Charity.

I was quickly swept-up in that life and found myself volunteering at Nirmal Hriday, the first home she ever opened—a hospice center in the heart of Kalighat. I'd spend my mornings exploring

Kolkata and my evenings with the dying women in Kalighat. There wasn't much I could do to truly help them—unlike the seasoned nurses and doctors who spent their time sewing cuts and picking maggots out of wounds—so I joined the other general volunteers in washing and disinfecting laundry and dishes. Before my shift ended, I'd make sure to spend a few hours just sitting with the patients, trying to communicate my concern and love for them using hand gestures and the universal language of smiling.

People from all walks of life saved up their money and traveled to Kolkata to serve. If you want a fun, memorable trip to India, you visit Goa or the Taj Mahal, but it's adventure philanthropists who head to Kolkata. I recall a conversation I had with a fellow volunteer from the Netherlands, wherein I asked her why she came to Kolkata.

"I'm missing something from my life. Can't put my finger on it, but I feel better when I'm here," she said, putting out a cigarette on the cement wall. We liked to sit on the roof in the evenings after our shift, taking in the sights and sounds of the market below.

"I am too, but I feel like... isn't it sort of selfish of us to have come here to serve these people because we're looking for something to make us feel better?" I asked.

She laughed out loud then. "Sweetheart," she said, "if someone says they're here for purely selfless reasons, they're lying. We all came here looking for something—even the nuns. We're not saints."

* * *

Soon enough, as often happens in these scenarios, I developed a slew of acquaintances and a couple of very dear friends.

There were the three backpackers from Seattle who regaled me with tales of their adventures around India, smoking the best hash they could find. There was a group of Korean missionaries looking for a chance to guide people to Jesus. There was the sweet Parisian girl, Célia, who taught me about Catholicism and was the very image of poise—until and unless someone on the street tried to cop a feel.

Kazuma was a Japanese college student volunteering at Kalighat with me, searching for the meaning of life on a more spiritual plane. He and I spent hours on the subway and at dinner every night having heated discussions about religion and spirituality, comparing his stark, pragmatic childhood in Japan to my vaguely Christian upbringing in the Midwest.

A full 6'2", Kazuma towered over nearly everyone. Foreign women like me were groped in passing several times a day in Kolkata, so it was nice to have him around to offer a barrier, both physical and otherwise. Men just didn't seem to bother the tourist women who traveled with men, assuming they were our husbands.

My closest friend, though, was Jane. A fellow American from Chicago, Jane came to India to serve as a nurse at the leper colony on the outskirts of the city. Several years my senior with a few pretty major life blunders under her belt, she tried to steer me away from the idiotic choices I seemed intent on making, usually with no success.

* * *

In Kolkata, I ran into young, talented soccer players from all over Africa, trying to make their name and fortune in India.

Many were attractive, but none compared to Samson.

A twenty-something man with the body of a god, Samson was from Lagos, Nigeria and was, like so many of the African footballers in the city, trapped in what one could justifiably call modern slavery.

Fresh out of high school, Samson was recruited by an Indian soccer scout. He was given a free one-way ticket to Kolkata and promised a lucrative contract, a career, and a fortune as a footballer in India. But as soon as he arrived, he found to his dismay that he had been duped. Sure, he was given room and board—two meals a day and a room shared with four other footballers in a rat- and cockroach-infested hostel—but his visa depended on a team signing a contract with him, and no teams in India actually signed such contracts with their outsourced African talent. Why pay for what you can steal, right?

Samson was smart, tall, and irresistible. The first time I saw him walk up the stairs of JoJo's restaurant, I wanted with all my heart to invite him over to my table. But my boyfriend was waiting for me back home.

A few days later, as Kazuma and I sat sipping our chai after dinner, Samson approached us.

"Hey! Sam!" Kazuma said. "Good to see you again! Can I introduce you to my friend, Kaighla? She's an American here volunteering in Kalighat."

"It's nice to meet you, Kaighla," he said, reaching across the table to shake my hand, his voice deep and rich. I liked the way my name sounded in his mouth, but I tried to hide my pleasure.

The two of them got into an animated conversation while I tried hard not to stare at him across the table. Everything about him, from his looks to his mannerisms, was electric, and I felt myself hoping he'd come to JoJo's more often.

13

Eventually, Kazuma had to return to Japan. The night before he left we had a small, private party for him at JoJo's. Sam was there, and so were several other footballers. Jane came in late and the restaurant erupted in cheers; having been away in Bangladesh for a medical mission, she was missed by all.

As we were walking home that night, Kazuma turned to me. "I don't want anything to happen to you like what happened on the train from Varanasi," he said, seriously. "Please, will you let Sam walk you home to the hostel at night? He's a good guy, trust me."

He was right. Just a few weeks earlier, he and I and Megumi, a fellow Japanese tourist friend of his, had taken a wonderful trip to the Hindu holy city, Varanasi (also called Benares). We spent several days wandering around the ancient alleys of the city, taking boat rides on the Ganges, being chased by monkeys, and watching the various Hindu ceremonies at the Burning Ghats. It was a trip to remember.

But on the multi-day train trip home to Kolkata, I had been sexually assaulted as I slept in my berth. The train stopped to rest for a few hours one night, and I awoke to a man fondling my breasts and butt. He was standing on the platform and reaching through the barred window, left open to let in the cool night air. I jolted awake and slapped his hands away, sending him running. As my eyes adjusted to the darkness, I saw men and women alike watching my reaction, but no one seemed surprised or bothered by the scene that had unfolded.

When Kazuma awoke and found me quietly crying, he was angry I hadn't woken him immediately so he could go find the guy responsible.

So, after Kazuma went back to Japan, Samson began walking me to my hostel at night and we developed a friendship. Initially, we'd chat about this and that on our walk directly back to my hostel, he'd leave me at the gate, and we'd go our separate ways. With time, however, we started wandering around in a more circuitous route so we could talk more, and he began shaking my hand before leaving me at the hostel gate. One night, Samson held my hand longer than necessary and looked deeply into my eyes, and I felt something deep drawing me to him, something beyond empty lust. From that point, there was no denying we were something much more than friends. I called Jin to tell him our relationship needed to be off-again forever.

Being around Sam was like being with an old friend you've known all your life. We understood one another with very few words, and I never felt like I needed to be anything other than Kaighla with him. It was the first relationship I'd ever been in where I felt so free and accepted and valued for who I was, no-strings-attached. That friendship and mutual compatibility evolved into a passionate intimacy of a caliber I'd not experienced before.

* * *

I began to feel nervous about how much I was feeling for Samson and decided to take a girls' trip with Jane and her Swiss friend to Darjeeling. The day we left Kolkata, Samson put me in the taxi and tried to kiss me, but I dodged him awkwardly and shut the door in his face.

The three of us spent a week enjoying the relative calm of Darjeeling. Situated in the Himalayan mountains, it's known for two things: tea and Buddhist temples. The number one thing I remember about Darjeeling was the quiet; it was *painfully* quiet there. Though the silence was a welcome relief from the noise and chaos of Kolkata, it was odd to be left alone with one's thoughts so easily.

We stayed in a quaint hostel that came highly recommended. There were heavy wool blankets on the beds and a perfect stoop on the roof for taking sunrise and sunset photos of Tiger Hill. Of course, Samson wasn't totally out out-of-sight, out-of-mind for me. I often found myself grinning from ear-to-ear when I saw something that reminded me of him. It didn't help that he was calling and texting Jane and asking her to convince me to come back soon. I called him once or twice during the week but mostly tried to avoid thinking of him. It didn't work.

The day we left Darjeeling, we headed down, down, down around the twisting, terrifying cliffs in a rented Jeep on the way to Siliguri, the nearest train station. Jane received a text from Samson asking me to meet him in Siliguri and stay a few days instead of heading straight back to Kolkata. He had a tournament there and wanted to spend some time with me.

"Girl, I have to get back to Kolkata," she said as she saw my mind starting to churn. "They've been waiting on me for a bit, and I need to get back. But, you could stay alone… "

The thought seemed both exciting and insane. For all the traveling I'd done alone in life, I hadn't actually spent any time alone in India. But my time away from Samson had only heightened my feelings for him, and the prospect of spending a few days with him was too enticing to pass up.

Jane tore out the pages about Siliguri from her *Lonely Planet: India* guidebook and handed them to me, hugged me tightly, and told me to be smart, winking as she pulled her backpack on and jumped onto her train.

The next morning, Samson came to get me from my hostel and we spent the next several days mostly at the soccer pitch for practices and games. His team won the tournament and he had me seated in the VIP section, telling a fib that I was his wife. We were young, in love, and soaring high. By the time we went back to Kolkata, we were engaged.

Not much later, we had a small, religious marriage ceremony at the Victoria Memorial in Kolkata, accompanied by Jane and several of the other footballers we'd become close to. Being two foreigners, we couldn't make it legally official, but I didn't mind. I was so deeply in love, and I was full of hope about our future together.

* * *

That fall, I came to understand God in a much larger, more inclusive way than I had in Bible college. When I wasn't spending every waking moment with Samson, I continued my spiritual journey in India, but now it was spiritual searching on steroids. The sights and sounds and people around me stirred my spirit in a way I had never experienced before.

I saw God's presence in the brokenness of the patients at Nirmal Hriday, and in the devotion of the worshippers bathing in the Ganges, and in the silence of the Buddhist temples in Darjeeling, and most of all in the easy way Samson loved me.

Ramadan had begun a few days before I left for Darjeeling. Though the population of Kolkata is predominantly Hindu, there is still a rather large Muslim population, and Ramadan meant things would be temporarily changing around Sudder Street—and not just for the Indians.

One of Samson's best friends, Sayeed, was a Muslim. In truth, he was the first Muslim I had ever met in my life, and he caught my attention right away. Relatively short compared to Samson,

Sayeed was also from Lagos, and he was striking in his beauty. He had acorn-shaped, wide-set, deep brown eyes, and his skin was dark and rich. But what struck me most about Sayeed was his smile: he never seemed to stop smiling—wide-mouthed, showing his white teeth all the way back to the molars.

In Ramadan, no one could ever seem to get in contact with Sayeed. Every time you turned around, he was leaving to go to the mosque. At every dinner, his absence was noted and dismissed with a "Yeah, it's Ramadan. He's praying in the mosque. He'll eat later."

During the three-day tournament he and Samson played together in Siliguri, Sayeed refused to have even a sip of water. It was easily one hundred degrees Fahrenheit, and the humidity level was at one hundred percent. He was drenched all the way through his clothes, just as his teammates were, but when they sat down to have a sip of water, he dumped his water bottle over his head to try to give him some relief from the muggy, infernal heat.

Once, back in the hotel room in Siliguri, Sayeed was too weak to walk to the *masjid* and had elected to pray one of the afternoon prayers in our hotel room. As he prayed, his voice was positively enchanting. The peace that settled on the room as he recited the Arabic verses overcame me, and I could tell it was affecting the others in the room, try as they did to seem unmoved.

Embarrassed by his own emotional response to the scene, one of the Christian men in the room—a footballer from the Congo—stood up and began to sing a hymn at full volume. It was some washed-up, overplayed American worship song from the 1980's Mega Church movement. His voice was off-key and jarring, and I wished he'd be quiet.

Later, over dinner, he egged Sayeed on more. "Your religion is evil!" he shouted at Sayeed. "You believe in killing innocent people! 9/11 was your fault!"

He launched into a tirade, leveling insult after insult at Sayeed, who sat nonplussed through the whole thing.

"Man, you don't know anything about my religion," Sayeed said. "Read the Qur'an or something and then we will talk."

Eventually, the argument died down, but I never forgot the way Sayeed carried himself with dignity and grace, even in the face of direct, intentional attacks against him and his religion. I recognized Jesus in Sayeed: he was embodying the command to "turn the other cheek," and I found him and his peaceful aura captivating.

* * *

I was raised in a generally non-religious but very typical Midwestern American home. If you asked my parents what their religion was, they would have responded "Christian," but quickly followed up with something about being "a good person" who loves God, but isn't interested in "all that church stuff or the rules or whatever."

Unlike my family, I had a very keen interest in connecting with God from a young age, and I became an evangelical Christian when I was fifteen years old. By the time I got around to college, I had found my calling: missions. I wanted to travel the world for Jesus, showing people his love by helping them with the practical things in life. Lincoln Christian University—then Lincoln Christian College—called this field "Bivocational Missions."

At Lincoln, we dove deeper into some of the tenets of the

19

Christian faith, including the belief that people were created in the image of God, but because of the choice of Adam and Eve to disobey God, humans were thereafter born with a sinful nature, doomed for Hell until and unless they decided to accept Jesus as one part of the triune God, and to become sanctified through his blood, via faith, repentance, confession, and baptism.

While most of my peers at Lincoln seemed to be thriving and coming closer to God the more they expanded their knowledge beyond Sunday School teachings, I was more confused than ever. No matter who I spoke to or how I reasoned with myself, I couldn't negotiate the inherent logical inconsistencies I found in Christianity.

I began to feel frustrated, for example, by the idea that God demanded the blood of a sinless being to forgive our sins. If God was all-powerful and all-knowing, why couldn't He just forgive me when He knew I was sincerely repentant? Why the blood? Why the cross? Why make part of His own self suffer for something *no one need suffer for*? And how could one part of God die while the other parts of Him lived on? These questions and more plagued me, and what I saw and felt in India only exacerbated them.

In India, I came to understand that morality was so much more than the black and white of sin and righteousness that I was taught at church and in Bible college. There was more nuance to life than I thought possible. I finally realized that the Bible wasn't meant to be used as a codebook for morality, but as a path to knowing God; the rules were never meant to be the end, but the *means* to the end, which was deep, life-altering connection with God.

I had literally scoured the earth across three countries and any number of boys' arms to find the affirmation only God could give me, and I came to believe that God couldn't possibly be the Old Testament blood-thirsty or the New Testament all-loving god I'd learned He was in Bible college. My experience in India was the final nail in the coffin that was my relationship with Jesus as Lord.

* * *

A few weeks after our wedding, I had to go home. We were totally out of money and Samson was still living as a literal slave to his soccer team. The plan was for me to go home, stay with my parents, work anywhere, save all my money, and come back to India a few months later. I couldn't have known when I left him there, crying on his knees in the airport, that I would never see him again—or that I was carrying his child.

A year later, Samson and I were divorced, our son, Ekundayo, was born, and my faith was dead. The distance between us was too much, and he insisted I stay in America since I was pregnant and he couldn't provide for us there, so we had given up on ever being reunited.

I had also been kicked out of Bible college because I was pregnant and they didn't believe my marriage was legitimate in the eyes of God since it wasn't legally recognized; Paul said, in Romans 13:2, that Christians must honor the laws of the land, after all. I shaved my head and refused to stop wearing my shalwar kameez sets, even in the middle of winter. I blame pregnancy. That shit makes you crazy.

Then, in January 2009, I slipped on ice and shattered my left ankle joint, fractured my tibia, and broke my fibula clean in half. Dayo was only six months old and we lived far away from my family, so my mom moved us into her home. I was on bedrest

21

for six months before I could even begin to learn to walk again. Of course, this gave me ample time to read and think and rage at God for the hand I'd been dealt.

I spent my time in bed reading book after book about alternative methods of Christianity. I was searching for something deeper, stronger, and more lasting than the evangelical fervor we sought at church, where the "holy spirit moving" was only apparent when we felt the swells of the worship music or the wisdom of the orator, and the goosebumps rose on our skin. I felt like I at least owed myself and God one last-ditch effort before giving up on Christianity forever.

By the time I was able to walk again, I had been hired to work for an NGO in downtown Chicago, so I took Dayo and moved north. Within two months, however, I lost that job because I was—as I mentioned earlier—ridiculously rebellious and inquisitive at all the wrong times and to all the wrong people. And so my baby and I found ourselves homeless, living in a motel room provided by Jin, the very same boyfriend I had left in order to marry Samson.

It was not my finest hour.

2

The Welcoming

Chicago, Illinois

Autumn 2009

On September 11th, 2001, I was a freshman in high school. Along with most white, Anglo-Saxon, Christian youth in America, I was fully brainwashed by the media lies that came out shortly thereafter, portraying Islam and Muslims as pure evil—the same lies our Congolese friend had leveled at Sayeed in Siliguri. But aside from these assumptions, I knew almost nothing about Islam. Having always been interested in world religions, I felt it was my responsibility, at the very least, to know enough about a religion to be able to state clearly why I didn't accept it.

Something about the mystery surrounding Islam made it enticing for me, and I could feel my heart being inexplicably drawn to it. I couldn't get Sayeed out of my mind, thinking

Islam must have *some* beautiful aspects to have given him such peace and stalwart grace.

And so, in our motel room in Chicago that summer, when I should have been looking for jobs online, I instead spent my time reading more and more about Islam. I began by reading *The Complete Idiot's Guide to Understanding Islam* by Yahya Emerick (who is a convert, himself) and watching videos on YouTube about people who had converted to the faith. Shocked with myself, I found I believed many of the tenets of Islam, and I was attracted to the extreme monotheism it pronounced, as well as the opportunity for a clean slate, as it were.

After reading everything I could get my hands on, I decided to call the local mosque. I wanted to speak with someone, in-person, who had embraced Islam. Unfortunately, in many of the mosques in America, even today, there is no one on staff to answer the phone, and if there is, they don't often speak fluent English. So, when I called and asked if I could speak with someone who was a convert to Islam, the message was mixed up and though they took my number, I was sure no one would call me back.

Imagine my surprise when I received a phone call later that same evening from a woman who said she'd received my info from the mosque. She said she was a Muslim convert, herself, and would love to answer any questions I had. We arranged to meet at her home the following day. I made an excuse to use Jin's car, and Dayo and I headed to her house.

She seemed like a normal person to me. She wore hijab and was very modest, but rather than being swathed in black like I imagined she would be, she was dressed in American-style clothing, albeit of the more modest variety.

Over tea and sweets, I told her what had gotten me into my

most recent predicament, and how I saw Islam as coming into my life at precisely the point I needed it.

"What sort of work experience do you have?" she asked.

"I guess mostly odd jobs," I said initially, before remembering my ESL-teaching experience in Korea three summers before, as well as all the kids and adults I'd tutored before and after.

"Wait, you're an English teacher?" she asked, standing up to grab her phone from the counter. "You know, I used to work at this Muslim boarding school an hour or so from here and I know they need an English teacher. Should we maybe see if I could get you an interview?" she asked.

Sensing my hesitation, she went on. "Don't worry. No one's going to force you to convert for the job. They need a teacher, you need a job. That's all," she added, smiling reassuringly.

I acquiesced, with great relief. She called the school and scheduled an interview for me the next day. I left Dayo with a day-care provider she had known for years and went to the school wearing borrowed clothes and a hijab, out of respect.

At the interview, things were odd. For one thing, the Pakistani principal of the school—Siraaj, or "Maulana," the title he was given—didn't look directly at me even once during the entire hour-long interview. His gaze rested somewhere just to the side of my shoe, or else just over my shoulder—something I found off-putting. But he was nonetheless polite and respectful, and he treated me with dignity. He also gave me the job almost immediately.

"One last thing, Ms. White," he said as we were wrapping things up. "I need to make it clear that your religion is none of my business. We're hiring you because we need an English teacher, and you're qualified for the job. Now, should you choose to be Muslim, we will help guide you if you'd like. But you are very free to live your life in whatever way you prefer, and it will have no effect whatsoever on your position here."

"But what is my business," he continued, "is that you are a single mother with a small child, and this is a hard city. It worries me that you're living off of your ex-boyfriend's generosity that, according to what you've said, could run out at any time. We have plenty of empty rooms here, and God would not forgive me if I had a safe place for you and your baby to stay and I turned you out into the street just because you didn't want to practice my religion. What kind of religion would that be?"

Yes. What kind, indeed, I thought, and I recognized God's love in him.

We agreed that Dayo and I would move into the boarding school that weekend. Classes would begin in a week, so he wanted us to have plenty of time to get settled in.

I went home and told Jin that I had found a great job and a place to stay, and I hoped he would not delve deeper. Jin was a staunch Christian and knew nothing about my recent interest in Islam. Unfortunately, he did delve deeper, and when he got the truth out of me, he lost his mind in anger. I had never seen him like that, screaming and cursing at me and calling me names.

"You will pay me back!" he screamed at me in the car while Dayo sat in his car seat behind us. "You will give me back every dime I spent on you and your baby. He isn't even mine! So help me God, I will fucking kill you if you don't pay me back!" he yelled. I believed him.

I called my new Muslim friend, and she and her husband cut their dinner short to come an hour out of their way to get us from the motel and drive us to their home. They insisted that Dayo and I sleep in their bed while they slept on an air mattress in their home office. She awoke early the next morning and drove me to the boarding school, where I finally, for the first time in months, breathed a sigh of relief that Dayo and I were safe.

A few days later, Ramadan started. The *Alima* students—who were my age and studying Islam in-depth—moved into the dorms, and I found myself surrounded by young, intelligent Muslim women who understood their religion and their role in their communities, which were rich and varied.

While we waited for the school year to start, I read whatever books I found in the school library, and eventually decided to read the English translation of the Qur'an. I came to the middle of the chapter called *Al-Maidah* ("The Table Laid With Food," referring to the Last Supper of Jesus and his disciples). In that chapter, God says about Jesus:

> *And [beware the Day] when God will say, "O Jesus, Son of Mary, did you say to the people, 'Take me and my mother as deities besides God?'" He (Jesus) will say, "Exalted are You! It was not for me to say that to which I have no right. If I had said it, You would have known it. You know what is within myself, and I do not know what is within Yourself. Indeed, it is You who is Knower of the unseen. I said to them nothing except what You commanded me, that is: 'Serve God, my Lord and your Lord.' I watched over them as long as I remained among them; and when You did recall me, then You Yourself became the Watcher over them. Indeed, You are Witness over everything."* (Surah Al-Maidah, *verses 116-117)*

That passage seemed to have been written specifically for me, openly addressing my deepest concerns. That was the day I knew, for sure, that Islam was the truth, at least as far as the basics. I couldn't have imagined that day how much my life would change in just a few short weeks.

* * *

"I will never see this face again," I said out loud, looking at myself in the mirror as I dried my hair and began putting on an ill-fitting prayer garment one of the other teachers had gifted me. I was about to be a new person.

When I came out of the bathroom, my new friend and fellow teacher, Mariam, led me into the small prayer room down the hall from our rooms.

I turned and looked behind me to check on Dayo. He was laughing rapturously as he bopped along on the shoulders of one of the *Alima* students.

In the prayer room before me sat and stood a few dozen women. Aside from Mariam and a few of the older *Alima* students, I recognized no one.

A woman I later learned was the Qur'an teacher sat at the front of the room with a wad of tissues in her right hand, drying the corners of her eyes. "Welcome, Ms. Kaighla. Shall we begin?" she asked.

I really had no idea so many people would be coming, and felt embarrassed and suddenly very, very naked in a crowd of hijabi'd women, my own head-cover loosely wrapped. *This is my business,* my heart said, *and I don't want these strangers to be part of it.* But my feelings and intuition had become suspect in the previous few weeks, the more I learned about the power of Shaitan, The Devil, to influence our feelings. "God's reasoning is not like ours, and His is higher," they taught me. "If something about Islam doesn't feel right, your feelings are wrong, not Islam."

Maybe this is how things are supposed to be for Muslims, I thought. *Maybe they have a right to witness my conversion, and who am I to take that from them?*

I sat down on the plush carpet and Dayo ran to me—or really tumbled into my arms, pulling the hijab down my shoulder. I hastily fixed it, though no men were in sight. Something told me I should always be perfectly covered while in the prayer room.

One of the women in the room plied Dayo with candy and he toddled in her direction, then sat contentedly sucking on a lollipop amidst his own veritable harem of adoring ladies.

"Okay, now sister, first I must ask you if this is wholly and completely your choice. Are you sure you understand what it is to be a Muslim?" the Qur'an teacher asked kindly, but seriously.

Did I know what it was to be a Muslim? I hadn't the slightest fucking clue.

I was sure of the most basic teachings of Islam, but many other aspects alluded and even confused me. But Mariam said I didn't need to fully understand Islam to embrace it. She said as long as I believed there was only one God and that Prophet Muhammad was his final messenger, I was technically already a Muslim. The rest, she assured me, would fall into place in time, and I needn't worry.

"Yes," I said, and I meant it. I did want to practice Islam—I wanted it very, very much. I was convinced of the Oneness of God and the prophethood of Muhammad more than I had been convinced of anything in my life. But deeper, way beneath this newfound faith, was a more profound aching: for a new life.

Islam—all the books, and Mariam, and the *Alima* program girls told me—promised me a new lease on life.

"*Insha'Allah*, let's get started, then," the Qur'an teacher said. "On this, the fourth day of the most blessed month of the year—Ramadan—all these people here, all of them, care deeply about you and Dayo and they want the best for you both. We are here to witness you saying your *shahada* and becoming Muslim—if you'll allow," she said, my pulse beating so loud I could barely hear her.

"Repeat after me," she said. "*Ashadu an la illaha il Allah, wa ashadu ana Muhammadan RasulAllah.*"

The Arabic words sounded strange and foreign, and they felt wildly uncomfortable in my mouth, but I tried. By the time we got to the English parts, the entire room was in tears.

"I bear witness that there is no God but God, and I bear witness that Muhammad is his final Prophet and Messenger," I said, and the room erupted in shouts of joy and "*Allahu akbar!*"s all around. Suddenly I was engulfed by a sea of women and girls I had never met, kissing me on both cheeks and basically throwing gifts at me.

By the end of it all, I had twelve large garbage bags full of various items of clothing from various countries. I stood in front of the mirror trying things on for what felt like years while Dayo slept in his playpen. Nothing fit right.

I also had been given a dozen books about Islam that seemed to have been written in another language and then poorly translated, and most had clearly never crossed the path of an editor or anyone who remotely understood modern English.

The next day was going to be Day One of my life as a Muslim, and also as a fasting person. Before Islam, I had only ever "fasted" in the Protestant fashion: giving up sugar or cursing

Surrey Libraries

eAudio, eBooks & eMagazines
@ surreylibraries.ca/books-media
Strawberry Hill Branch
14 Jan 2020 02:41PM

TITLE: Things that shatter : a memoir /

CALL NO: 297.092 UMD 2019
Barcode: 39090040584720
Due Date: 04 Feb 2020

TOTAL: 1

FOR RENEWALS, DUE DATES, HOLDS & FINES
CHECK YOUR ACCOUNT ONLINE AT
WWW.SURREYLIBRARIES.CA
OR CALL TELECIRC: 604-502-6333
****

We can let you know by email about your

holds and overdues. Ask for details.
****

during Lent, but now I would be going without both food and water from dawn to sunset. To say I was intimidated is an understatement. But I was determined to start my new life off on the right foot.

I crawled into bed and listened as Maulana Siraaj and his brother took turns on the microphone reciting Qur'an for the extra *Taraweeh* prayers of Ramadan. Their voices, distinctly Indian as they rang through the speaker system in the school, gave me an odd sort of feeling. Not comfort, really, but a kind of curious focus. *What can they be saying,* I wondered, *and why can't they say it in their own language?*

As I drifted off I heard Dayo waking up, so I brought him to my bed, where we snuggled as we both fell asleep.

In the morning, or rather before the morning, one of the *Alima* program girls I had become friends with came to wake me gently, reminding me it was time to eat before dawn crept on us. I stumbled excitedly toward the dining room, leaving Dayo still asleep in my bed. We sat on the floor and ate various things, all of which were spicy and made my stomach hurt. I eyed a box of Cinnamon Toast Crunch and grabbed myself a big bowl.

"Don't forget to drink more water, sister," one of the girls reminded me.

Sister. What a strange and far-fetched idea that just because less than twenty-four hours ago I had declared that I had faith in God the same way she had faith in God, now I was her family. I didn't buy it, but it was nice enough.

I drank as much water as my body could hold, then went down the hall to the bathroom to learn to make *wudu* correctly, preparing myself for prayer by running warm water over my hands, face, nose, mouth, arms, head, and feet before joining my friends in the prayer room.

* * *

It was a tough month, but I slowly began to sort of under-stand why everyone had looked forward to thirty days of self-deprivation. I felt lighter and less bogged down by worry, and I was more sure of my decision than ever. Withholding food and water from myself for upwards of fourteen hours a day for almost a month made me feel like I could resist sin much more easily than I believed I could before.

One of the things they talked about that month was how great 'Eid was going to be. One of two official celebrations in the Islamic calendar, 'Eid al Fitr is the celebration of the end of Ramadan, wherein one slaughters an animal to feed the hungry, or else gives some form of obligatory charity. There are parties and family gatherings and presents; it's a veritable Muslim Christmas.

Imagine my surprise when I woke on the morning of 'Eid and found... nothing. No streamers, no lights, no presents—nothing. The entire building was vacant but for Dayo and me, and the other convert—the elderly dorm mom.

Two hours after we woke up, everyone came back to the school and found us shocked and confused. "Oh, you missed the prayers!" they said. "You were sleeping and we didn't want to wake you."

Thus went my first 'Eid ever: spent alone with another equally confused new Muslim in an empty building.

After 'Eid, my time was spent mostly teaching English and preparing for class, but in my spare time, I continued on my hungry search for more knowledge about my new religion. The school library the Maulana had invited me to use was full of mostly Arabic and Urdu commentaries on the Qur'an, as well as various types of Islamic Law books. There was a tiny corner for English books, but like the ones gifted to me the day I said *shahada*, these books were very poorly translated and were full of typos and strange words like "vicegerent" and "ablution."

So, in lieu of my preferred medium, I watched as many videos online as I could, having no filter whatsoever to help me discern what parts were authentic Islam and what parts were cultural baggage.

I also found a creative outlet in the blogging world. A few weeks after my conversion, I created a Blogger account and called my blog "Struggles of an American Muslimah." I chronicled not only my struggles but also the parts of my new life that I was pleased with and wished I'd found sooner. Within a few weeks, I garnered several hundred followers. Most were kind, welcoming Muslims, and there were even a few converts like me—women struggling to reconcile their new faith with their culture and identity. I would develop a strong friendship with several of them over the years to come.

* * *

As a Christian, prayer came naturally to me and felt like something I didn't have to force myself to do. I loved to drive down one of the country roads near my childhood home, park my car, and sit on the trunk worshipping God. I'd sing and paint and cry and rage at God, and I felt sure—as sure as the corn and soybeans would grow and be harvested and be replanted—that God loved me and heard me and delighted in my worship.

But as a Muslim, prayer felt anything but natural. For one

thing, what I'd been doing all my life—talking to God anytime, anywhere I wanted, about anything at all—was called *du'a*, and was different than the five ritual prayers I was required to perform now, called *Salah*. "Perform" is certainly the right word, too, considering how many special movements and incantations I had to learn in order to complete the ritual in the accepted manner.

Before praying my *Salah*, I had to wash in a specific way before I could even begin the ritual prayer, and with a toddler running everywhere, such a thing was often hard to accomplish within a reasonable amount of time. That extra step alone meant praying as a Muslim prays would require more from me than the casual relationship I enjoyed with God before.

Then there was the fact that I didn't speak or understand Arabic, but I had to memorize the specific wording and Qur'anic excerpts to be able to pray my *Salah*. I was gifted a coloring book meant for teaching children to pray, which I laid on the floor next to me as I prayed. Later, I was given a laminated, pocket-sized, folding card containing the same instructions, which I could take with me everywhere.

When I missed a prayer—which happened for any number of reasons, but mostly the logistics of being a single, working mother, as well as a new Muslim with no self-discipline—I felt like trash. I was given conflicting advice on what to do in such a situation.

"You must pray the prayer you missed before you can pray the current one," Mariam told me.

"Okay, but what if I've missed… several prayers. How on earth can I pray three or four entire prayer sets at once?! And doesn't that sort of nullify the whole 'communicating and connecting with God throughout your day' argument?" I asked. "If God isn't in need of my worship, and it's not about *owing* God my prayers, making them up just doesn't make sense."

Mariam didn't often have answers to my questions, but she tried, God bless her.

Eventually, someone told me about a ruling in Islamic Law that says if you've missed four prayers or more, you need to just start over and try to make up those prayers later. So if I missed a prayer or two, I began skipping prayers intentionally to add up to the four so I could just start over the next day because I felt so overwhelmed.

And yet, at the same time, someone else told me about the legal opinion that missing three consecutive days of prayers nullifies your Islam and means you have to say the *shahada* if you want to be considered Muslim again.

This—and many other issues—confused and frustrated me. The plethora of legal opinions—all based on the beliefs of men (always men) from primarily Arab and Desi cultures—made me feel like I would never have a clear idea of what God wanted. Where some saw freedom of thought, I felt lost without structure and clear guidance. I needed a teacher.

3

The Bait

Chicago, Illinois

Autumn 2009

Less than a month after I said my *shahada,* as I finished up my *Dhuhr* prayer—the noon prayer—I found the Qur'an teacher sitting at the back of the prayer room, silently reading to herself. I hoped the day would come that I would be able to read and understand the Qur'an as she did.

"*Asalaamu alaykum,*" she said warmly after I finished my prayer, closing her Qur'an. "How are things going, sister Kaighla?" she asked, fumbling with my name, just like everyone else always has.

"*Alhamdulillah,*" I said, thanking God in the customary way. "Things are going okay, I guess. It's hard with Dayo, though. Being a single mom, I mean. It's tough."

She smiled. "You know, I have been meaning to talk with you

about something, but it's sensitive..." she said, hesitating.

"Ahhh, ok. Go ahead then," I replied, feeling curious.

"Sister Kaighla, God created Muslim women for Muslim men and Muslim men for Muslim women, and we are not designed to be alone," she said, touching my arm gently. "Have you considered finding a husband to help you raise Dayo?"

A husband?! I thought.

Seeing the shock on my face, she laughed. "We Muslims don't marry the way people do here in America, sister," she continued. "No dating for years, living together, trying things out first before you commit. Muslim women who fear God are introduced to a man through their father or brother or uncle, and they only meet with him along with these chaperones," she explained.

"You talk about things," she continued, "like what you want in a marriage and such, and when everything is said and done, if you like him and his level of religious devotion and you feel he's compatible with you, and if your guardian agrees, you marry. No delaying!"

She said all this like it was the simplest thing in the world, like walking into the grocery store and picking up a cantaloupe.

I'd already been approached a few days before this by Maulana Siraaj. He told me I had several offers of marriage, all from men who had never even seen a picture of me. They knew I was a new Muslim, they knew I had a small son, and they knew I was a white American, and that's all they needed to know to offer me marriage, apparently. He advised me to ignore them, though, which I was thankful for.

"I have never thought about it," I said honestly. "I am only twenty-two and I loved my son's father very much. I had hoped to return to India someday so we can raise Dayo together, me and him, or else go to Nigeria together," I replied. "It's got a lot of Muslims."

She smiled. "Yes, but is his father a Muslim?" she asked.

No. No, he wasn't a Muslim and no, he would never imagine being a Muslim, as he told me himself when I mentioned it a few weeks before my conversion.

Sensing my reluctance to answer, she continued, "Sister Kaighla, a Muslim woman cannot ever marry a non-Muslim man. Unless Dayo's father is interested in being a Muslim, you must break any emotional attachment you have to him and begin looking for a better man."

"A *better* man," she'd said—meaning "a Muslim man."

"Then I'd rather stay single, thank you," I replied, suddenly aware that there was not only a cultural gap, but an age gap between us, and I did not truly know that woman, nor did she know me. I wondered why she seemed so comfortable talking to me about my private life.

She hugged me and grabbed her things, said "*Salaam*," and assured me that she would be there for me if I changed my mind, then left.

But Mariam said she was right. A first-generation Palestinian-American, Mariam was divorced. After ten years married to an abusive man who refused to divorce her, he kept his hold on her even while she took refuge in her father's house.

"Muslim women can't initiate divorce because women are naturally more emotional than men," she told me, so that sort of decision is entrusted to the "stronger sex." Women can ask for an annulment, or *khula*, but only if they give back their *mahr*, or bride-gift—which can sometimes be valued at upwards of the thousands—and only if they have "just cause."

Mariam definitely had just cause, but the sheikhs she went

to seeking an annulment didn't feel that way. "Muslim women should be patient with abuse and pray that their husbands stop hurting them," they said. "Plus, really, you need to consider what you could be doing to deserve it."

She had to go all the way to Syria to find a sheikh willing to absolve her of her marriage vows. Three years later, she was still single, being too broken and traumatized to entrust her heart to another man.

A Muslim woman, and especially one with a child, has no business being single, according to Mariam, the Qur'an teacher, and the sheikhs I listened to on YouTube.

"What better way to learn the religion than to live with a good Muslim who could teach you?" That's what they said, and I bought every word of it because I thought they knew better than I did.

* * *

September 30th, 2009

Dayo woke me this morning around the time to pray the Fajr *prayer, so I took him with me to the bathroom and* wudu *area, then to the prayer room. He just stands there and watches my movements curiously, but I know that each time I do this, he is learning how to view me. I am his mother, the person who loves him most, and I choose to submit myself to God in my human frailty. The pillar of strength in Dayo's life crumbles before the Living God.*

He's my prayer clock now, waking me just before the end of the designated time. Now that Ramadan is over, the ladies don't come to wake me for prayer, assuming I have mastered it by now, just a month in.

Between teaching my classes, I diligently check my email inbox for any messages from Ameer. His flight should be arriving at 6 p.m. Mariam's father, Abu Mohamed, is supposed to be picking him up from O'Hare to drive him to her house where we will meet, in person, for the first time.

So yeah, you could say I am a little bit excited.

All of this, all of it, is new to me, and all of it is part-thrilling and part-terrifying. I have no idea what the future holds, but I feel so sure God can only intend good for me by bringing me this man as a husband.

I was shocked to find him, really. I'm glad I finally gave in and decided to open a profile on a few Muslim marriage sites. The school is heavily segregated, so I never have a chance to interact with men—aside from the Maulana, and that's infrequent—so it seemed like the only way I'd ever find someone that I could choose for myself. If I am going to be pushed into marriage, I at least want to find and choose the guy myself.

When he first messaged me, his profile said he was a "professor," so that intrigued me—eternal intellectual that I am. But I quickly learned that his English is wildly sub-par for a professor at any university in America. Plus, he kept talking about "us" like "we" were already a thing. Within five minutes or so, I was bored and weirded out, so I closed the chat box.

A few days later, though, he messaged me again, but this time it was different; he was polite and asked me about my day, wanted to talk about my little son, and asked about how my prayers were going.

We talked a little about some of the concerns I have, and I noticed that when he wrote about things related to the religion, his English seemed to improve a bit, like it was the topic in which he was most often engaged in conversation. By the end of our discussion, he asked if he could have my wali's number, so I gave him Abu Mohamed's info.

Since I've been married before, I don't technically have to have a wali *to help me choose a good guy—or to kick his ass if he's not such a good guy after all—but Abu Mohamed said it's a good idea. So anytime a brother has shown interest in me, I've sent him first to Abu Mohamed so he can give me his opinion.*

I really love this family, Mariam's family. Ever since my first week as a Muslim, they have welcomed me and Dayo into their home. It's become a ritual for us to ride with Mariam to the city and spend all weekend enjoying her mother's delicious dinners.

During Ramadan, they had me sleep in Mariam's old room on the main floor while she slept with her family upstairs. Before dawn, her mom used to wake me gently to eat the pre-fasting meal, suhoor, *and she was careful not to wake Dayo. I can still smell the freshly baked pita bread and the oil and* zataar *on the table, eggs boiling away on the stove as the rest of the house prepared themselves for prayer.*

Abu Mohamed gave me the okay to talk more with Ameer, but said he was nervous about Ameer's age and his previous marriage situation, calling it "worrisome." Ameer told us that his ex-wife lives in Egypt now with their kids. She lived in Brooklyn for a few years with him, but she apparently eventually went home because they weren't able to bring all their kids to America yet and she missed the others. Ultimately, they divorced because the distance was just too much, and because they never got along before anyway.

And yeah, he is older than me, around twelve years older actually, but I find it attractive. I hate men my own age, or, God forbid, younger. Why in hell would any woman want a man she has to raise? A man she has to teach how to be a man? No thank you.

* * *

During a conversation one day, Ameer said he needed to go pray. Just as we were about to hang up the phone, I overheard someone in the background say, "*Ya* sheikh, are you coming? It's time to pray."

Sheikh? I hadn't been Muslim long, but I knew what that word meant. He was a religious leader: a highly-educated minister in the mosque—not a professor at all.

The next time he called me, I asked him outright why he had been lying to me about his profession. "If you're a religious leader, why not be proud?" I asked.

"It's not a lie, *ya* Keee-la," he said, hatcheting my name. "I said 'professor' because I'm a teacher, you know? I did teach some classes in the local college on Islam, actually. But if I told you I am a sheikh, I thought you would not be interested. Sheikhs are usually old and boring," he said.

He didn't apologize for the deception, just explained why he was justified in it.

"You're wrong to have lied, but you're also wrong about me," I replied. "I love that you're a sheikh. You are educated about

Islam, the thing I know nothing about, but love the most, and I am excited at the idea of being your wife."

And so, things went on like that for several weeks until he actually asked me over webcam to marry him. He even bought me a ring and mailed it to me. Sure, it was only $100 and fake in every sense of the word, but it seemed a sweet gesture at the time.

A few more weeks went by and I was beginning to feel attached to this man I still hadn't met. Mariam told me to make sure I was careful, that not all men are as good as they seem, but I was not stupid. I knew religious leaders could be evil, but surely not a Muslim cleric of his acumen, I thought. He had two master's degrees from the greatest Muslim university in the world—*Al-Azhar* in Cairo—and he seemed to know so much about Islam. I assumed he wouldn't violate God's laws, knowing better than most what the consequences are.

Everything seemed to be going swimmingly until one day during a Skype call, he brought up his ex-wife.

"She is my second cousin, and her brother is married to my sister," he explained. "The divorce really destroyed our family and especially my kids. They love us so much, and it hurts them when I come to visit and their mother can't even sit like normal with me, having to wear hijab and act very formally since we are not married anymore. I only go to Egypt once a year for about a month, but other than that I will be always with you and only you..."

"But...?" I asked, sensing his hesitation.

"But I think it is very likely I will marry her again," he said. "She is the mother of my kids and our families are very connected, and I cannot handle the pain it is putting my kids through. It would not affect our marriage at all, I promise."

43

A thousand things ran through my mind in an instant, and I turned away from the screen and paused, waiting for the feeling to pass before I responded. When I felt adequately put together again, I smiled and said, "If that is what you intend to do, I have no interest in being your wife. May God give you and her the best."

I could see the shock on his face. He thought I was bluffing.

I truly wanted to be with him, but polygyny was something I knew I couldn't handle. In fact, for weeks before I finally said the *shahada* and became Muslim, I struggled with exactly this issue: how can God say a man is allowed to cheat on his wife—love and sleep with another woman—regardless of how his wife feels about it?

"Why does God care more about the sexual pleasure of a man than the real and tangible pain of a woman? How can I hope for peace and stability and love with a man who is divided in two, or, God forbid, three or four?!" I asked Mariam.

"It's not like *that*," she said, clearly uncomfortable with the power of my passion against the idea. "Look, sister Kaighla. God knows what's good for us, and what seems like a bad idea to us may be the best thing for us in the end," she said.

She wasn't wrong. The Qur'an itself says that we may hate a thing when it's good for us, and we may love a thing that's bad for us, and God knows best (2:216). Of course, what they failed to tell me was the context surrounding that verse—it's about people feeling reluctant to go to war to defend themselves—but random verses from the Qur'an, like this one, were often used to explain and defend things that didn't make sense in a 21st-century context.

"Please, be reasonable," he implored me. "Think of how she feels, seeing me there and not even being able to touch me. I don't love her, and I never did. But she does care for me, and I don't hate her. She is the mother of my children, and she is my family, so I respect her. And she doesn't even need to know about you."

I was disgusted. "You think tricking your wife, making her think you're here alone, and all the while living and sleeping with me, is an okay thing to do?! If you'd do that to a woman who was faithful to you for all those years, what sort of lies would you feed me?!" I spat back, surprised by the surge of rage I felt.

One of the other teachers cracked the door of my office then, having heard me shouting as she was walking down the hall.

"No. I am sorry, but I am not interested. Please, leave me alone," I said calmly.

I closed my laptop and cried. I wasn't sure why I cried so much, considering I had only known Ameer a few weeks at that point and had never met him in person, but I had gotten so excited about marrying him. I had worn his cheap-ass, fake engagement ring with such pride.

* * *

The next day, I had ten missed calls from Ameer, so I blocked his number. A week later, Mariam told me that he had been calling her father day and night, night and day, begging him to convince me to reconsider.

I was flattered and annoyed at the same time. Growing up, I was taught that if a boy really likes you, he won't take "no" for an answer. The more he persists, the more he cares for you, regardless of your own apprehensions and rejections. *Trust his dedication to winning you more than your own feelings,* was the message I'd been given as a young woman. So, I called him.

"Listen, I am willing to talk to you about this if you will leave that poor man alone," I said, pretending to be annoyed but smiling into the phone.

He promised me that he would not remarry her without first telling me about it and making sure I was okay with it, and if I was never okay with it, he would never do it.

After a week or so, I agreed. There was no wedding planning necessary, as Ameer and the other sheikhs at the school said American-style weddings were *haraam*—forbidden—as they were "copying the *kaafirs*' ways." All we needed to do was sign religiously-binding marriage papers with a sheikh and two other male witnesses (or four female witnesses) and we would be married.

Ameer said legal marriage wasn't necessary, either. "God doesn't respect the laws of the non-Muslims, just as they don't respect His laws," he said. Considering how many men openly admitted they were only interested in marrying me for the chance to get a Green Card, this was good for me, this not-being-legally-married thing.

We decided to meet at Mariam's father's house, and if the chemistry was right in person, we'd sign the papers, then he'd fly home and, in a few months, Dayo and I would go visit him in NYC. After several months of these visits, we would move in with him there. We'd do things slowly, carefully.

* * *

Ameer's flight landed an hour later than we thought it would. Chicago, that city of the wind, tried to keep him from getting to me, but God had other plans.

46

When he arrived at Mariam's house, he was greeted and rushed into the formal sitting room, where Mariam's father and brothers and even her uncles and cousins had come to meet the sheikh who would be marrying the new Muslim in their care.

After what felt like years, the door between the kitchen and dining room slid open and the men welcomed me in. My little sister, Ariel—whom everyone called "AJ"—was eighteen at the time. She had driven up to Chicago and was even donning one of my hijabs for the occasion. When they invited me in, she squeezed my hand with her free hand, the other holding Dayo on her shoulder, long since asleep.

Shortly after they arrived, I had sent Dayo waddling into the men's sitting room in his new *shalwar kameez* set we bought him for the wedding. He looked adorable, and I wanted to know how Ameer would react to him interrupting their male bonding session. If he was annoyed with Dayo or sent him back to me, marriage was out of the question.

The men gasped and laughed animatedly when Dayo entered the room, and suddenly everyone was stumbling over one another to get to him, then picking him up and kissing his cheeks and offering him snacks.

I heard Ameer's distinct, deep voice calling to him. "*Yalla, ya* Dayo! Come sit on my lap. *Masha'Allah*, may God bless you, *habibi*. You are so handsome in these clothes!" he said, laughing. I heard Dayo giggling, too, as Ameer tickled him. Soon, he came toddling back to me, hands laden with sweets, with a big smile spread across his face.

So, when they called me into the room to talk with Ameer, I was happy. I felt confident. I was sure he was the man I wanted to be with.

"When will the official wedding be? The legal one, I mean," Abu Mohamed asked Ameer casually, pouring him more tea.

"Ah, *akhi* there is no need for that. We will sign the papers tonight and be married. No need to make it legal," he said, smiling across the table at me.

Abu Mohamed laughed uncomfortably. "And you are comfortable with this, sister Kaighla?" he asked.

Of course, I was. I was *very comfortable* with it, in fact.

"If she accepts that, it's her right, but it makes me uncomfortable, *ya* sheikh, if I am being honest," he said, turning back to Ameer. "Is there some reason you don't want to be legally married to the sister?"

Ameer shifted in his seat. "Actually, brothers, unfortunately, I am still legally married to my previous wife, the American convert I was married to for a few years. We divorced earlier this year, but she has agreed not to file the legal papers yet so I can get my Green Card, which is still processing," he said.

The air in the room changed, tense electric energy filling the space around us. Abu Mohamed smiled awkwardly, and the men asked to be excused to talk more in private, leaving me and Ameer alone together—though Mariam, my sister, and Mariam's mother, Um Mohamed, were just a few feet away from us, listening behind the sliding door.

He smiled at me, I smiled at him, and I visualized what it would be like to make love to him after tearing off his silly tie with my teeth. *Astaghfirullah, God forgive me,* I thought to myself. *He's not even your husband yet.*

After ten minutes, the group of men came back into the sitting room and Abu Mohamed spoke. "We're sorry to say this—with our full respect, *ya* sheikh—but we cannot authorize this marriage," he said.

Ameer's face changed.

"This sister is our daughter in Islam, and we worry for her. We don't understand the ins and outs of this marriage situation you have, or about your ex-wife in Egypt, and we worry this is not a good environment for our new Muslim sister," Abu Mohamed's brother said. "It's too complicated and too dangerous for her very weak, new faith. We humbly request that you hold off the engagement until your divorce from the other sister goes through and we can meet again."

The room was silent then.

Ameer took a sip of his tea, looking unfazed. "I appreciate your concern, brothers, I do, and I care for the sister as much as you can imagine," he said. "But I will marry her tonight."

When he sensed their resistance, he went into full lecture mode.

"I don't see what right you have to stop this marriage. You know that it is a major *fitnah* when you stop two people from marrying. Our Prophet Muhammad said...," and here he broke off and went back to Arabic—all of the men in the room being Palestinian—before switching back to English for my sake. "Prophet Muhammad said that if a man comes asking after your daughter and you are satisfied with his religious devotion, and if she accepts the proposal, you cannot stop them from marrying each other or else you are creating a great *fitnah,* a great trial, on the earth."

I could see their faces changing.

"Okay, *ya* sheikh, I understand your point, and we will not stand in her way if she is adamant," Abu Mohamed said, "but surely you cannot hope to marry her tonight as Um Mohamed tells us that Um Dayo is... ahem... *not praying.*"

Intercourse is forbidden when a woman is on her period, and

most Muslims believe women are forbidden from praying the ritual *Salah* prayers when they're on their period, too, so the polite way of saying I was not "open for business," as it were, was to say that I "wasn't praying."

Ameer chuckled to himself. "Brothers, do you imagine that is all I came here for—for some sex? Maybe I would like to take my new wife to the hotel and talk to her, get to know her more!"

Everyone laughed then, and the mood changed slightly.

"Okay, Sheikh Ameer. We see your point. But the reality is the same: we cannot authorize this marriage until you divorce your first American wife so you are free to legally marry our sister, Um Dayo. This way she will be given her due rights as a Muslim wife—both in the eyes of God and in the eyes of the government."

He became truly angry then. "I will marry her tonight, and you will not stop me," he said firmly. "I will take her to any *masjid* I find and make some other sheikh marry us, and shame on all of you for trying to stop us," he nearly yelled. Then he excused himself to the bathroom.

The men in the room looked at each other, and several of them whispered quietly.

None of them looked in my direction; none of them asked what I thought. It felt strange. I knew that my consent was required for the marriage to go forward, and I was also uncomfortable deep down, especially when I saw the way Ameer was reacting to their apprehensions. But I ignored these nagging feelings in my mind. I trusted Ameer.

Just then, Mariam rapped softly on the sliding wood door and handed me a tray of fresh coffee and sweets to give to the men. As the respected daughter of the host, she would not stand in the room with those men—her own uncles and cousins—handing them treats, and certainly not so long as there was a non-relative among them. She would simply knock quietly on the door in a pattern her father was accustomed to hearing, pass him the tray, and shut it again quietly, as if she was never there at all.

When Ameer returned, he asked if someone could find him some paper and a pen. He hastily wrote out the marriage contract in Arabic, signed it, and handed it to the men in the room who all signed it quietly. Abu Mohamed signed last and passed it to me with a grave look on his face.

The contract was written in Arabic, so I had no idea what it said or where I was supposed to sign, and they forgot to hand me a pen. Ameer pulled one from his shirt pocket and handed it to me, careful not to touch my skin.

"What does it say? Where should I sign?" I asked.

Ameer pointed out where to sign and asked if perhaps Mariam could translate the contract and write one in English for us to sign, just for me to keep.

Everyone signed the contract, and the brothers gave us empty congratulations as we walked to the rental car. My sister stood among the crowd, holding Dayo as he smiled and waved at us, happy to be with his auntie for the weekend.

Before we left, Ameer grabbed my hand and kissed it gently, then snapped a selfie, and we were off, the car full of sexual energy that no "not praying" status could halt.

4

The Honeymoon

Brooklyn, New York

Winter 2009

I burned the rice. I also burned the chicken, but that was Ameer's fault.

It was just after *Asr* prayer. Dayo was down for his afternoon nap and I was cooking lunch (lunch, he called it, at 3 p.m.!) and had not mixed the frying vermicelli and rice often enough. I was trying to wash dishes at the same time and forgot about it. When I turned to look, it was a pile of black, oily muck.

Just then, he walked in from the mosque and laughed at the sight. "Be careful, baby, or the entire *masjid* will know you are burning the sheikh's food," he teased and grabbed me from behind, grinding himself up against me.

"I know! I know, I'm sorry. It was an accident," I laughed,

welcoming his embrace.

"This wall is paper thin, so all the smells escape right into the *masjid* area," he said. "And all the sounds, too, so *yalla* and let me take you to our living room," he whispered in my ear.

"But I'm cooking chicken right now in the broiler, *habibi*. It'll burn. Let me turn it off really quick," I said, but he was hauling me to the living room, tearing off my clothes.

By the time we were in the bathroom washing up, the house smelled like the sheikh had indeed married a silly American girl, after all, unable to keep his food from burning.

"Don't be sad, *hayati*," he smiled as we both surveyed the charcoal chicken. "I will take you for Chinese at that *halal* place, *mashy?* Let's clean this up and wait for Abdullah to wake up from his nap, then we'll go."

Abdullah. Dayo was called "Abdullah" now. I was Um Abdullah. But I did not give birth to an Abdullah; I gave birth to my Dayo baby. But Ameer said I had to call him "Abdullah" because "Dayo" was "too African."

"If the people in the *masjid* knew you had a baby with a black man before Islam, they would think you were not a good girl before," he explained.

"Ameer, he's clearly a mixed child," I replied.

"People don't know he's half-black. He looks pretty Egyptian, actually," he said.

"Maybe, but what on earth does having a black man's baby have to do with being good?! Your ex-wife Aishah had two children with a Jamaican... " I asked, angry now.

"Come on, Kaighla. You know why. Good white girls don't have sex with black men. Everyone knows white women only sleep with black men for drugs and stuff like that," he replied, scoffing. "And yeah, her kids were half-Jamaican, but they were dark-skinned and much older, so there was nothing I could do about it. Everyone knew they weren't my daughters. They just assumed Aishah had made some bad choices many years before she converted. We can just ignore their questions about who his father is. They'll assume he was another Arab or something."

I threw my hands in the air in frustration. Islam's stance on racial equality was pretty clear, but I had never seen or heard more racism than I did among Arab Muslims.

Seeing my agitation, he softened up a bit. "*Habibti*, my reputation is our livelihood. If people think badly about you, they think worse about me for marrying you, and you can't let some Nigerian boy you slept with in India all those years ago ruin our lives," he said.

"My *husband*. He was my husband," I corrected him. "And we did not 'have sex' like I was some common girl on the street. We loved each other very much," I said, tears beginning to fill my eyes, remembering the love we had shared and how much it hurt to lose him.

Ameer let it go then, and after that, I called my son "Abdullah" in front of Ameer and in public, but when it was just us, I always called him Dayo.

But Sheikh Ameer's obsession with image seemed to know no bounds. One rainy morning, we were walking down Manhattan Avenue and I had walked a few feet ahead of him, as he was holding Dayo's hand, making sure he didn't fall or jet out into traffic.

"Abdullah!" I heard him yell from behind me. Thinking Dayo had hurt himself, I turned on my heel to see what was wrong. But Dayo seemed fine, and Ameer was just standing there staring at me with a perturbed look on his face.

"What's wrong? What happened to Abdullah? Did he try to

run into the street?" I asked as I stooped down to check on him. But Ameer didn't answer me. He calmly took Dayo's hand again and kept walking.

When we got home, I asked him again what was wrong.

"Nothing happened to Abdullah, *ya Kaighla*. I was trying to get your attention because you were walking in front of me. You shouldn't ever walk in front of me," he said.

"… Okay … leaving aside why you think there is something wrong with me walking in front of you, why'd you call me 'Abdullah'?" I asked, confounded.

He seemed irritated now.

"You're my wife. That's why you don't walk in front of me. I am the sheikh. I don't walk behind anyone, least of all a woman, and certainly not my own wife," he said. "And I didn't use your name because your name is part of your *'awra*—it's private. No one on the street needs to know your name. It's no one's business," he explained.

He later told me that the worst insult any boy could give another boy in his village in Egypt was to say, "I know your mother's name."

"It's like saying you've seen her naked," he said, shuddering.

* * *

In my free time, I hung out with some of the younger Yemeni ladies who attended the mosque. Most of them were talented, intelligent, posh women who lived life to the fullest, but still understood the importance of obeying their fathers and honoring their cultural heritage. There was a major cultural difference between us, to say the least, but I found myself admiring them. After all, they loved God deeply, but they were nothing like what Ameer said a Muslim woman should be: they wore makeup and jewelry and high heels and they even laughed out loud, right in the street.

"Some Muslim women don't understand the importance of modesty, *habibti*," he said. "Even the way a Muslim woman walks should be modest, subdued, and as quiet as possible. A Muslim woman shouldn't draw attention to herself. And she should look at the ground when she walks, not up and around at people and the sky and stuff. God told believing women to lower their gaze."

They invited me to a *halaqa* circle, which as far as I could tell was basically like Bible study group, but with the Qur'an and stories about Prophet Muhammad. When Dayo was napping, I'd turn on the baby monitor and head down to the basement where they held their classes, in the dank recesses of the women's prayer area. We talked about Prophet Muhammad, about the rights of our husbands on us and ours on them, and about what constitutes *halal* and *haraam*. I noticed there was little discussion about the spiritual side of things, but no one seemed bothered by that.

I also started taking free online classes about Islam, including one where I learned how to read and write in Arabic. I almost had the prayer words memorized, but I still needed to use my little laminated pamphlet from time to time, laying it down on the ground right where I'd make prostration so I could see the transliteration clearly.

Overall, things were great. I was growing and learning and it seemed like I had made the right decision, after all—both in choosing to embrace Islam and in marrying the sheikh.

5

The Revealing

Brooklyn, New York

Winter 2009

After a grocery run one chilly December evening that year, we pulled into the *masjid* parking lot and Ameer began unloading the groceries as Dayo slept in his car seat in the still-warm car.

"Be careful, eh? Because of the ice," he said as I got out of the car. It had been less than a year since I'd slipped on ice and shattered the lower part of my left leg, and since the time I spent on bed rest recovering from that fall pushed me headlong into a more intimate connection with God.

As I began walking inside, I remembered to grab Ameer's clothes off the line so they wouldn't get wet again overnight. I went in through the side door, grabbed a laundry basket from the bedroom, and stepped out onto our back porch to get his nearly-frozen *jilbabs* off the line. Ameer went back outside to get Dayo, and laid him, still sleeping, on the couch.

When I came inside, laundry-basket in hand, I accidentally knocked Ameer's phone off the kitchen counter. It fell to the ground with a sound that was probably not as loud as I imagined, but every noise is a cataclysmic event when your toddler is sleeping. When I bent down to pick it up, I saw he had received a few messages from Aishah, his American ex-wife. I tried to resist the urge, but the temptation was too strong, and I grabbed the phone, threw it in the laundry basket, and went to our room. I could hear him turning on the shower, so I knew I still had some time.

I sat quietly on the bed, leaving the door open, my ears sharp for the sound of his footfall.

"I know you miss me, habibi," the text read, *"but what's done is done. I married him, you married her, and it's done."*

I took a deep breath and scrolled through weeks of conversation. There were texts of passion, of begging, of yearning—always on his end. She was dignified and never seemed coerced into accepting his pleas to fix things between them. I could feel the heat radiating around my head, and hot, angry tears starting to form. Something wasn't right about it. Many things were not right about it.

Aishah was the convert Ameer had married before me—or one of them, anyway. Truth be told, Ameer had a penchant for marrying converts. That three-year-long marriage which ended in divorce, he told me, was an overall happy one, but he couldn't handle raising her daughters. Though he had several children of his own by then, he hadn't ever had to actually help raise them, so he knew next to nothing about what it took to be a good father. Plus, his racism often got the better of him.

They ended things well, he told me, mutually agreeing it was best, back in June.

But before her and even while he was married to her, he'd had multiple other wives.

First, there was a pretty Ukrainian. Ameer said she came from a Muslim family, but she refused to wear hijab, and as much as he liked her, he could not accept her resistance. Sure, perhaps he could be patient with her and give her time to grow into wearing hijab, but the *masjid* community would not, he said.

He told me a story about her during an argument we had once about my "disobedient spirit," a few weeks after Dayo and I moved to Brooklyn. Apparently, she and Ameer had been shopping for a coat for her one day and she got pissy with him, so he slapped her in the face, right there in the middle of the department store. When another customer tried to intervene, she was livid.

"Don't you dare touch my husband, you bastard. We are Muslims, and he can hit me when he wants to! Mind your business!" he told me she'd said.

"This is the level of respect a Muslim woman should give to her husband," he taught me. "She should be understanding with him and ask herself what she is doing to cause his anger, and she should protect him and his reputation from harm."

Ameer often lectured me about a man's rights on his wife. Every conversation we had seemed to somehow turn into one of his *khutbas*.

"Prophet Muhammad, peace and blessings be upon him, said, 'If the husband had an ulcer covering his entire body, and it was oozing blood and pus, and his wife came to lick the blood and puss off for him, she would still not have fulfilled his right,'" Ameer said.

Of course, many years later, I would learn that this *hadith* was most likely fabricated by men seeking to control their wives with religion—especially when one considers the extremely serious commands Prophet Muhammad gave to men, time and time again, to treat their wives and daughters with the utmost respect and dignity.

Ameer eventually divorced that Ukrainian Muslim, assuring me they never consummated things, so it "didn't count."

Then there was the first-generation Irish convert who covered her entire body, including her face, but cursed like a sailor and wouldn't stop her smoking habit. When things began to turn sour in his marriage with Aishah, he married the Irish girl, but apparently, it didn't go as he'd hoped with her, either.

"I am sorry to say it, but her private parts smelled so bad it made me sick, and I divorced her right there on the bed without sleeping with her," he told me.

But these messages were from Aishah: the ex-wife he respected, the woman who worked hard in the mosque to help bring up his reputation, the good American convert who went with him to all the social events in the city, and to all the interfaith councils. I came across a newspaper picture of the two of them standing at a pulpit in a cathedral when I Googled him before we married. She was beautiful, and she presented herself as the dignified, refined woman that Islam had turned her into.

I called her, breathing shallowly, my pulse beating in my throat. I had always avoided conflict as often as possible—good midwestern girl that I was—so I was nervous. She answered with a sweet "*Asalaamu alaykum, ya* sheikh," assuming it was him since I used his phone to make the call.

"*Wa alaykum salaam*, sister. This is the sheikh's wife, Kaighla.

I'm sorry to bother you, but I just wondered why you are messaging my husband," I said, barely able to keep the tears back. I always cried when I was nervous.

There was a long period of silence on the line before I heard her tell someone in the background she would be right back; she had to take this call.

"*Asalaamu alaykum*, sister Kaighla. How are you, hun?" she asked kindly.

"Don't call me that. I am not your friend. I am the wife of the man you're messaging, calling him '*habibi*.' Please, tell me what is going on," I said, all seriousness.

She chuckled a bit to herself and asked, "Do you know who I am, sister?" Yes, I knew who she was. "Okay, so you know that Sheikh Ameer and I were married for three years and only divorced in September, just a month before you married him. I believe he started talking to you on that site when we were separated but still married," she said.

"He told me you were divorced back in June," I told her.

"No, that's not true," she replied. "Anyway, I apologize for messaging him, and I promise it won't happen again."

I relaxed a little.

"I thought he was going to be visiting his wife in Egypt like he usually does at this time, so I was surprised when I saw him calling. I thought something may be wrong with his visa. That's the only reason I answered," she said.

"Wait. His wife?!" I asked, confused. The ringing in my ears right then was so loud that I didn't hear Ameer come into the bedroom, standing next to the bed in only a towel. I pushed past him, running through our apartment to the metal door that separated our tiny home from the mosque area. It was well after 9 p.m. that winter night, so the building was completely empty. I went straight up the stairs to the second-floor prayer area and sat down against the wall. It was the furthest I could get from him and still be within the warmth of the building.

"What?!" I asked, tears streaming down my face. "He said they were divorced!"

There was a long silence on the line again.

"*Ya Allah.* Oh my God. Honey, I am so sorry. I genuinely did not mean to create a problem. You're telling me you don't know about his first wife, Shahida, in Egypt? The woman he has been married to since he was twenty? The mother of his six kids, one who is not even a year old yet?" she asked.

"No, sister. He didn't tell me any of that. He said he was divorced! He said he had five kids, not six," I cried.

"Wait, he divorced Shahida? When did that happen?" she asked, sounding honestly shocked.

"He said he divorced her years ago when she left him here to go be with the kids, before he ever married you," I explained.

"Oh, sister. Please forgive me," she said quietly, the regret evident in her voice. "I truly had no idea he had lied to you about her. He told me about her the day we met. But you have to believe me: I promise you, they are very much married. He has never and he will never divorce Shahida. Aside from being the mother of his children, she is also his cousin, so it would wreck their family if they divorced. Plus, her brother has promised to divorce his sister, Lena, if he ever divorces Shahida. I can't understand why he would tell you he was divorced."

But I knew why. I knew full well why he lied. "Because I refused to marry him when he said he would 'maybe remarry her' in the future. That's why. He knew I would not marry him if I knew the truth," I cried, snot running down my face onto my t-shirt.

Just then, I heard him coming up the stairs. When he reached the top, he stood impatiently, staring at me in my pitiful state.

"Hang up the phone and come inside, Um Abdullah. Right now," he said, serious as death.

"I will hang up when I am good and ready, you asshole!" I yelled through the empty mosque.

"You will hang up NOW and come downstairs into our home at once," he said.

The sheikh almost never yelled at me. He spoke so calmly it was unnerving, but his words could kill.

"Sister, listen to him. Trust me. Hang up the phone and I will come to see you in the *masjid* in a few weeks and we can talk more. He cannot stop me from coming to the mosque. *Asalaamu alaykum*, for now," she said, hanging up the phone.

I picked myself up off the floor and walked past him, down the stairs, into the house, and sat down on the couch. He moved Dayo into his crib and sat down on the love seat opposite of me.

"So, what now? You will divorce me now and go back to living in the boarding school with your son?" he asked, chuckling.

He was right. I had nowhere else to go—and that was assuming they would even take me back. When we married in October, the plan was for me to stay on at my position until the summer. But I had come to visit him in early November and when he asked me to stay and break my promise to Siraaj, I acquiesced, and happily. I wanted to be his wife, and I wanted to live with him. "I have a greater right to you," he assured me after his phone call informing Maulana Siraaj of our decision. "You're my wife. You and Dayo belong with me. He can find another teacher."

Sitting there in our warm living room, in a posh neighborhood in Brooklyn, as the snow fell outside, I tried to think rationally.

Ameer was good to us. Dayo and I were provided for. We didn't have to worry about having food or rent money, and Ameer was an attentive step-father. Plus, we had nowhere else to go. My own mother had asked me to leave her house after my fall when I was barely capable of walking from one room to the next, prompting my move to Chicago in the first place. I knew we wouldn't be welcome in her home again.

But, then, how could I stay, knowing what I knew? All I wanted to do was run and cry and vomit out all the fear and panic I felt inside.

"You lied to me! You tricked me into marrying you! You swore you were divorced and promised not to marry her again unless I was okay with it! I trusted you and you lied to me!" I cried, tears pouring hot from my eyes.

"May Allah give you what you deserve for calling Aishah and making a problem between us, *ya* Kaighla," he said. "She and I have respect for one another and you're making things ugly."

"*That's* your concern? If your ex-wife thinks badly of you for tricking me?!" I asked, truly surprised by his messed-up priorities.

"Yes, I lied about divorcing Shahida. So? What you wanna do? You want a divorce? I'll divorce you right now if you want. As you see, I can clearly have any woman I want, whenever I want one. You want me to book your ticket? No one is trapping you here," he said, not a trace of sadness or regret in his voice.

How could he be willing to throw me and my son away so easily—my son, whom he forced me to call "Abdullah" after his own stillborn son? My son, whom he swore he loved as his very own?

"And what about Dayo?" I asked, crying. "You said you loved him. You said you loved me!" I yelled.

64

"His name is *Abdullah*, and he is *my son*," he corrected me. "I am raising him, I am providing for him, and I love him. His dog of a father in India or Nigeria or Liberia or wherever he is, he is not a man," he said, spitting on the carpet next to him to convey his disgust.

"Does she know about me, your wife in Egypt?" I asked.

"Of course not," he answered. "I don't have any obligation to tell her, and I won't until and unless I believe it's necessary. But that doesn't matter," he continued, "We're talking about you and me now. Do you want a divorce? Or can you accept this situation?"

When I didn't respond, he asked again. "You gonna break up our family and go back to being homeless, all because I have a wife in Egypt? A wife I never see, a wife I spend maybe three weeks with each year? A wife you will never meet who doesn't affect your life at all? Huh? You wanna do that to me, to us—to Abdullah?" he asked, his voice becoming gentler now.

"I don't know what I want! But I don't trust you! You are a liar! How can I ever trust you again?!" I cried, the fear and the anger mixing with the bile in my throat.

And with that, he scoffed and stood up. Just as he was heading into the bedroom, he turned again. "Remember," he said, pointing at me, "if you die tonight and the angels take your soul, you will be thrown into the Hellfire because your husband is angry with you. We must remember that we are here to please God, and you please God by pleasing me," he said.

"Prophet Muhammad," he continued, "said that a woman who dies when her husband is happy with her will be given paradise, and I am very, very unhappy with you for your actions, so there is nowhere for you but Hell until you fix things between us and apologize for the way you talked to me."

With that, he walked into the bedroom, closing the door behind him.

* * *

New Year's came and went without fanfare and Ameer and I fell into an easy, comfortable routine. Of course, I hadn't forgotten what had happened, but for Dayo's sake—for the stability he deserved—I stayed.

Each morning, we made breakfast together, opened all the windows to let in the fresh air, and sat on the roof of the mosque, sipping tea and watching Dayo scoot around on his little bike. We often talked about his life back home, and about his childhood.

"When my father died," he said, "my mother was only twenty-five, and she was still beautiful. She had four children, though, and she knew how hard it would be for another man to love us as much as our dad did, so she refused to remarry."

That choice would prove to be fateful for the entire family, but none so much as Ameer. Suddenly, at sixteen, he found himself responsible for caring for his mother and three little sisters. His father's male relatives descended on them within weeks of the burial and began to portion off parts of his inherited land for themselves.

"It got so bad that me and my younger sister, Ihsan, decided to stand guard at one of the land markers they had been moving. I was taking karate classes at the time, so I taught her some basic moves and together, back-to-back, we fought off my cousins and uncles," he explained.

Learning so much about his childhood helped me understand some of his quirks better, and I wondered what else I would uncover in time.

* * *

A few weeks later, we still hadn't heard anything about what was holding up Ameer's Green Card, so he made an appointment with the immigration office in New Jersey. When I asked him what could be causing the delay, he was vague, insisting there was nothing to worry about and it would all be resolved soon.

I wasn't legally his wife, of course, so I had no right to go inside the building with him. Dayo slept in the backseat as I waited in the car, looking out across the cityscape and listening to the rain. I had some time to spare, so I decided to call Aishah again. We had seen one another several times since our first conversation, as she headed up the *halaqa* I attended in the basement of the *masjid*. I liked her more and more with time and felt I could trust her.

When I called, she picked up on the first ring, sounding out of breath. *"Wa alaykum salaam*, sister Kaighla!" she said cheerily. "Just finishing up my morning classes and headed to lunch. What's up?"

"I just... I need to know more about why you left Ameer," I said. "There is just something about him and his penchant for lying that makes me really nervous, and I want to know more."

She sighed heavily into the phone. "I... I really don't feel comfortable talking about it. It's like I said: I just felt like it was the best thing for myself and my daughters."

"But why can't you tell me more?" I asked, wondering why she was being so secretive. "I'm not asking you to bad-mouth him or something, *authu billah*—I seek refuge in God from Shaitan. I just need to understand more about his character and who he was before I met him."

"Listen, you're already married. If you'd come to me before marrying him, I'd have been obligated to tell you everything I could about his character, but it's not appropriate for me to talk about him now in a way that could create problems in your marriage," she said.

"Aha! So whatever the reason you left him, you're afraid if I knew, it would cause problems in our marriage, yes? Then aren't you supposed to tell me?!" I asked.

"No, no I am not. And I'm not saying it would. I'm saying God hates divorce, and it's not my place to cause friction between you and the sheikh, and all I can tell you is what I have: he just wasn't the right man for me."

Ameer came to the car just then, and I acted like I was talking to a friend back home. "What did they say?" I asked, hoping he'd brought good news. He was planning a trip to visit his family in Egypt soon and needed everything to be smoothed over, immigration-wise, beforehand.

"*Insha'Allah khair,*" he said, like he always did when he hadn't the slightest clue how things would work out, but didn't want to admit it.

"Ok then…" I said, stepping out of the driver's seat so he could drive us home.

* * *

That spring, Ameer went to Egypt to visit his family.

One morning, I woke up feeling woozy, so I took a pregnancy test, hoping against logic that I was pregnant. I had taken countless pregnancy tests in my young life, but it was the first time that I actually wanted the test to be positive, so it was a new sensation. When it blinked "Pregnant" after a mere 10 seconds, I couldn't believe it. I loaded Dayo up and walked to the Rite-Aid on Manhattan Avenue to buy another test. When I came back in the side door of the *masjid*, the phone in Ameer's office was ringing.

"*Asalaamu alaykum, ya habibti!*" he said. "Why are you out of breath? Is everything okay?"

"*Wa alaykum salaam.* Yes!" I beamed. "Things are great! Can you give me just a second? I need to use the bathroom," I said, running to the toilet to take the second test. When this one confirmed the result, I picked up the phone again.

"Ameer, I'm pregnant!" I cried happily.

"What? Really?! Are you sure?" he asked, sounding as thrilled as I was.

"Yes! I really am! I just came back from buying another test. That's why I was out of breath. And it's positive! We're going to have a baby!"

"Oh honey, this is the best news. *Wallahi* you have made my day! *Masha'Allah*, may God bless you, baby," he said. "Please, by Allah, don't tell anyone except your mom and sister. We don't want anyone giving us the Evil Eye in their jealousy."

Our excitement didn't last long, though. A few weeks later, Aishah and her new husband came to the mosque to deliver the letter she had received from USCIS.

Ameer was found out. The immigration office knew he hadn't ever actually legally divorced Shahida. He had committed marriage fraud in trying to get residency papers through his marriage to Aishah. Now, he had no right to stay in the States, and USCIS would soon begin deportation proceedings.

The same morning they came to deliver the message, Ameer called me to say he received the news from his lawyer and would be coming home right away.

"My best advice?" his lawyer said when we went to his office a few days later. "Run away. Move out of state and don't report your new address. They can't deport you if they can't find you."

A few months later, Ameer was offered a position as the sheikh of a new *masjid* and cultural center in Dearborn, Michigan. It was the perfect opportunity to make a little more money for our new addition—and to escape the American government for as long as we could.

6

The Brainwashing

Dearborn, Michigan

Summer 2010

Driving around Dearborn, Michigan felt like cruising on Muslim Mars. Every other store was Muslim-owned, and most restaurants had a *Halal*-certified sticker on their door. I saw more hijabi'd women than uncovered ones in our little neighborhood, so I finally felt somewhat at home in my skin for the first time since I began wearing hijab.

Before we'd even settled into the house we rented, we went to visit the mosque. Ameer sent me upstairs to the women's prayer area while he had a meeting with the mosque board downstairs in his new office.

When I went up to the women's prayer area, I was pleasantly surprised. I'd only ever been to a few mosques since I converted, and none had such a large, nicely-furnished area for sisters—if they had a women's prayer area at all, that is.

Even though Prophet Muhammad never ordered the genders to be segregated in the *masjid*—beyond a general admonition that women should pray behind men—the majority of mosques around the world keep men and women segregated in one way or another. Since Prophet Muhammad ordered all men to attend the Friday prayers in the *masjid*, but didn't give the same admonition to women, building resources are most often invested into creating serene, elegant prayer spaces for men while women are given whatever space is leftover—like corners, basements, and rooms not much larger than broom closets.

The *masjid* Ameer was hired to work for in Dearborn was newly built and, thank God, some women there had clearly advocated for themselves. I found a few sisters—mostly older women—sitting at the front of the room, discussing something or other in Arabic. They had Qur'an copies sitting open in front of them, so I assumed it was some sort of *halaqa* study group. When they saw me enter, they smiled and invited me to sit with them.

"*Asalaamu alaykum,*" they greeted me. "*Ahlan wa sahlan! Marhaba!*"

"*Wa alaykum salaam!* I'm sorry, but I don't speak Arabic," I replied, embarrassed. All the "new Muslim" books said I should have learned at least some basic Arabic by then.

"Oh, you are not Arab?" one of the younger ladies asked. "You are American then? You look Syrian."

"Ha! No. I'm just a white girl from Illinois," I responded, fidgeting with my *abaya*.

"Oh, *masha'Allah,*" she said, seeming less happy now to talk to me. "What brings you here then? We have a few converts, but not many," she said, the suspicion heavy in her voice.

"My husband is the new sheikh of this *masjid*," I explained.

Their eyes got large as the younger sister translated for the older ladies. "*Masha'Allah* sister!" she said, changing her tone immediately. "You are most welcome here!"

I sat with them as Dayo ran around in circles before finally sitting in my lap and sucking his thumb. They asked me all manner of personal questions about my life before Islam, and I answered them as best I could. Time seemed to rush by, and soon I heard Ameer calling to me from the top of the stairs.

During the car ride home, he seemed annoyed. "Let them think whatever they want about you, okay?" he said. "Don't tell them anything about you except what we agreed on: you have been Muslim three years now, and I am Abdullah's father. *Khalas*, that's all. Nothing more. They don't need to know anything at all about your family or background."

Ameer said it was my honor he was protecting, though I didn't care if they gossiped about me being odd. But every time we went to any gathering, I got the same lecture beforehand: "Don't share anything personal. Avoid questions about your education, age, and experiences. Pretty much don't talk about yourself at all, no matter how they dig."

He also constantly lectured me about not talking about our marital problems with anyone. He said telling anyone our business was tantamount to *gheebah*—backbiting, the punishment of which in Hell is to be forced to eat the literal flesh of the person you gossiped about.

By teaching me that it was *haraam* to tell my closest friends and family about what was happening in our marriage and home, the sheikh effectively cut me off from my support system—a key component in what was to come.

* * *

July 20th, 2010

We found out today that our baby will be a girl, and I can't believe it. I'm so sad, I don't even have words. Personally, I don't really care, but Ameer is so devastated, it makes me feel like a failure.

Last night, he was downstairs talking to Shahida and I forgot, so I sent Dayo down to get a toy he'd forgotten. When I realized it, I ran down the stairs myself to get him before he interrupted their call. Ameer didn't even mind him coming down, apparently, but was so angry that I'd come to get him.

I am feeling more and more fed up with his increasingly tense treatment of the multiple-wives situation.

We fought all morning, and we fought more when we dropped Dayo off at our friend Sadia's house. We were terse with each other as we walked into the doctor's office and sat down in the waiting room. Once in the exam room, it took all my willpower to bite my tongue as we sat waiting for the technician to finish getting her measurements. He wouldn't stop bothering her about the sex of the baby and it was so embarrassing.

"I understand you really want to know, but that's not the purpose of today's scan, sir," she finally told him. A few minutes later, though, she turned the screen around so we could see it. "That's your baby daughter," she said. "It's a girl."

Ameer's face went white and he stood up, put his jacket

on, and told me to get dressed. He is usually really nice to doctors, but he didn't even tell her "thank you" or "goodbye."

I can't believe this. I know how badly he wants a boy, a brother for his son, Khalid. I mean, he has Dayo, sort of, but not really. Ameer is so worried Khalid will be in the same position he was when his dad died.

So then just now, after he climbed into bed, I tried to kiss him and he pecked me on the cheek before sighing, rolling over, and saying, "Next time it will be a boy, insha'Allah.*"*

* * *

Our life in Dearborn was wonderful, in so many ways. Aside from all the *halal* eateries and the many hijabi'd women that made me feel less out of place, it was the first time in my life I'd lived so financially well. We were not rich, by any means, and Ameer was still sending upwards of $1,000 a month to Egypt, but we were comfortable. More than this, I'd made some convert friends for the first time.

There was Sherry: a convert who, at that point, had only just informed her parents of her choice to convert, and who was forced to pray in secret lest her alcoholic father interrupt and tear her hijab off. There were also a few Arab ladies I enjoyed spending time with, who taught me how to make food from their parents' home countries, and helped me navigate the strange dynamics of the predominantly Yemeni and Palestinian community at our mosque.

My best friend in Dearborn was Jamilah. She was an African-American convert of ten years or so, and she was a single mom. She and her ex-husband had converted together in college, and she was now raising their five children largely on her own. They visited their dad, but she had the bulk of the parenting and financing responsibilities.

She and her kids lived in a beautiful home half an hour's drive from our house. She even had her own prayer room, full of the books she'd collected during her time as a Muslim, as well as an impressive collection of Islamic art she'd purchased on her travels to Turkey and Morocco. We often prayed there together with the elder kids while the younger ones ran around the house.

Jamilah was, without question, my first *real Muslim friend*, and being with Jamilah was fun, relaxing, and beneficial to us both. I enjoyed listening to all her stories, but some were less-than-happy. Not only did she have to deal with the same bigotry I did in the world—thanks to hijab—but she had the more pervasive issues that accompanied being a black woman in America. But she was proud to be a Muslim and equally proud to be a black American woman, and it never seemed like those aspects of her personality conflicted with one another.

"You need to read some more books, Kaighla," she'd say when I spouted off something Ameer had said that rubbed me the wrong way. "I mean, he's the sheikh, yeah, but... I dunno. I think you should read more," is all she'd say. Of course, I didn't tell Ameer when she seemed to disagree with him on something he'd told me, or else he would have tried to stop me from spending time with her.

In the mosque, Jamilah seemed comfortable, cool, and collected. Unlike me, she didn't seem to feel out of place at all. She was able to manage herself and her kids, all while being courteous and respectful to the older Arab women in the mosque. They called it a "mosque and cultural center" and made a point to have lots of interfaith and larger community gatherings in our pocket of Dearborn, and Jamilah and I spent as much time together at those events as possible.

Watching Jamilah was both inspiring and intimidating. I wondered how she had developed such a proud, unshaken identity in a world where if she wasn't being discriminated against for being black, she was facing backlash for being Muslim. But her world felt like a million light years away from mine. I was constantly being reprimanded for being too American, too "western," too "free," so I was never able to fully settle into my identity as a Muslim American.

* * *

One evening that fall, Ameer and I went out to dinner at our favorite *halal* American diner—yes! Glory of Glories, there was such a thing in Dearbornistan!—while Dayo hung out with Jamilah and her kids.

As we waited for our food to arrive, we got into a discussion about how each of us would feel if one of our kids grew up and decided they didn't want to be Muslim.

"I'd love them anyway," I said. "You can't make someone love God, after all, and the Qur'an says 'There is no compulsion in religion.'"

Without flinching, he said, "No, I would kill them. I would kill any of my children who tried to leave Islam," and continued eating his burger as if we were simply discussing the weather.

I was very pregnant with his child, and he had no qualms admitting he would kill her if she wanted to apostate.

That conversation—and the fact that I was being forced to lie about my entire past and the parentage of my son—caused a deep resentment to grow in my belly.

We also fought more than before, too. He was never home, always busy in the mosque, always helping everyone else—never with me and Dayo. He said it was the sacrifice we had to make to be honored by the community.

"Allah chose me to be the leader of the people, and that means doing everything I can to help them, anytime, day or night," he would say. "You need to stop being so selfish."

Selfish. That was a common theme. I—his very pregnant wife—was *selfish* if I wanted my husband home sometimes, or if I wanted us to have some time with him before our new baby was born. I needed to work harder on killing my *nafs*—my inner, sinful self—if I had any hope of gaining Paradise, he'd say.

And yet the anger was growing in me. The more I saw him behaving in public as a kind, caring man, and in our home as a domineering overlord, the more I lost respect for him, and it was getting harder and harder to fake it.

* * *

October 14th, 2010

> *Last night, after I got Dayo down to sleep, I was sitting in the office sewing a cloth diaper for Sajidah—stockpiling before she's born—while Ameer sat in the lounge chair reading in preparation for his* khutba.
>
> *I read something yesterday from a blog I was following, all about a Muslim woman's right to her own religious opinions, regardless of how her husband feels. So I asked*

Ameer what he thought, and he told me that a woman should have the same religious opinions as her husband to prevent arguments in the household. He said that even if he were a normal guy, I should follow his school of thought, but since he is a sheikh, I really should.

"We need to show solidarity to the people, set a good example of a strong marriage," he said.

I vehemently disagreed. "So, what? Only men can have opinions? Women should just drop their brains at the marriage table? No thank you, sir," I laughed.

But he didn't think it was funny. "Don't laugh at me," he replied. "I am serious. You cannot be telling women it's okay for them to argue with their husbands, or to have different religious opinions. The husband is the head of the house. Why can't you understand that? You're the wife of the sheikh, Kaighla. You should know better."

I was frustrated and felt tired of his endless rules. "Yeah well... maybe if you cared more about what goes on in your own house than what happens in their marriages, you'd be better informed about what your wife thinks and feels..." I popped off.

In a flash, he stood up, walked toward me, slammed my office chair against the wall, and held my shoulders back against the chair, squeezing hard. "I am your husband and you will not speak to me like that. Do you understand me?" he asked in a calm voice, tightening his grip on me.

I was too terrified to cry and too stubborn to admit defeat, so I simply sat staring at him, wide-eyed. He finally let me go, looking down at my burgeoning belly, holding his daughter. Then he casually sat back down to read.

I'm just grateful Dayo was asleep.

***

It's not every week you give birth, nearly die, and then get into a serious car accident.

Sajidah was born just after midnight on Christmas day, which was both funny and odd on so many levels. People forever after would hear her birthday—like at doctor's offices and school registrations—and be all "Oohh!! A Christmas baby! Lucky you!" and Saji would just stare at them blankly.

But laboring and giving birth in a heavily-Muslim community during Christmas meant everyone in the room—from the midwife to the nurses and the orderlies—was Muslim. Everyone else was off-call, after all.

At one point during the worst of my labor, I passed through a pretty rough contraction and turned to see Ameer recording me.

"WILL YOU PUT THAT DAMNED CAMERA AWAY?!" I shouted.

Two nurses looked into the curtained-off area, apparently to see how my husband, the sheikh, would react. No wonder, because just as soon as they turned back around, he looked right at me and made one of the most frightening faces I had ever seen him make.

To try to lighten the mood, I quipped, "Hey, one day you'll be in a load of pain and I will pull out my camera to record you! Maybe then you'll know how I feel!"

That made him chuckle a bit, and I even heard an Arab orderly snickering as she changed out the garbage in the attached bathroom.

A few hours later, the pain was beginning to be unbearable. Just like with Dayo, they induced my labor because she was "measuring large," and now I needed more chemicals to cope with the pain my body's natural mechanisms should have been soothing. It was the classic "Pitocin-Epidural-Cesarean Cycle" happening in real time, and I hoped I could beat the odds once more when they came around to give the spinal epidural.

But after sitting stark still for ten minutes while the anesthesiologist inserted a long, hollow needle into my spine—and I was contracting every 2 minutes—he finished up, primed the pump and... *nothing happened.* I could still feel everything, but now my legs and hips were too weak to walk or stand, making labor all that much harder without the benefit of gravity and pain relief.

Things began to go south when her heart rate started to spike and fall rapidly with every contraction. Thankfully, my midwife had the experience to suggest I get onto my hands and knees, with two nurses and Ameer supporting me on both sides so I wouldn't topple over.

Right around midnight, our first baby was born. We named her Sajidah, meaning "the one who prays," in the hope that she would be a devoted worshipper of God. Because of her difficult labor, she was born with a reddish-pink birthmark on her forehead that looked very much like the dark mark some people develop from prostrating on their prayer rugs so often—a signal they're devout. It was all too perfect. She was jaundiced and would need to be placed under the phototherapy lights, but was otherwise healthy.

The same could not be said of me. I was hemorrhaging out of control. In an instant, two nurses came alongside me and popped two Pitocin shots, one on each side, deep into my thighs. Just after that, someone snapped a picture of Ameer holding Sajidah, smiling from ear-to-ear. Just to the left of him in the photo, over his right shoulder, there was a mountain of bloody towels and utensils.

* * *

The next four days were a blur as we had to leave Sajidah at the hospital to receive phototherapy until her Bilirubin levels dropped to a healthy level. I tried to sleep but kept waking up every few hours to call the hospital and check on her. During the day, we would sit in the nursery with her, watching her, kissing her hands, and wishing we could hold her. I was pumping milk to get my supply going, and it hurt not to be able to nurse her.

Finally, on the fourth night, they released her and bundled us into our van. As we exited the hospital, we entered the ramp to the freeway, but because it was rush hour and there had been a recent blizzard, traffic was backed up, so we had to wait at the bottom of the entry ramp for a chance to inch into the flow of traffic.

Suddenly, I felt our van lurch forward, out of control, and slam into the right side barrier. The impact threw me hard against the back of Ameer's seat. When we came to an abrupt stop, Ameer was moaning, and it felt like someone had bashed my upper chest with a crowbar. Sajidah, in her car seat next to me, had screamed out at the point of impact and then didn't make another sound.

I tried not to move too much, knowing it was likely I could have injured my spine, but I was reaching for the overhead light so I could check on Saji. My seatbelt was jammed, though, so reaching with all my might, I still couldn't turn on the light.

"Kaighla, *habibti*, are you okay?" Ameer said then, his voice raspy, as if he were holding back, trying to save his energy.

"Oh my God, Ameer! Yes! I'm okay. Are you okay? Does anything hurt?" I cried, reaching my arms around to touch his shoulder.

"*Insha'Allah khair*," he said. "My neck and my back hurt so much. But stop moving, okay? You may hurt yourself."

"No, no, *wallahi*, I'm fine," I cried. "My chest hurts, but I'm okay. But Sajidah isn't crying or making any sounds. I can't see her or hear her breathing. Oh God, please let her be okay!"

Thankfully, a nurse just finishing her shift had been behind the car that rear-ended us, and she saw the whole thing. Having first checked on the driver that hit us, who was unharmed, she ran around to the passenger side of the van and yanked it open. "Is everyone okay?" she asked, turning on a flashlight she had taken with her when she jumped out of her car. She shined the light up, so as to not blind us.

"My husband has hurt his back and neck pretty badly, but I am okay. Please, check on our baby! She's… she's not making any noise at all!" I cried.

The nurse placed her hand on my arm and guided my hand to Sajidah's little chest, which was moving up and down, slowly. She was asleep, miraculously.

The ambulance pulled around then and the paramedics carefully situated Ameer onto the gurney before wheeling him into the ambulance. Sajidah and I rode in the back next to him.

Two hours later, after they'd checked out both Sajidah and me and declared we both were just fine, albeit shocked, the news came about Ameer: he'd broken his neck and fractured his back in two places.

As he lay there in the hospital room—just two floors down from the one I labored in less than a week ago—I pulled out my phone and began recording. "So, Sheikh Ameer… it looks like you're in quite a bit of pain," I laughed. "You have anything to say?"

He laughed loudly then, a big belly laugh, but that hurt his back, so he tried to stifle it. "Ohhhh *ya baqarah!* You think you're so funny, eh? Your husband is in pain and you're having fun?" he laughed, taking my hand in one of his and kissing it. "I love you so much, and I love our babies."

Sajidah was asleep, having woken up briefly to nurse and then fallen back into a deep slumber again. I was so thankful Dayo had stayed behind at Jamilah's house. Who knows what would have happened to him if he had been with us.

That experience—giving birth to my daughter with him beside me and then being in the car accident right after—seemed to solidify our bond. I began to love him more deeply, even as I struggled with his abuse and my own identity crisis.

For the level of disappointment he felt over her being a girl when I was still pregnant, Ameer was absolutely taken with Sajidah from the moment she was born. They had so much in common, from their welcoming smiles to their distinctly Egyptian noses, and from that point on, they were inseparable.

* * *

May 10th, 2011

> *It's been a year since we moved to Dearborn, and I never want to leave this house. I am standing in my kitchen looking out the window into the backyard. There are four beautiful trees which previously had charming white and pink blossoms covering them. Now big green leaves have*

taken their place. Ameer says they are cherry and apple trees, but that is yet to be seen. There is also a cement patio with a trellis overhead, covered in grapevines with big leaves which will soon be used for cooking mah'shi, but for now, they're shading the patio beneath.

My favorite room in the house is our shared office on the main floor, next to the bathroom. Never in my wildest dreams did I imagine I would get to live in a house with more than one bathroom, let alone an entire room dedicated to study and peace and quiet! But Ameer demands it. He says he can't live in a house without a private place to go study his many fiqh and hadith books.

When Saji was born last December, the fridge was stuffed with food. After everyone heard about the sheikh's new baby, they came rushing over to see her and to bring us food. But it wasn't really about her being born. Sure, maybe they would have come one or two days and offered to help me if that were the case. Maybe I'd have had a few containers of food in the fridge. But when they heard about the accident on the way home from the hospital that broke both Ameer's back and his neck, that's when their floodgates of mercy opened wide.

The people in our mosque treat me like an honored guest, though, of course, they only treat me that way because I am the wife of Sheikh Ameer. It's got nothing to do with me as a person. None of them have any idea that I was a real person once. They have no clue that I really and truly lived once. It seems like in their eyes, I was born into the world fully-grown on the day I became Muslim, and all else before that moment can burn.

Then, I have to lie about how long I have been Muslim.

The irony! But the only way people will believe Dayo is his son is if I say I converted to Islam long before he was born. Because of course the sheikh would never have committed fornication, and certainly never would have married a Christian.

The Qur'an is very clear that we should call people by the names their fathers gave them, their family names. Lying about paternity is a pretty serious sin, but Ameer says I misunderstand the verse.

"I am not legally claiming he is my son. That would be outright haraam. *But for the everyday people around us, it's no one's business, so it's okay for me to say he is my son, and he is. I love him with all my heart. He was only a baby when we married and his worthless dog father will never meet him or even support him, so I am the only father he has," he says.*

So now he thinks God cares if Muslims respect the "laws of the kaafirs," *but he didn't when we married and he said we didn't need to make it legally official...*

I hate him for making me lie. I can't get mom's voice out of my head. I remember sitting with her on the front porch of our house, listening to the rain falling and watching the cars speed by. I see her in my mind, sitting there next to me with a glass of sweet tea, smoking cigarette after cigarette.

"Kaighla Dawn, listen to me," she'd say, taking a drag off her cigarette. "Men will take every chance they can to take advantage of you if you let 'em. Don't you ever let a man tell you what to do."

Aside from never letting men control me, she taught me that lying is the most serious sin of all. "If you get comfortable with lying, honey, you get comfortable with being somebody you're not, and that brings a whole slew of problems where problems don't need to be," she'd say.

And here, now, I am absolutely letting a man control me, and I'm lying to everyone, acting like someone I am not.

I am the sheikh's wife, so more is expected of me, Ameer says. "You must strive to be like the wives of the Prophet," he says. "You're not like other women. You're honored among women for being chosen to be a sheikh's wife," he says. "God is pleased with you when you change yourself in order to please me. It's a woman's greatest jihad to willingly change the things about herself that shame her husband's reputation."

I hate him for forcing me to kill the deepest parts of me. I hate him for making me lie. But most of all, I hate him for making me change my son's name. He wasn't there when I was alone in that shit-hole town, leaving my terrible bill-collecting job every day and going straight to the bookstore, looking through each and every single baby name book they had, searching for the perfect name for my boy. I was bound and determined that my son would have a beautiful, powerful name with a deep meaning.

When I came across it, I knew it was for my son: Ekundayo, meaning "my sorrow has become joy." I cried when I read it and that was it. My son would be Dayo, my proof that joy does, indeed, come after sorrow.

And now he doesn't even answer to that name. He is Abdullah, the handsome son of Sheikh Ameer, running everywhere in the mosque and crying to anyone who will listen and give him candy and ice cream.

I think the problem is expectations. Ameer imagined I was a fresh, vibrant new Muslim, a nice addition to his life *of dry, boring old ideas. He imagined I would be eager to please him, and that I would stop at nothing to make him happy. I think he hoped I would be an updated version of his first American wife; younger, fresher, more refined, with one less child, and that one child a baby boy.*

He never anticipated me in all my Kaighla-ness. I am nearly the furthest thing in his mind from what a woman should be, let alone a good, modest Muslim woman. Sure, I wear hijab. I pray—thank God—most of the time. But when it comes to the everyday manners of a good Muslim woman—her countenance, the way she carries herself—I am surprisingly disappointing. To be fair, though, I have only been a Muslim for less than two years.

It feels like every time I turn around, there's a new rule he has for me to follow, and he always has daleel *to justify his bogus rules. I want to be a Muslim. I want to serve God and obey the messenger of God, and I want to have peace in my heart because of this. But I don't have peace, because 99% of my time and energy is taken up struggling with my identity as an American among Arabs. I miss the days when all I wanted to be was a good Muslim—when I laid awake at night feeling insufficient as a Muslim rather than as a wife, just because I'm not Arab enough.*

I want to be loved and appreciated by my new community for who I really am, flaws and all. No one has the right to know my sins, for sure. But my past, my experiences—these make me who I am! I am tired of lying about myself, about how long I've been Muslim, about my family and such, about my son and his parentage, and about my life. I am tired of having to keep track of who I have lied to and what about. I can't even tell Jamilah the truth, though I think she probably suspects it.

My name is not Um Abdullah. I have a real name, and so does my son. I am Kaighla, and he is Dayo. I am more than my son's mother, and I am more than my husband's wife.

Some days, honest to God, I wish I knew half of what I know now before I converted, not because I would not have converted if I did, but at least exploring the questions and the fears would not have the terrifying fear of committing some big sin attached as it does now. At least back then I was neither Christian nor Muslim and any information I received about either religion was absorbed and considered without bias. Now I am only allowed to consider some options and some viewpoints for fear of shirk—giving partners to God—which is the only unforgivable sin if you die doing it.

* * *

The day I found out I was pregnant again, Sajidah was only seven months old. She had just cut her first tooth and was whiny and miserable. I felt strange and off-balance, but my period wasn't even late. I happened to have a pregnancy test in the medicine cabinet, so I took it, and when the result came back positive, I spent the entire day crying, wringing my hands, and trying to find any way out of it. Not that I would have considered abortion, truly, but I did entertain the idea of taking the kids and running away from Ameer. The last thing I needed was one more rope binding me to him.

Ameer came home that night to find me sitting in my usual

place in the living room, looking at my computer. My eyes were all puffed up and red. Worried, he asked me what on earth could be wrong.

"I'm pregnant! Again!" I cried. "And I don't want to be! I don't want to be pregnant again! Saji is still a baby!"

He was surprisingly calm, considering what I'd said, and he listened and held me while I cried. "I know, honey. I really understand. Saji is so young still. I know it will be hard for you. But I will help you. Let's try to see this as the blessing it is. Maybe God will give us a son this time!" he said, eyes beaming, trying to comfort me.

That was his plan: to keep me perpetually pregnant until I finally produced the son he needed. Already I had been unable to fast two Ramadans in a row because of pregnancy and nursing. Now I'd be adding another, maybe two more Ramadans to that list.

* * *

I loved our home and the comfortable life we enjoyed, but I couldn't relax fully into it. I wanted to plant flowers and paint the walls, but I held off because it felt futile to decorate a home I knew wasn't truly mine. I knew that Ameer and I would be forced to give up the life and home we enjoyed one day, sooner or later. Moving to Dearborn would not protect him from the All-Seeing Eye that is the American government forever; we both knew that it was only a matter of time before we would receive a letter saying his deportation hearing had been scheduled.

I began to think we should voluntarily leave the country. In my mind, it was better to willingly give up our comfortable home, our friends, and the average American life we were enjoying than to have it torn from us whenever the government decided to evict us. As I had done so many times before in my life, I elected to give up what I loved, in my own time, rather than let someone tear it away from me without notice.

Beyond this, a thought began to take root deep within me that God would not bless us or our marriage, no matter how much I prayed. I felt sure He would allow pain and suffering to come our way, and it was all Ameer's fault. He was the one, after all, with two wives he wasn't being fair to; he was the one who would face God on Judgment Day with half his body paralyzed because he did not give his first wife her marital rights, or so the *hadith* says.

At that point, his family in Egypt knew about me and our kids, but he kept us from ever speaking to one another and insisted on calling them only when he was outside or else far from where they could hear me or the kids. I had never spoken to his wife, Shahida, and I didn't necessarily want to, but I was a woman and she was a woman, and I knew how I would feel if my husband had a secret wife he intentionally worked to keep from me for months.

When I first found out about the fake divorce, all I thought about was how she would affect my life or not. I didn't care about her or her kids, and I didn't know anything about what God expects of a man with more than one wife. But as time went on and my faith in God increased, and as I read more and more, I came to understand the seriousness of what Ameer was doing to her in leaving her there alone with all those kids. She was without care and affection for eleven months of the year, and that could definitely not be okay with God.

Even before I was Muslim, I knew that God was just and good, and He loved justice and goodness. I believed that God blessed those who chose to pursue the most just path and that God allowed those who chose to participate in or support injustice to stumble and suffer. And so, the thought began to take hold of me that if we wanted God to bless our life together, I couldn't keep living comfortably with my husband, acting like there was nothing amiss. I would surely be held accountable before God for being complicit in Ameer's treatment of his other wife if I didn't at least speak my mind.

Prophet Muhammad taught us to change injustice with our hands if we could, with our words if not, and to hate it with all of our hearts if we couldn't even speak against it. So, I did what I could do: I told my husband that I thought if we really wanted a good, blessed life, he must be fair to his other wife; we must move to Egypt.

Of course, he fought me on it. He hated Egypt and told me he didn't love his wife. He refused to go and said it wouldn't be like I imagined. "It will be hard, and the people are closed-minded. It will be too hot all summer, and too cold all winter," he said.

"But," I asked, "isn't it worth all that to know we are pleasing God and earning His favor? Would you sacrifice the happiness of your *akhirah,* your afterlife, for the love of this temporary world, this *dunya, ya* sheikh?"

He laughed at me then. "Kaighla, it's totally fine, Islamically, to leave her there like this. She has happily and readily accepted the situation for what it is. Yeah, she has to give up her right to time with me and her sexual needs being met, but she is patient and she understands that I have to be here if I am to provide all that money they enjoy. Plus, she knows I will always come back to visit. She is okay with it, I promise," he said.

But I didn't buy it for a second. What sane woman would

willingly leave her husband in a place like America, knowing he was sleeping with another woman, all year long—just for money? *No,* I thought, *he must have coerced her, just like he coerces me, and I won't stand for it.* Prophet Muhammad said someone will never be a true believer until he or she wants for his or her fellow Muslims the same happiness and blessings he or she wants for himself or herself. I didn't know Shahida, but she was a human being and my sister in Islam, regardless of who she was as a person, and I wanted her to have her rights and to have the same sense of normalcy that I enjoyed.

Within a few months, we'd begun making plans to move to Egypt, and announced it to the *masjid.* There was no backing out now. My fate was sealed.

* * *

The closer we came to moving day, the more uncomfortable I became. I knew we were doing the right thing—and the inevitable thing, after all—but I was beginning to have second thoughts.

One afternoon, Ameer and I got into a pretty big argument about the fears I was having, so I decided it was time to go visit my family, to get a break from things. The more time I spent away from Ameer, the more I began to feel a deep inner resistance to not only the idea of going with him to Egypt but also of remaining married to him at all. I spent a few days with the kids at my mom's house, but I still felt out of place and strange, with my massive black abaya and my swooping hijabs.

I saw clearly that I couldn't stay with my mom long term—primarily because she was of the opinion that one should do anything and everything to provide for one's children, including removing my hijab and lying about my religion—so I did the only thing I could think to do: I loaded up the kids and drove three hours north to the boarding school to speak with Maulana Siraaj. Thankfully, he wasn't busy and invited me and the kids right in.

"*Asalaamu alaykum*, sister!" he said, not looking directly at me, but focusing his attention on Dayo. "*Salaam*, Dayo! You remember me?"

Dayo looked at him perplexed, having forgotten him entirely. "My name is Abdullah," he said.

The Maulana smiled awkwardly and offered him a lollipop as I sat down in the chair in front of his desk. "How can I help you? Is everything okay? How is the sheikh? Congratulations on your new baby!" he said, smiling.

"He's... the sheikh is fine. He's in Dearborn, getting ready to go to Hajj," I said, but the tears started falling before I could continue. "I am sorry to surprise you like this, but I didn't have anywhere else to turn and I am scared."

"Yes, I'm sorry to hear about your situation," he said, seeming genuinely worried for me. "Mariam's father told me a little about your marriage problems. It's a shame, really," he said, handing me a box of tissues.

"Yes, it is. I was tricked. The sheikh is not the man we thought he was, and now we are moving to Egypt because of his choices. I feel a terrible, deep certainty that things will not go well. And the worst part is that it was my idea! I'm the one who convinced him to move back there so he could be fair to his first wife," I replied, drying the corners of my eyes.

"We will make *du'a* for you and your family, including Abdullah and your little girl here," he said, gesturing to Sajidah.

"Please, brother. Please help us. I know you don't owe us

anything, but if you know of any way I can get out of this marriage, please help me," I said, giving up on my hopes that he would pick up the clues I was dropping.

He sat in his chair now, looking out the window of his office at the darkening sky, and sighed. "I wish we could help you, sister, but unfortunately, we just don't have any way to help. When you lived here before, it was just you and Dayo, but now you have this little one, too, and we don't have any openings for teachers," he said.

"Well, I'm pregnant again, too," I added, for good measure.

He sighed again and then smiled in my general direction. "I believe the best thing for you and your children is to go to Egypt with your husband. Just be patient and make *du'a* that Allah will protect you all," he said. "And you are doing the right thing in supporting your husband to be fair to his other wife. Rest assured God is with you."

Now, I actually began to full-on cry. I wouldn't shame myself further by asking for help again, but it took all my might to walk calmly to my car, turn the ignition, and drive back to Dearborn.

* * *

October 12th, 2011

> *Ameer has been gone for two weeks. He went first to visit his family in Egypt, then he's going to the* Hajj *before he goes back to Egypt to get an apartment ready for us. He left me here alone to pack everything up and finish the lease. It's so hard managing it all alone with two kids, and pregnant.*

Today I met an American convert from Maine. Sara has six kids, from the age of twelve on down to a one-year-old baby. Her husband apparently splits his time three ways between her, his wife in Egypt, and his new Russian wife in Brooklyn.

When she married her husband, he wasn't even practicing. They fell in love when she was only nineteen years old and got married soon after. Islam didn't even become a thing for them until a few years later when he began practicing pretty sincerely. The way she describes her husband, he is an angry man and religion has only made him angrier.

A few years later, she converted to Islam of her own accord and they put their eldest kids in with a Qur'an teacher who was later deported back to Egypt. When that happened, they made the life-changing decision to follow the Qur'an teacher to his small city in Egypt so their kids could continue to learn under him.

Someone from the mosque heard we were moving to Egypt and suggested I meet Sara. Her house was chilly—almost as cold as it was outside—and she had no furniture at all. She said her husband didn't send money very often because his international shipping business was suffering, and because of his multiples wives and children.

As we drank tea, I told her a little about myself and my situation. She listened as her children ran circles around us, her eldest bringing more tea and more snacks. I told her of our plan to move, and how it was my idea because I really wanted God's blessing in our lives and in our marriage. She listened politely, though it became apparent she was uncomfortable.

"So, how did you like Egypt? Were you happy?" I asked

her, casually—this woman whom I had never met.

"I hated it," she said, tears filling her eyes and falling down her cheeks. "Every day of my life, for four years, was hard and painful, and I felt very, very alone."

What could I say? The thoughts were circling around in my head, and my ears were buzzing. It felt too perfect to be coincidence, me meeting her like this, mere weeks before we're supposed to leave. "Wow. That bad?" I asked as I handed her tissues.

She said it really was that bad, and that things got ten times worse when he married his Egyptian wife. She had been the kids' Arabic tutor and had been courting him right under her nose. One day, with the Arabic tutor-cum-wife sitting there all innocent and doe-eyed, he told Sara that they were married now.

"She was his world after that. It was all about her family and her needs, her world," she said. "Everything was about making sure he didn't do wrong to his sheikh's only daughter."

She saw how I was beginning to worry and tried to reassure me that my experience probably wouldn't be anything like hers.

"I'm not trying to scare you! Sorry I got so emotional. It was just a really hard time for us. But I know several sisters who have had very positive experiences in Egypt! Don't worry. Insha'Allah khair," she said.

But I can't shake her words or her face from my mind, try as I may. I've been watching "Sister Wives" episodes lately, trying to remind myself that there really are people practicing polygyny who are not miserable.

Shahida and I don't have to be miserable, either. Ameer

says she isn't exactly thrilled that we're coming, but she is happy to have her husband back and she is very willing to help me adjust to my new life.

With all my heart, I want the best. I just want the best for all of us, for her kids and my kids—our family, our combined family. The wives of the sheikh, the mothers of his sons, Insha'Allah, *if this baby is a boy.*

7

The Silent Treatment

Sharqia Governorate, Egypt

Winter 2011

The most shocking part of living in Egypt: finding out that roosters don't just crow at dawn. It turns out that roosters everywhere crow whenever they feel like it, apparently, but I had never lived among them before.

Then, for the first few weeks, I was convinced ambulances and police cars were constantly on the run, their sirens waking me in the middle of the night, every night. But when I asked Ameer how there could be so much crime in such a small town, he laughed. "Those are not sirens, *hayati*, they're *tuk-tuk* horns!" he said.

In true Egyptian-boy style, those teenagers thought it was funny to use American-sounding emergency sirens as the horns on their *tuk-tuks*—a sort of motorcycle with a covered buggy attached, like mini-taxis for getting around town. They'd blast their horns at all hours of the night, as a sort of signal to potential customers that they were in the area and available. Good Muslim boys on their way to the mosque blared 50 Cent and Eminem, shouting out the filthy words of English songs they didn't understand.

The first time I went to Ameer's mother's house, I was struck by the size and splendor of it. A full two stories of solid rock and concrete, it was beautifully designed in the Baroque style, with marble columns twisting up around themselves. There were three massive balconies on the front of the house and a trellis above the front courtyard. A massive iron gate stood in front, connected to eight-foot walls of concrete and brick that protected the house from burglars, and the women from onlookers.

Like many of the other buildings in town, there were tall, thick iron stability wires sticking out of the columns in the top floor, waiting to be added to when they had the money to finish building the third floor of the house. Looking out across the horizon, it looked like the entire upper third of the homes in our area had been blown off by some sort of explosion, leaving only the bottom two floors in-tact, and these stability poles in place.

Inside, there were three bedrooms on the first floor, as well as two living room areas and a kitchen, and the second floor had another three bedrooms, two bathrooms, a second kitchen, and two more living room areas, the floor-plan mirroring the first floor almost exactly, except for the extended balcony areas off of the front two bedrooms and living room.

The house, like many in upper-middle-class rural Egypt, was decorated in a gaudy, French-inspired style. There were fake plants and vines everywhere, and frilly, excessively feminine curtains and couch pillows. It looked like either a very, very poor French noblemen and his family, or else a very, very wealthy wannabe-French family, lived there. It was nauseating for me, but they were clearly proud of themselves and their "super lux" style, as they called it.

More than the overall scale and grandeur of the house, I was surprised by what I saw when I first walked into the first-floor *salon*: a giant, 4'x2' portrait of Ameer, hanging on the wall just above the couch.

The real Ameer sat down under his portrait like a king on his throne, sending his children, wife, and mother scurrying this way and that to bring him water, coffee, tea, snacks, and more. Suddenly his name made a bit of poetic sense—he was clearly the *ameer* of his home, the regal prince, and all hustled to do his bidding.

* * *

Ameer took me one day to buy *abayas,* and Shahida and his mother—whom everyone called either Mama Bushra, or *Hajja,* depending on if they were family or not—insisted on coming along to help us haggle prices. In the car on the way to the center of the city, the *medina,* Mama Bushra was shouting at Ameer, her rapid-fire Arabic interspersed with sad gasps and sighs.

It amazed me that Egyptian women didn't collapse and die from heart attacks daily as much as they screamed about literally everything. Happy, sad, whatever—they never seemed to speak at a normal volume, so it was impossible to detect anger. My nerves were constantly on edge from the noise level.

Considering how much Ameer had lectured me on the proper way for a Muslim woman to behave, I found their behavior confusing.

When we parked, he told me what they were arguing about: me, covering my face. His mom insisted that I begin wearing *niqab* immediately, saying displaying even a tiny portion of my white skin was "just an invitation for men to flirt with me." We had actually discussed the topic before we left Michigan, and I wasn't against it. *How can being more modest be a bad thing? I thought. How can copying the wives of Prophet Muhammad be a bad idea?*

As we were driving home from the market, *niqabs* and *abayas* in hand, Shahida noticed my arms sticking out from my *abaya* and ran her hand along my skin, saying something in Arabic with a look of disgust on her face.

I didn't understand her and smiled uncomfortably.

"She's asking why you don't shave your arms," Ameer translated, looking at us both in the rearview mirror.

"My arms?" I asked, surprised.

She spoke again, pointing at the baby-fine down that grows on the sides of my face.

"She says you should shave that too," he said.

"But why?" I asked again.

"She said 'Ameer hates it, so you should remove it for him,'" he laughed. "I don't really care, though. You know that," he reassured me.

Why does she care if our husband likes the way I look? I wondered. I'd soon learn just how much she enjoyed "advising" me on ways to please Ameer, intended more to shame me than to sincerely help.

* * *

I initially felt ambivalent about Shahida. It was as if she was just another of his family members. It hadn't sunk in yet that she was also his wife, and I didn't feel jealous, probably because Ameer had always been adamant with me that he did not love Shahida. He told me that they married each other just to please his mom. He was in love with a different cousin, from his mom's side, but she refused to allow them to marry over some petty family squabble. But she saw it was time for Ameer to be wed, so she convinced him to marry Shahida—his great-uncle's daughter.

They were initially good together, he said, but over time, her lack of religious devotion or interest in learning more, as well as her total lack of interest in pleasing him in the bedroom, made things sour between them.

So, when we arrived in Egypt, I believed the time he spent with her was a duty for him—both conjugal and otherwise.

"I am not going there because I want to, baby. And don't think about it like that. I have to sleep with her because it is her right, but I swear to you I have never enjoyed being with her, and I never will," he said, holding my hands in his on the first night he left me alone in Egypt to be with her. "Girls from good Muslim families here are taught from a young age that sex is dirty and bad, so they never learn to enjoy it, even when they get married. I love being with you because I love watching you enjoy yourself with me," he said, nibbling on my neck.

I was sure it had more to do with what they *didn't* teach good, well-behaved Muslim boys in Egypt: how to please their women. Oh and... their unfortunate tradition of snipping off part of a girl's clitoris when she's just completed puberty; that seemed to be a pretty effective means of ensuring she doesn't enjoy herself in bed.

* * *

Mama Bushra was an incredibly strong and intimidating woman. She towered over me and was almost twice my size in girth, too. Her laugh was loud, her anger was hot, and her love was overwhelming in its unwavering magnitude. One minute she was throwing her sandals at a kid's head and calling them an *ibn al kalb*—literally, "son of a bitch"—and the next she was rubbing the spot with her hand and shushing their cries.

She had been a very beautiful woman in her youth, and everyone in Ameer's ancestral village remembered it. Like many girls in her village in the late 1960s, she was married off to Ameer's father when she was only fourteen years old and he was fifty-seven, and then she had to raise four kids alone when he died less than ten years later.

Over time, as she grew older and her children married and moved out, she came to be a respected elder in her community—a *Hajja*. Her home was always open to the neighbor kids, and her love and anger were dished out equally, regardless of their parentage.

I wanted so much to impress Mama Bushra, but she always seemed both perplexed and irritated with me. One of the first days we spent in the big house—the home Ameer had built for his son, Khalid, using the money he sent back from Brooklyn in the early 2000s—I offended her in such a profound way, she would never let me live it down.

We were all sitting on the couches in the *salon*—the main living room area with western style couches, where guests were welcomed before the men were ushered into the more formal *majlis* area, full of Arabic-style cushions laid directly on the floor. I had my legs crossed in front of me, sitting comfortably.

Suddenly, she began shouting at me in Arabic and gesturing wildly to my legs. Hearing the commotion, Ameer came running into the room to see what could be wrong.

"Oh, Kaighla. No. You can't cross your legs like that in front of an elder, or really anyone other than me," he explained.

"But... I... why?" I asked.

He shrugged and said it must have something to do with seeming too comfortable in her presence. "You should look like you could, at any moment, hop up and grab something for an elder should they ask. If you sit with your legs crossed, you look like you're too much at ease," he said.

Then there was the time we all sat on the floor and I made the mistake of sitting with my legs out in front of me, meaning the soles of my feet were pointing toward her. This, too, was wildly offensive, it turns out, so I ultimately followed Shahida's example and sat with my legs folded to the side, hidden under my flowing *abaya*, so as to not upset the delicate emotions of the *Hajja*.

* * *

A few weeks after we arrived, Ameer went out of town for one reason or another. The second day he was away, some relatives of theirs came into town from the *balad*. I knew it was a large group of people because I heard them piling out of the minibus all the way from my balcony, a block away.

Hoping to perhaps create some sort of bond between us, I asked a friend of mine, who was also married to an Egyptian, how to say "Can I help you cook?" in Arabic. I practiced it a few times before getting dressed and heading over to her house.

When we arrived, Mama Bushra was running around frantically, trying to get the house cleaned up while her guests sat under the trellis in the front courtyard, sipping lemonade with mint and waiting to be invited in. Apparently, they'd had no warning before the arrival of their guests, so the house was in disarray.

I walked into the kitchen and saw Shahida and her eldest daughters running around just as frantically as Mama Bushra was. After saying "*Salaam*," I got up the nerve to try my new phrase.

"*Mumkin ana asa3dik fil matbakh?*" I asked. "Perhaps I can help you in the kitchen?"

At first, they seemed confused, so I assumed I must have said it wrong. I repeated myself, trying to say each syllable clearly. They started laughing, then, as Egyptians always did when I first began trying to speak Arabic. Shahida laughed the loudest before asking me something in Arabic I didn't understand.

"Mama asks, 'Did Ameer tell you to say that?'" Jennah translated.

I was taken aback. They thought I was sent there with my new phrase at Ameer's beckoning.

"No, *habibti*. No, your Baba didn't send me. Please tell your Mama that I really would like to help her cook for the family," I said, feeling hurt by her assumption. I removed my hijab and placing it, along with my bag, in the *majlis* room, just off the kitchen.

Soon enough, I was planted in front of a cutting board and asked to cut onions and tomatoes. I began slicing and dicing as I'd always done, but their laughter started up again. Mama Bushra came in to scold us for laughing instead of cooking, but when she saw me cutting up the vegetables, she, too, joined in the laughter.

"Why are they laughing, Jennah?" I asked, trying to seem jovial, too. If they were laughing *with me* instead of *at me*, it hurt less.

"Nothing, *Tante!*" she said, trying to mask her own giggling. "It's just... the way you cut vegetables is so funny!"

Just then, Shahida stopped washing dishes and picked up an onion and the knife I'd left on the cutting board. She deftly sliced all the way through it, while holding it in her hand like an apple. When she'd sliced it several times, all the way to her own skin, she flipped the whole sliced onion sideways and began slicing it the other way, holding it over the bowl so the freshly diced onion pieces fell in. It was impressive.

I busied myself cutting the tomatoes, instead, getting the juices everywhere. I thought it was as good a time as any to practice some vocabulary I'd memorized before we left Michigan. I didn't know how to say "tomato" in Arabic yet, so I turned to Shahida and asked her, "*Ma haatha? Bil Arabiy?*" "What is this? In Arabic?" I asked.

The laughter erupted again.

"No, that's not how we speak here," Jennah explained when she stopped laughing. "That's old Arabic—*fusha*. Here, we say '*Eh dah?*' not '*Ma hatha?*'"

From that day forward, I did all I could to avoid having to speak Arabic in front of them until I had a better grasp on things. I also tried not to work in the kitchen with them because they never stopped making fun of the way I did things.

* * *

107

December 30th, 2011

As much as I am jealous, I know this is the right way. And this was my idea, after all. Plus, if I am honest with myself, polygyny is actually proving to be really good for me.

Polygyny requires a level of selflessness I've never experienced in any other lifestyle I have lived. It means considering the needs of another human being who doesn't actually benefit you at all, and it means forcing your ego to take a back seat. It means planning your future in pencil because there is the real possibility another person (or many persons) will be affected negatively by your plans.

This lifestyle also gives me the space I need to be grateful. Without fail, every time I get away from my husband for even a little while, all the silly things we used to bicker about day-in and day-out fall by the wayside, and I am able to give thanks for the parts of him and our marriage that are wonderful.

More than anything, though, this lifestyle is a mirror for the deepest parts of me. It shows me what I need to change about myself.

It also forces me to release my illusion of permanence. We want to believe love is forever, that true love is everlasting. This is a silly delusion propagated by Disney movies and by stories read to us as little children. Sure, true love exists, and marriages can last, and those involved can actually be happy for a lifetime. But eternity? No way. Nothing is eternal but God. That's what makes him God: there is nothing like Him and everything will vanish but Him. I am forced to accept that all is ethereal, all will die, all will pass, and no state will remain as it is.

I can only hope that things continue on this path, and I am certain that if things start to fall off track, Ameer will put it all back in order. It really feels like everyone here is interested in what's good for the entire family.

* * *

Considering all the different places I had lived in my life by that point, you'd think I would have learned how to recognize culture shock when it happened. Still, a few months in, I found myself feeling completely off-kilter in Egypt, and unsure of how to remedy the situation.

Life in Egypt (and many places around the world, in fact) is based on the family unit; one makes decisions based on what is best for the whole, even if some individuals within the whole suffer for it.

I grew up in a culture in which I was not accountable to anyone for my actions unless someone was directly affected by them. Once I turned eighteen, I was an adult; I did not have to have the approval of every family member down the line to make a choice, and I did not have to explain my decisions. I lived twenty-five years in a "my way or the highway" mindset, but I had been in Egypt for three months and was expected to let all of it go.

In fact, long before we went to Egypt—since the day I converted, really—I was exposed to a sort of forced assimilation, like an age-old game of retaliation. It was as if the suffering my ancestors inflicted on their ancestors gave Arab and Asian Muslims the right to force me to assimilate to their culture or risk both social alienation and the wrath of God. If I asked to be welcomed into the fold without having to kill my cultural identity, it seemed to them like I was demanding white privilege in the only safe space these immigrants had in an otherwise hostile country. The message was clear: "This is our religion, and you're a guest, just a passing shadow, until and unless you begin to dress, behave, and think like us."

I would never give unsolicited advice to a woman I didn't know, and rarely even to my friends. But Egyptian women—or at least those I met in our small town—just *had to nag*. It seemed like it was almost a social requirement to harass other women, especially if those women were "below" you in age, status, rank, class, or if they were a foreigner—the worst position to hold, by far.

Just like back home in my own small town, people assumed if someone didn't understand the local language and customs, they didn't understand how to live in general. If someone did things differently than most, they were doing it *wrong*. People patronized and talked down to me at every opportunity, and I couldn't tell if it was because I was still young or because they thought I was lacking in intelligence just because I didn't speak Arabic.

I had women telling me every day how to live my life. I was harassed for everything I said and did—and many things I *should* have said or done but did not. I was criticized for not putting enough layers on my kids, while they let theirs run around without shoes. I was harassed and mocked for insisting on car seats for my kids, but it was fine for them to let theirs jump around a moving vehicle. But did I criticize them for being really shitty parents sometimes, according to my cultural standards? No. Because it wasn't my business, and I was in their country.

And then there was the total lack of privacy. Unlike Shahida, I was not allowed to cry too loudly, yell, or show any sort of frustration at all, in my own home, for fear the neighbors would hear and the sheikh's family would be shamed. This was an absurdity to me. In my home growing up, the acceptable way to deal with pain and anger was to cry, yell, scream, throw things, slam the door, stomp out of the house, and drive away—and then never speak of it again once you'd returned. Of course, such behavior isn't healthy, but it's what was modeled for me.

But in our small Egyptian town, no matter what my husband did to me, I was not allowed to physically express my pain or anger in any way. I was expected to state calmly that I was upset and if this did not move him, did not affect him, did not make him see that he really hurt me—well, tough cookies, sister. I personally witnessed Shahida screaming at him on more than one occasion, but since she lived in a separate house, rather than an apartment, she had more freedom.

In that place where I had no friends or family, very rarely had internet to talk with my friends and family back home, and no ability to go out anywhere—since I didn't speak even basic Arabic and no one was willing to go with me—my only method of relief was talking with my husband, and when he was too tired/bored/busy/uninterested to listen, I had no relief. So, I cried. I screamed. I slammed doors, and this made him angrier and things between us got worse.

Since I didn't understand or speak Arabic, I was forced to either trust Ameer's word for it, or else imagine how Shahida and Mama Bushra were feeling about things, and that was almost never a positive experience. Shahida looked at me as if I had come to usurp her throne as his wife, and our mother-in-law just stared at me with a mixture of pity and annoyance.

111

I knew then that we would never be a priority in my husband's life until my kids were very ill, or until I gave birth, or until my kids were school-age, or until one of us was literally dying. Otherwise, we were an after-thought in every practical way.

If anyone in the village needed anything at all that Ameer could provide, he would go, post-haste. If Shahida or her kids needed anything at all, they would have it right then. I waited all day for him to bring basic groceries because he was busy taking his mom all over God's green earth getting things she wanted; we waited for *food* because she was getting things she *wanted*.

It was the same with his money. Mama Bushra held the money bags, so he always had to ask her to give him some of his own money. Every time the kids or I needed something, he had to ask permission from his mother to buy it. When I pointed out how insane that was, he said he kept his money with her so that he didn't lose it.

"But Ameer, Shahida buys anything she wants, anytime. She asks Mama Bushra and she never tells Shahida no. How is that fair?" I asked.

"*Insha'Allah khair,*" he said. End of discussion.

For the first few months, we lived entirely off of the money he saved while living in the States since his salary as a sheikh in Egypt was very, very small. What would happen when that money ran out? No one knew, and no one seemed concerned. With two wives and eight kids, and another baby on the way, he had no idea how to lead the family. No one had a plan.

February 23rd, 2012

Today I hate this life. Today I am deeply angry and bitter that this is the lot handed to me after so brilliant a youth. I can't believe that God in His wisdom decided to put me in a situation that is so full of disappointment after disappointment, small and large.

What is a husband? What is a wife, if you have two? I did not imagine that being married to a man with two wives would feel the same as being a girlfriend, only in prison. When I spend all day alone wondering where he is and calling his phone repeatedly, only to find that he has turned it off on purpose, I feel like less than a girlfriend.

It feels like the pain will never abate, like Islam really is oppressive to women, after all, like the rules are intentionally designed to keep us feeling powerless and dependent on men. How can something so painful, so completely horrid as polygyny be halal, *and even recommended, according to Ameer, the sheikh?*

There are days here that I feel sorry that poor Sajidah was born. I love her so much, but when I think of her likely lot in life if she marries someone from her father's culture, it almost breaks my heart.

The sunlight streaming through my balcony shutter, sitting here in this chair, the tea in my hand, the journal on my lap—all these things should give me joy, and did give me joy before. The sunlight should feed my soul. But my world feels very small right now, and it's dark—like the walls are closing in.

When I think about the life I have led, the places I have seen, the people I have known and the Kaighlas I have been,

I cannot believe or understand how I got myself in this predicament. How could so brave, so bold, so curious, so adventurous and thirsty a soul become a woman so cold, bitter, and hopeless as I am?

It's only been four years since I was pregnant with Dayo, and now I am pregnant with a third child. He says God gave him the right to keep me pregnant as long and as often as he wants, that God made me his "land to till," according to the hadith, *and that one of the rights of a husband is children. One of the responsibilities of all able-bodied Muslims is to make as many babies as possible, he says. Now I have another life to worry about, another mouth to feed and another innocent child is suffering inside of me because my husband, the sheikh is making me suffer.*

It seems to me that the only way for any of us to be happy here is for me to give up my rights permanently and allow him to come and go whenever he feels like it. This way Shahida, his beloved Um Khalid—the mother of his only son, Khalid—can keep believing she is his only wife, his kids can go on believing they are his only children, and I can hope that when he comes to my house, he actually wants to be here. But when a woman gives up her rights to her husband permanently and allows another woman to take over those rights, that's not polygyny anymore—it's called "divorce."

My deepest need is to have a stable life. I want to have the same husband forever, to live in the same home for a long, long time, to develop and sustain the same friendships for years, and to contribute to the building up of the same community across decades. He cannot or will not give me any of these things.

I wonder what it must feel like to know that if everything else fails, and if your husband isn't making you happy, you can always be sure you have your family to rely on. If he makes her so miserable she feels like killing herself (like he has made me feel), she does not have to get to that point. She can leave and go back to her father's home, knowing that he will help take care of her and her children. I have no one to run to. Not here in Egypt, not in America—not anywhere.

I have never felt so lonely in all my life. I am sitting next to my phone waiting for a man to call me, a man that is supposed to be my husband, a man I should be able to trust to always be there for me when I need him. But that man is busy coddling and mending things with another woman—a selfish woman who ruins everything with her selfish choices.

While my husband, the man I have given everything for, is kissing the ass of another woman, I am sitting here. Waiting. Pregnant, alone with two small kids, and waiting. Watching my life pass me by.

He says when I am sad or angry that I forget everything good that has happened between us. But when will good things happen again? When will I be able to enjoy time with him without someone somewhere calling and demanding that he leave us and go to them? How long does he think I can survive on a few good memories that happened years ago?

He needs me to be the sort of woman no Arab woman would ever be expected to be, and he needs me to give up things no Arab woman would ever be expected to give up. I never had a wedding with him, a party, a celebration. I *had a $100* mahr *for God's sake! I never got the chance to even pick out my furniture or kitchen utensils, since he just moved me into the apartment he and Aishah had lived in, and then we moved all that stuff to Dearborn without changing a thing, and then he and his family bought the furnishings for this place before we ever even came here. Now, he expects me to be okay with always being his second priority so that she is never inconvenienced.*

* * *

Of course, it wasn't just Ameer and his family that drove me insane in Egypt. I realized later that a good portion of my frustration stemmed from the ridiculous expectations I had before I came to Egypt.

I believed, for example, that I would get the chance to live a more natural, organic life because that's the picture Ameer painted for me. But I found to my dismay that the vast majority of Egyptians I met were living anything but a natural life.

The highest calling for most people in Egypt is to become a doctor. Regardless if it's what you truly want—to save lives—if your final high school test scores are among the highest in the country, that's the field that is chosen for you, followed by engineering students, and on down through the professions until, shockingly, those with the lowest test scores are funneled into the teaching profession.

Most people in rural Egypt had adopted the idea, spread by America in the 1950s, that when it comes to illness, doctors know best; only idiots question their doctor. There was no sense of personal responsibility for one's health and wellness.

My insistence that Ameer ask questions of the doctors we took the kids to seemed absurd to them, and more than once they looked at both of us with a quizzical brow when I simply asked why a medication needed to be prescribed, or how a certain illness could cause this or that symptom.

Women also seemed perplexed and entertained when they learned that I had chosen to cloth diaper Dayo and Saji. "Pampers are so much easier!" they'd laugh at me. "Why make more work for yourself?!" Though there were multiple brands of diapers in Egypt, everyone called them "Pampers"—a clear indication of western commercialism.

Aunties and elderly women alike criticized me for exclusively breastfeeding my babies, too. "Your baby is so skinny! Give her formula!" strangers would say, regardless of the fact that I kept careful track of their weights and compared them to growth charts I found online. But anything other than a clearly obese baby, covered in rolls of fat, was "too skinny!" for their taste. I was also criticized for choosing to delay giving my babies solid foods and to withhold sugary sweets from them in favor of more natural sugars, like fruits.

Under all this, there was a shocking, pervasive lack of critical-thinking skills. Having lived thousands of years in a tribal society, full of strong traditions—one of which was a deferment to elders, as well as to the most educated and wealthiest members of the tribe—they listened to the people they believed knew better. Most people did what their culture dictated without asking why. Western colonizers took advantage of this tendency time after time, seeing that if they could get the oldest, most educated, and wealthiest members of a society to accept an aspect of colonization, the rest would follow. This tactic had worked fantastically.

* * *

March 30th, 2012

Dayo is vomiting again and he's covered in pox. It's midnight. It's not my night so my husband is with his other wife. I am pregnant and alone with a sick toddler and another baby. I can only dry perhaps eight articles of clothing at a time on the line on my balcony (if it's not too windy or cold) so almost every article of clothing for Saji and Dayo is dirty. What am I supposed to put on him after he has thrown up for the third time and there is nothing left?!

There was another sandstorm today, and my house was coated in a fine yellow dust that made us cough all day, which didn't help the kids sickness at all, and it makes doing laundry even harder.

On nights like this, I cannot forgive Ameer for putting me in this situation. Both of my children are sick, and I have no idea how to make them feel better. I cannot give them a warm bed to sleep in at night because he won't buy another heater. I cannot give Dayo clean clothes or fresh sheets on his bed every time he vomits because I don't have a way to wash all the dirty laundry, then hang them, dry them, and ensure they are ready for him when he needs them.

I have a huge belly and here I am trying to haul buckets of water into my half-automatic washer and drag blankets and laundry to and from the line outside, all by myself. Because my husband has another family to care for.

Can Ameer even imagine how hard this is as a mother?! To not have the ability to help your children feel comfortable when they are sick? I am pregnant with another of his babies, another that he will leave because it isn't her mother's night. Vomiting, crying, sick—who cares? It's like he saying to them, "It isn't mommy's night, so suffer, honey."

We will never be an emergency for him. If it were Saji would he care? Would he rush over in the middle of the night? I know that if it were Juwariya, Shahida's little daughter, he would leave my house anytime, day or night, and rush her to the hospital. But not for Dayo.

I'm so angry I'm crying! He has given me half a husband, half a life, and twice the heartache! I can't trust him. I cannot trust a word that comes out of his mouth because most of the time, he doesn't mean anything he says. He doesn't value my feelings. He doesn't care if I trust him. He only cares about my pain if it makes him look bad. So, I am forced to sit around thinking of ways to make him look bad publicly so that he will see how badly he is hurting me. Is this love?

Sajidah has stopped nursing completely. One day, she was nursing six times a day, and the next day, she wouldn't even come near my breast. It's like she instinctively knows my milk is poisoned with pain and fear. I miss that closeness with her, but I don't want to hurt her. She's old enough for cow's milk now, so that's the good news.

Ameer's most recent promise has been that he will make up all these days and nights he has spent with her after the baby is born. He swears, by God, on the Qur'an, and even on the life of his father, that when our new daughter is born, he will stay with me for two solid weeks as I heal.

* * *

That spring, Ameer took me to visit the *balad* for the first time—the rustic, country village where he grew up. There was a family event, and rather than leaving me at home like he usually did, he invited me to come along with the family.

Of course, before we could get going, there was the scramble to see how we could fit four adults, eight children, two ducks, a bag of rice, and two bags of clothes in our minivan.

When I strapped Saji into her car seat, Mama Bushra was fuming. "Why doesn't your wife want to hold her baby?!" she yelled at Ameer. "Let me hold her if Um Abdullah's too lazy!"

"Mama, calm down," he said. "It's not because she's lazy. The car seat is safer for the baby, okay?"

She laughed then and carried on in Arabic, and from what I could understand, she was basically deriding me and calling me selfish.

Of course, she knew full well that Ameer and I were only still alive because we'd been wearing our seatbelts in the car accident, and he'd told her before, more than once, how Sajidah's car seat had saved her. Nonetheless, they never stopped harassing me about insisting on the car seat. It took up the space of a full adult, and most people in rural Egypt held one or even two babies on their lap to make room for everyone.

Squeezed in like sardines, we arrived at Shahida's parents' home an hour later and were greeted, seated next to the fire, and given cups of hot tea. Soon enough, Dayo was lost with the other boys, running around and getting dirty. Saji mostly sat with her Baba, sucking her thumb and looking around curiously.

Someone walked in just then and invited Ameer and his father-in-law to drink coffee at their house, so he left me there with Shahida and her family. It wasn't long before the house was full of women, chatting and generally being curious about the sheikh's new American wife.

They asked me all sorts of questions that were wildly inappropriate by my cultural standards—like whether or not Ameer and I loved one another, and why I didn't want my parents and siblings to go to Heaven since it had to be my fault that they hadn't found Islam attractive yet. When they had finished digging into me—or Ameer's eldest daughter, Jennah, had given up translating for me—I was left sitting in a corner, in a home, in a village, in a country I didn't feel comfortable in, just an afterthought in the sheikh's already busy life.

There was one bright spot, though, in our trips to the *balad*: getting to spend time with Ameer's younger sister, Ihsan. Her smile could light up any room, and she hugged me like I was a dear friend. As tall as her brother and just as broad, she somehow managed to appear meek and discrete in her *niqab* and *abaya* whenever men were in the room. But as soon as they left, Ihsan was the life of the party.

Her husband, Idris, was just as jubilant, and just as welcoming. He spoke a bit of English and loved to sit with me in their modest *salon*, discussing anything and everything about my life back home. Idris was a taxi driver, shuttling people back and forth to Cairo and Port Said, and he had broken both legs several times, all in car accidents.

For a while, Ihsan and Idris treated me like a novelty to be fawned over but never actually known, just like everyone else did, but with time, they came to be some of the few people in

Egypt I truly felt loved by.

* * *

I continued my blogging during those first months in Egypt. By now, it was my foremost outlet for the pain, frustration, and confusion I felt. In lieu of friends to talk with, I poured my heart out online to perfect strangers, exposing my own deepest feelings to people who may or may not have had good intentions in reading and commenting. When the internet was out—and it usually was—I would write post after post and save them for later.

Most of the people who followed my blog were kind-hearted fellow Muslims who felt helpless in the face of my suffering—much like my friend Jamilah had when she decided a few months into our stay that she couldn't listen to me wailing on the phone anymore.

But some followers just came to watch the three-ring shit-show that was my life, and they enjoyed the show. I was the gladiator, Shahida and Mama Bushra the lions, and the internet our audience. Some of the commenters were downright vicious.

"You should have your children taken away for putting them in this situation," one said.

"Your weakness is disgusting. No wonder your husband prefers his other wife," another quipped.

"If you loved your kids, sister, you would have divorced him the moment you found out about his other wife. Instead, you have chosen to be a home-wrecker. You're getting what you deserve. Accept your situation. You dug your grave, so die in it," another said.

Many years later, I would be appalled at the level of vulnerability I expressed to strangers—even "Muslim" ones like these commenters. In 2014, I stopped blogging and began writing only for paid online and print publications after I finally understood that no one had a right to watch my circus without paying the admission fee.

* * *

It started with a kitchen cabinet. I could literally blame a great majority of my later problems in Egypt on a set of kitchen cabinets.

Unlike in the States, houses and apartments in rural Egypt are typically not built with a permanent cabinet system in the kitchen. When a woman gets married, her family purchases kitchen cabinets for her. For the rest of her life, they go with her wherever she goes, like all the other furniture. They're temporarily hung and sealed in every house she lives in.

I had waited months for Ameer to buy kitchen cabinets for me. Of course, it wasn't supposed to be so long before I got them, but Sheikh Ameer was always too busy. There was always a wedding, always a funeral, always a baby being born, always a party to attend, always people to see and host. Even if the event happened on my allotted day with him, he still took Um Khalid instead. Sure, I could tag along if I wanted to, but I was never treated like his wife that day, just the American mother of one of his many daughters, there as entertainment or as a tourist.

For weeks he'd been coming to my house after *Maghrib* prayers, going back to the mosque for *Isha*, and then sleeping in my house, only to wake up, go to the mosque for *Fajr* prayers, and head immediately to her house before going off to work for the day. Every waking moment of every day that he was not praying or working, he was spending time with her—or in her house, anyway—and I did not sign up for that shit.

When I imagined her feelings, as a woman, I thought it was likely that she probably wasn't having a great time with him, really. The times I had seen them together, they argued and seemed frustrated with one another constantly. All marriages have secrets, so it made sense to imagine that things were not all rosy on her end, either, but it was hard to see past the many ways she seemed to always worm her way into my private time with him. It was starting to weigh heavily on me.

So, when the week finally came that Ameer agreed we would, *insha'Allah*, get my cabinets, I was stoked. Of course, right on schedule, Shahida called early on the morning we planned to buy the cabinets, complaining of being sick yet again. She was so sick, apparently, that she couldn't go to a doctor in town and she couldn't go to the hospital. No, she needed a specialist in exactly the town we were intending to travel to. How convenient.

Three days before this, I was sick and needed to see a doctor for the pregnancy, anyway, so he made an appointment in Faqqous for me. Did he take me alone, or even with the kids? No. He took Shahida with us because it was her day with him. Any time I tried to talk to him in the car, she sighed dramatically and said she needed him to translate if we were going to speak in English. So, he turned on the Qur'an.

But, on this day, she claimed to be sick. She was my sister in Islam, and I wasn't a monster, so I sent him on his way to her. He took her to her doctor's appointment and then went back to her house to spend the rest of my evening with her, then her night. Since he had spent my day with her, it was understood and agreed upon that the following day—her day—would be spent with me, finally going to get the damned cabinets.

I got up in the morning, dressed, and prepared the children, then sat waiting for him to come. I called and he assured me he was on his way. But an hour, then two hours, then three hours went by and he still hadn't shown. I began to get anxious and worried he wouldn't come. They lived only a block away. What was taking so long?

By the time he pulled up to the apartment and began furiously honking at me to hurry up, I was livid. It was the hundredth time he had done that same thing: called us, told us to get ready, then made us wait hours, and then acted annoyed when I had to re-dress the kids who had, of course, taken off their shoes and jacket after the first hour of waiting. *I threw away my happy life in Dearborn to come to this situation and he can't just be fair with the time?* I thought, throwing myself a pity party. I was ranting and raving when he came upstairs to grab the car seats.

As we passed through the front gate, I turned to my left and saw, right there in the backseat, none other than Shahida. *In my car. On my day.*

I lost my mind. I screamed at him in front of our apartment building, right there in public—something one never, ever does in Egypt. "What is she doing in the car on my day, Ameer?! Again?! Will I never have time with my husband without her?!" I yelled.

He seemed just as surprised as I was to see her, but it was too late. I was unhinged.

"Divorce me! Divorce me now! I am going home tomorrow!" I screamed as I stomped back up the stairs with Saji on one hip and Dayo trailing behind. I was shaking and crying and screaming when we got into the apartment. I knew she could hear me yelling at him, and I hoped so. I looked out the balcony window and saw her get out of the car and walk home.

125

He tried all he could to calm me down. I was seven months pregnant, for God's sake—that ranting and raving weren't good for me, or the baby. I stood in front of the front door and refused to let him go, but eventually, he did leave.

When it was time to pray, some hours later, I knew exactly what I would pray for. I had had enough of her and her family and her country, and of her stealing my time with my husband. On my face in *sujood*—the position of prayer wherein one places their face on the floor, and wherein one is closest to God and is encouraged to ask anything of Him—I begged God to curse her. I begged Allah to give Shahida pain-upon-pain. I begged Him to hurt her like she was hurting me. I begged Him to make her suffer like I was suffering.

She had intentionally, deceitfully stolen from me something I willingly gave up for her: time with our husband. She had taken advantage of my kindness. She knew I had no one but him in the entire country, and she had stomped all over my willingness to throw my life away so she could have fair time—not all of his time, *fair time*.

On my face in prayer, when I could have been begging God for peace, I tainted and poisoned my own heart with hatred and malice for her.

8

The Mercy

Sharqia Governorate, Egypt

June 2012

We decided on a home-birth, but it had nothing to do with my more natural sensibilities. No, it was because Ameer refused to spend the money on a clean, safe hospital birth. We spent the previous few months going to every doctor's office, clinic, and hospital within an hour's drive that was within his allotted budget.

At one clinic, women formed a long line in a cramped, stinky hallway as others gave birth in the few rooms available. I even saw one woman screaming and squatting, about to give birth right there in the hallway of that building—which had not been cleaned in years, surely—because there were no beds open just yet. At another, I grabbed Saji just in time to stop her from picking up a used syringe off the floor, lying among bloody

Bandaids littering the area around the overflowing trashcan.

And of course, there was the hospital in town, where doctors smoked cigarettes in the hallway and watched movies in the nurse's station as their patients died.

"What do you expect them to do?" Ameer had asked, shrugging. "The hospital doesn't have the tools or technology to save most people who come with emergencies, so they often have no choice but to send them home to die or let them die right there."

Blankets were shared without ever being washed, sheets were non-existent, and people brought their own food in containers from home. There was no soap in most bathrooms, many sinks had no running water, and most bathrooms were actually locked to prevent anyone using and dirtying them since the hospital couldn't afford to pay more cleaning people.

I was not a delicate flower. I had lived in the poorest parts of Kolkata, India, and had slept among my fair share of bed bugs, lice, and cockroaches. I could handle filth, and it usually hadn't bothered me. But I didn't have children back then, and I was not looking at the prospect of giving birth there.

Finally, after the last visit we had with a doctor in the village, I demanded to be taken to Ismailia to meet with a well-known and respected doctor who was at the top of our price range.

Her office was clean and nice, her nurses and assistants were polite, and they spoke decent English, so I was very hopeful. If there's ever a time you want your doctor to speak and understand your language, it's in the labor and delivery room.

We sat down at her desk and she made small talk with Ameer in Arabic while she filled out paperwork and handed it to her nurse, who quietly left the room, shutting the door behind her. When we were finally alone, the three of us, the doctor smiled at me and asked if I had any questions for her.

"I do, actually. Several," I said. She kindly invited me to go on. I gave her a quick breakdown of all I had seen that terrified me about Egyptian hospitals and such, and she agreed the state of things was atrocious, even from her perspective.

"I was just wondering if you're in the practice of delayed cord clamping," I said.

She looked perplexed, so I went on.

"I mean, do you wait until the umbilical cord stops throbbing and pulsing before you clamp it and snip it?" I asked. "Since the umbilical cord is full of nutrient-rich, oxygenated blood, I mean."

She took her glasses off in a dramatic way and stared at me long and hard. "Oh, oh, oh, no. No, you can leave, *madame*, right now. You think you know more than I know? You think you are the doctor? You think because you are an American, you know more than I know about delivering babies?" she asked, in shock.

I could not believe the way she was talking to me, this woman who was literally being interviewed for a job. I was confused and speechless.

"Let me make one thing perfectly clear to you, Um Abdullah: *I am the doctor, and this is Egypt, not America.* If I think you need a drug, I will inject you with that drug without even telling you, let alone asking your permission. If I need to do something to you to get your baby out alive, I will not wait for your approval," she said as I sat there, mouth agape. "When you are giving birth, your life and the life of that precious baby are in my hands, so I make all the decisions, and if you have a problem with that, you can seek care elsewhere."

With that, she stood up, slammed my file on her desk, and

walked out of the room.

I was shaking and crying. Ameer helped me stand up from the low chair, and we walked out of her office.

"I don't know what to say, honey," he said on the drive home. "She is the best of the best within our price range. Maybe we should see if we can convince her to reconsider?"

I stared out the window at the drab surroundings, wishing with all my heart I had the money to go home.

* * *

From that day forward, I spent all my time learning about home-birth and even what to do in case of an accidental unassisted home-birth. We hired the village midwife from Ameer's *balad*, mostly because she had a government-issued oxygen tank that we may have needed should things have gone awry. We paid her a deposit to be sure she would be on call and ready to come to our town whenever I gave birth.

Of course, Ameer's entire family thought I was crazy. Doctors are next to God in Egypt, so my refusal to allow a doctor to do whatever he or she liked to me without any concern for informed consent… well, it smacked of white arrogance.

Vaginal birth at all—whether in the hospital or at home—was the exception in rural Egypt. The women I spoke with actually preferred to have C-sections because they knew that people would wait on them hand-and-foot for a month or more afterward. When a woman gave birth vaginally, though, she was typically able to care for herself within a few days, so no one hung around to help.

With all that was expected of women there, all the work they had to do constantly, could anything different be expected?

That's how desperate they were for a break: they were willing to get their abdomen sliced open—tearing muscles and ligaments that may never heal, having their organs removed and their uterus cut open, risking their lives and those of their babies—just for the chance to rest for a few precious weeks!

No, I would not be going to any of those filthy places to bring my child into the world. I knew the germs in my house were mine and my children's, and I knew how to clean really well. I knew my baby would be much safer there than in some hospital laced with Hepatitis, and worse. Ameer had contracted Hepatitis B from a blood transfusion at that very same hospital, back in the 90's—long before they were screening blood donations for diseases other than HIV.

Let them think what they will, but I know my body best, I thought. I had given birth twice already. I knew how to tell when something was going wrong, and if I was going to die, or God forbid the baby was, I preferred that it happen in my quiet, clean home than in some God-forsaken, rural Egyptian hospital.

* * *

Our baby, Rahmah, finally came into the world one hot June day, but she didn't have a name for a solid week. Like everything else in my life in Egypt, the choice of what to call her had to be agreed on by twelve other people before things could be finalized. Even then, they rarely called her by her name, preferring, instead, to call her by her pet name—Rumi.

I had been having contractions all day in an irregular but increasingly painful pattern. Around *Maghrib* time, the contractions had gotten more painful and slightly more regular, so I decided to take a walk in the park across the street from

Ameer's house to relieve my anxiety about another false alarm, and to clear my mind. I reminded myself my body was perfectly designed to give birth, and that birth was usually not an emergency.

The family was concerned when they saw my level of discomfort and began harassing me to go to the hospital or see a doctor to "make sure everything is okay."

"*Ya Nayna*," I said to Mama Bushra after she'd given me a glass of cool lemonade and sat me down in the *salon*, "everything is fine, and no, I am not going to a doctor because I am not sick. I am just going to have a baby."

"But *binti*, why?" Mama Bushra started to ask. I hugged her and thanked her for her concern and then went home and immediately began nesting.

I cleaned and swept and mopped and set out what I thought the midwife may need: towels, a bucket for the placenta, a small table, a comfortable chair, etc. I set out candles and lit incense and turned on some Qur'an in an effort to calm my nerves.

Finally, the contractions began coming at regular 10-minute intervals and stayed that way until I was in active labor around midnight. We had called the midwife after *Maghrib* to tell her of the situation, but she told us she imagined I would make it until at least *Fajr* the next day.

The kids were asleep by 9:30 p.m. and Ameer and I enjoyed our time alone, laughing and joking between contractions. All it took to get uninterrupted quality time with him was for me to go into labor—go figure.

I took a shower to help relieve the tension in my lower back and he helped me with the shower head, making sure I didn't slip in the wet bathroom. He went to lay down for a few hours, and I woke him at midnight to tell him things were serious and

132

it was time to call the midwife back.

We called and called but there was no answer. By the time we reached her at 1:00 a.m., I knew I was in the transition phase. I was moaning through the contractions. My husband told her she needed to come right now.

"*Ya* sheikh, you know I cannot come in the middle of the night. It's just not safe to travel so far at night, you know," she explained. "If your wife is in too much pain, tell her to go to the hospital," she said flippantly.

I threw myself against my armoire in tears, remembering the comfort she had given us before, her confident reassurances that she would come from the *balad* anytime, day or night, and would bring everything we needed—especially the oxygen tank.

"Honey, please be calm. She will come as soon as it's light out, okay? Plus, she is sure you will not give birth before that," he said, clearly believing her experience over mine.

My previous weeks' worth of reading and watching videos proved fruitful. I knew enough to explain the shoe-string method of tying off the umbilical cord and cutting it with very sharp scissors cleaned with rubbing alcohol. Ameer listened carefully but insisted we would be fine, confident that she would make it in time.

I felt hopeless, like it may never end. Manic, mammalian grunts and yells emanated from somewhere deep inside me, against my will, pouring out into the quiet apartment and the dark street below.

Ameer decided then that he needed to go get Mama Bushra for help since the midwife was probably not going to make it—like I'd been saying for hours. But neither of us had any idea the delivery was so close at hand. Having been induced both times, with Dayo and Saji, I didn't know what normal labor felt like—or, rather, what normal, un-intervened progression felt like, anyway.

After he left to get Mama Bushra, I had one more horrid contraction and then suddenly the pain stopped for a few minutes and something inside told me to get out of the bathroom as soon as possible.

I grabbed a towel I had placed on the table in the *salon* and went into my bedroom. I got onto my bed with the towel beneath me and put myself in the most comfortable position I could find: on my hands and knees, in the same fashion by which I had birthed Saji. I had one more final contraction before her head emerged along with the rest of her body, easing out in one swift flow. I moved a few inches forward on the bed, just in time to balance on one arm and catch her.

She was tiny, six pounds at best, but her color was normal, and she was covered in vernix. I stood on the bare floor, picked her up and placed her on my chest.

Just then, Ameer, Mama Bushra, and Shahida all came bursting through the door. Imagine their shock to find me standing there in a pool of blood and amniotic fluid with my newborn in my arms! The look on their faces was priceless.

I was overcome by the most overwhelming feeling of peace and accomplishment I had ever experienced in my life. I did it all by myself! There was no one there to help or inhibit me, no one to tell me to push like this or lay like that, and there was no one to encourage me or assure me that everything would be fine. I had only God, only remembrance of my Lord and His perfect design. I had the knowledge I had gained telling me that my body had a beautiful way of making this amazing miracle a reality.

I felt a rush of joy as I held her little vernix-covered body against mine. I was hit with a complex dance of chemicals and hormones working together to make me fall desperately in love with the same screaming, bloody creature who had caused me so much pain moments earlier.

The only problem? My audience.

Mama Bushra and Ameer were in shock, trying to figure out what to do first, how to do it, and who should do it. Shahida just stood in the corner of the room gawking at the sight of my bloody nakedness, a sight I know she would have never wanted to endure, poor thing.

I was confused with the language barrier, and I didn't understand their reactions to the beautiful, miraculous happening I'd just experienced. Mama Bushra kept insisting I needed to lie down so she could massage out the placenta. I complied and around twenty minutes later, the placenta came out without a problem.

Reasonably speaking, I would have been lost without them. In an hour, they accomplished what Ameer and I couldn't have all day: the bed was cleaned up, the floor mopped, the sheets changed on top of plastic sheeting, my filthy body scrubbed by Mama Bushra, the baby cleaned up by Ameer, and my house spotless. I thanked Mama Bushra and Shahida again and again for their selfless service to me in the face of absurdly awkward circumstances. I reminded myself that the cost of our polygynous lifestyle was high, but the benefits were outrageous at times.

9

The Cracking

Sharqia Governorate, Egypt

Summer 2012

Managing two toddlers and a newborn alone, with no family or friends around to help, is hard anywhere. Doing so in a foreign country was no picnic, to say the least. Also, it was hot—really, *really* hot, like late-June-in-the-desert-without-air-conditioning hot.

The combination of both of my young kids needing me at the same time that the baby and I needed sleep, along with a heat that made me feel like my brains were frying, was pushing me to my breaking point.

Ameer came home at all hours of the night because he was busy dealing with family issues—*her* family, their shared family. Whenever he decided to show up at night, I'd have to get up, get fully dressed, go down two flights of stairs, unlock the inner gate, and then the outer courtyard gate. Our landlord only gave us one key and Ameer was afraid to lose it, so he usually left it with me.

That night, I vowed in my heart that if he didn't come by 11:30 p.m., I was closing the doors and windows and turning off my phone, and even if he called my name for an hour outside, I would not let him in.

"Ameer, you have two choices," I said when he sat down in the *salon* at 11:15 that night. "You can either be fair with your wives or divorce one of us. These are the only two options God gave a man, and you know it, *ya* sheikh. There is no third option of shaming one of them into having her rights robbed from her."

"*Inshallah khair,*" he said. "God-willing, it will be okay." That was always his cop-out, his way of assuaging my worries while effectively avoiding an actual promise to make any actual changes.

The next morning, I woke up just before dawn and found him ironing his *jilbab* in the *salon*.

"Why are you awake so early?" I asked, rubbing my eyes as they adjusted to the light.

"I forgot I have to take Siham to her exams in Zagazig today. I'll be gone until after *Maghrib* tonight," he said before unplugging the iron.

It was always them—always *her*, always *her kids*. I had been neglected by him during the entirety of that pregnancy, so he promised to spend two solid weeks with me after I gave birth to our daughter. Unlike Shahida, I didn't have anyone to come help take care of me and the kids after my delivery. I *needed* him.

Now, Rahmah was only four days old and he was still serving their every whim and neglecting us, though technically sleeping in my apartment, if only for a few hours each night.

"You mean to tell me that for eleven years, the kids got to their exams okay without you, but *now*—when my baby is four days old—they need you to take them?" I asked incredulously.

"Yes. That's what I'm saying. They went without me for many years, so I need to be there for them now," he said.

I began crying then. The idea of being left alone in that apartment—alone with my thoughts and fears and emotions, and alone with my new baby and my two young kids—frightened me. It was all too much. I was overwhelmed with the needs of my children, and feeling like I couldn't take care of them made me feel ashamed and lonely, so I cried more. And none of that was my fault, anyway. I hadn't kept him away from Egypt for eleven years.

"*Habibti*, this crying only wastes your energy and doesn't fix anything. Get up, feed yourself and the kids. Then do something else, then something else, and before you know it, you'll have accomplished a lot. Cry while you are working if you have to, but do something," he advised me.

Dayo and Saji woke up a bit later, so I cooked breakfast and then nursed Rumi back to sleep. Afterward, we all sat on the floor around our low table. Right when I was starting to feel better, after getting some much-needed nourishment, Ameer dropped some news on me.

"I just need to tell you I'll not be here tonight. I'm staying there," he said before shoving another handful of bread and *fool* into his mouth.

When my face gave away my shock and frustration over yet another broken promise, he offered an explanation.

"You seem fine, Kaighla. You don't really need my help. You didn't have surgery, so there is no reason I need to stay longer.

I've been here every night for four days, and I need to go back now so we can start the two-day cycle again," he said. "Plus, she's sick."

"So just forget all the times I was sick when I was pregnant and you never broke your schedule to come and be with me, right?!" I yelled. "And I cannot believe her selfishness! I gave up my whole life to bring you back here so she could have her rights fulfilled, and this is how she treats me? Really, she is so sick that Mama Bushra and all Um Khalid's daughters aren't enough to help her?! She requires you... the only person I have in this entire country!"

He sat, unmoved, munching on his food with his mouth open.

"You know what, Ameer? *Khalas,* I am done. If you want to only care for and honor and respect one wife, then have one wife. I will not be your glorified girlfriend anymore, and it's clear you prefer Shahida. I am finished!" I yelled.

I walked calmly into the kitchen and calmly placed the dishes on the counter. But as I turned to go back into the *salon*, I felt a wave of white-hot rage come over me. In the blink of an eye, I lost my mind. I was screaming, throwing dishes everywhere, sending glass and ceramic pieces flying all over the room. I slammed the electric kettle on the ground, breaking it, then threw all the silverware in their case on the ground. When that didn't make me feel better, I grabbed the dish drainer on the wall, shaking it violently in an attempt to remove it, but only managing to knock off several glasses, shattering them all over the floor and the sink.

Exhausted, I fell to the ground, hyperventilating. And the kids saw the whole thing.

Ameer had run to the kitchen when he heard me breaking things, but stood in shock in the doorway protecting the kids, lest they come in and get hurt. After I collapsed on the floor, he tried to help me get up, but I couldn't move. The world was going black and breathing felt like enormous work.

He left me there crying on the floor and put the kids in their room to stop them from cutting themselves on the glass. Rumi wailed from our bedroom where I'd laid her down to sleep after nursing her.

He carefully picked up the glass and swept up the rice, and at one point, I got up and moved to the *salon*. When he finished cleaning up, he came and sat down next to me, holding Rumi.

I was horrid-looking, covered in snot and tears and dried breastmilk and baby drool and urine. My face was red and puffy and my hair disheveled.

Ameer handed me Rumi and just sat with his face in his hands, sighing deeply several times. After a few minutes, he got up and changed his clothes.

"I have to take Siham to her exams. I'll come back after *Maghrib* and we'll talk then," he said, and then took the keys with him when he left.

I had never felt such powerful animosity before my marriage to Ameer. As time marched on, I felt myself becoming more and more volatile, like I was covered with a thin veneer of calm that could be easily pierced at the smallest annoyance. I also didn't know what the incident meant for my marriage, and I worried about what Ameer was thinking and planning.

My poor kids generally tried to avoid me that day. They played together and watched "Aladdin" for the hundredth time in the *salon*, while I mostly laid in bed with the baby and walked around the tiny apartment in a daze.

When Ameer did eventually come, we sat on our bed talking.

"Just explain to me why you did what you did today, Kaighla.

I have many things on my heart to say, but I want to hear from you first," he said.

"I'm just in so much pain, Ameer, and I'm so lonely. You're never here!" I cried. "I have no one but you in this entire country and you're always taking care of everyone else. And I just want a family! Why don't you ever invite your family here when they come to town to visit? Why do you always bring them to her house? Because she's your *real wife!* I don't understand why you decided to have two wives if you couldn't manage us both!"

"You know the big house is the family house. Everyone knows it's my home. And let's be honest: you have no idea how to be hospitable to Egyptians, ok? That's why I don't bring people here. Shahida knows how to make them feel welcome, and you don't," he said.

"And having two wives is not impossible. The trick is having wives who are mature and independent," he added, no emotion in his voice.

Once again, he was placing the blame for the decrepit state of both of our marriages on my shoulders—*me*, the young convert he had tricked into marrying him, saying he was divorced. Yes, it was all *my* fault. If only *I* were more mature, we wouldn't suffer so much. If only *I* would allow him to wreck my life and lie and cheat me always, abandoning me to the cavernous apartment and my own thoughts, things would be peachy.

"Ameer, you *always* do what she wants. You serve her, at every turn! You are so afraid to offend her family that you are willing to disobey God and break my heart! Why, Ameer? Why do you let them dominate you like this? When did you decide you were more afraid of them than of God?!"

He was angry then, but he didn't let it show, ignoring everything I'd said and instead focusing again on what I'd done wrong.

"Is this how things are gonna be now? Hmm? You just gonna throw a tantrum when I have to adjust my plans?" he asked.

"I cannot believe that you really think it was just your decision to go to her tonight that made me lose all control of myself—and with my children right there, too," I said. "I have endured this for months. Your lies, your broken promises, your neglect, and your abuse. You're crushing me!" I cried.

He waved away my words from his face, annoyed.

"*Abuse?* Please, Kaighla. You know what? One of my sheikh friends has three wives, and he slaps them in the face any time they dare to question him. You should thank Allah that I haven't ever hit you," he said smugly.

"You've shoved me up against walls, Ameer, when I was pregnant. You've threatened me, you've convinced me God doesn't love me just because you're angry! That's worse than hitting me! Even before we came here, you took everything from me and killed all the joy inside me!" I yelled.

"I've never shoved you up against a wall, Kaighla. *Haraam alayk.* Shame on you for lying. And please, by Allah, lower your voice," he said.

I couldn't believe what I was hearing. I remembered as clearly as if it had happened just the day before: he'd shoved me hard up against the wall and pinned my shoulders there when I was pregnant with Sajidah, back in Dearborn.

"Yes, you have, Ameer. In Dearborn," I said calmly.

"You're crazy, Kaighla, seriously. That never happened," he said.

I threw my hands in the air. "I am not crazy! And I can't trust you! You're the only person I have here, and I can't trust you!" I cried.

He sighed loudly then and stood up to open the balcony door. For a few minutes, he sat on one of the lounge chairs outside, looking out across the darkening horizon and enjoying the cool night air while I stood just inside the apartment.

"You know I hate that word, Kaighla. You can't tell your husband you don't trust him. That makes it sound like you think I'm evil or something," he said. "Why can't you just be patient?"

I wanted to scream. Back in America, when women came to him seeking help at his office in the mosque, complaining of abuse and problems in their marriage, that was almost always his advice: "Sister, be patient." It was the seemingly universal sheikh-y phrase for "Let your husband keep doing what he wants to do and stop whining so much about it. Have some freaking class."

Just as he was getting up to come inside, our neighbor came walking in through the courtyard gate and waved up at him. They engaged in some small talk from the balcony before he shut the door and came inside. He sat down on the couch next to me.

"Listen. I didn't intentionally break my promise, okay? Um Khalid came to me yesterday and said she believes I love you more and I'm unfair with her. She asked me to divorce her," he said, rubbing his hands together, trying to warm them.

He's being unfair to her? I thought. I felt sure there must have been an objective truth inside the strange, opposing realities she and I were living. He wasn't capable of being in two places at once, after all, and the thought that he could be at a third location never occurred to either of us in the isolated, Ameer-centered lives we lead.

"Well, you didn't divorce her, apparently, so what on earth did you promise her that made her say 'Okay, fine, I won't divorce you.' Was it enough for you to agree to go to her tonight and break your promise to me?" I asked.

He chuckled to himself sardonically.

"No, I didn't promise her anything and no, she won't divorce me. Ever," he said, voice dripping with the sort of confidence only an Arab man in his home element could possess.

Apparently, Shahida's father and brothers came to Ameer's house the previous night and insisted he come back to her house and start our normal two-days with me, two-days with her schedule again—just four days after our baby was born.

"Yes, of course," I said. "I should have known. If your special wife, Shahida Um Khalid, doesn't get what she wants, she cries to daddy and he saves her every time, right?" I asked, scoffing.

"Actually, he defended you," he said.

"What?! Why? What happened?" I asked, shocked.

"I explained about the time I owe you for all your days and nights I spent with her during your pregnancy, and they listened. But then *Hajj* Muhammad asked her to explain her side of the story," he explained. "She said that you think because you're young and beautiful, you just get whatever you want. And she said you shame the family and don't honor our traditions. Then she asked me to divorce her, so her father slapped her across the face."

"Oh my God!" I replied out loud. "But why? Why did he slap her?"

"Oh, he did worse than that," he continued. "He called her all sorts of names and reminded her that you weren't there to defend yourself, so she shouldn't insult you."

I couldn't believe what I was hearing. I had met *Hajj* Muhammad—Shahida's father, and Ameer's great-uncle—a handful of times, and he was always warm and welcoming in an Egyptian-hospitality sort of way, but I never got the impression he cared for me at all, let alone enough to abuse his own daughter in my defense.

"I told her that I would always tend to your needs first because you don't have a father or anyone here to help you," he said, taking my hands in his.

I wondered when that whole "always tend to your needs first" bit would start...

Just then, the *athan* for *Isha* prayers began, prompting him to stand up and put his shoes on so he could go lead prayers at his mosque.

"Let's get to the point, okay? I don't care if you both cry. You and Um Khalid can kill yourselves with your sadness for all I care. I am a man, not a child, and I will go and come as I like. I won't answer to you, and I won't answer to her," he said sternly.

"No, I don't accept that, and it's wrong. You have a responsibility to us both to be fair with your time and money, and you're not even trying," I replied.

He ignored me, opened the door, and left.

* * *

July 6th, 2012

> *I became a real adult today! Again! Ameer has been in the* balad *the past two days, doing God knows what, and our food supplies were running low. I was feeling down and out anyway and felt sure that cooking spaghetti would make me feel less... incompetent in every way, I guess. I*

mean, it's hard to mess up something like spaghetti. I told Ameer I needed some ground beef weeks ago, but he always "forgets" to bring it (read: it's expensive and we're not his priority).

I am so tired of depending on other people to care for me. I'm an adult, for God's sake! I miss running-away-to-California-at-seventeen Kaighla and traveling-the-world alone Kaighla! No matter what anyone told me in India, I went where I wanted to go, and I didn't worry, even after that unfortunate incident on the train. But here, I feel absolutely handicapped.

Ameer had accidentally left a few guineas on the coffee table, and I knew he had a running tab with the market on the corner in the medina, *so I did the unthinkable: I sent the older kids to Mama Bushra, loaded up the baby, and went looking for a* tuk-tuk *to take us into town. Several neighbors stared, and several more whispered, but I was unfazed.*

Ameer always says you can tell which tuk-tuk *drivers are bad news based on the music they're blasting—or the lack thereof. And it's well known that the best drivers are actually the eleven- and twelve-year-old kids. I let a few handsome drivers who looked my age and were blasting some rap music go on by, and finally hailed one with a driver who looked to be roughly in his fifties, and who wasn't playing anything, neither music nor Qur'an recitation.*

I'd practiced what to say over and over again, but I still felt nervous when he pulled up. I leaned closer and said, in my best preschooler Arabic, "As-souq fil medina." He smiled and said it would be three guineas, which was pretty

146

lucky since I only had eight with me and needed to get back home.

When we arrived at the grocery store, the man behind the counter first smiled at me and then looked down in shame when he recognized me. I only stopped wearing niqab *a few months ago, so people are just now beginning to recognize me as the American wife of Sheikh Ameer. I was tired of not being able to breathe, and of having to fumble around with it, plus my* abaya, *when someone came to the door, just in case it was a man.*

I grabbed my few items—the meat and some apricot jam—brought them to the front of the store, and began taking them out of my basket. The middle-aged clerk started ringing things up, never making eye contact with me. When he'd finished bagging my groceries, he wrote down the total Ameer would owe next time he came in and handed me the bag, careful not let our hands touch. I made the mistake of smiling at him. Old habits, man. It's just... unnatural not to smile at retail people. It's impolite.

When I finished, the same tuk-tuk *driver was waiting outside for us. He asked me where I'd like to go next, and I fumbled the general address of our apartment. I think he asked if I meant the same place we'd just come from, but I didn't understand so I kept repeating the location of my house until he smiled and took the bag from my hand, inviting me to step in.*

When we arrived safely at the gate to our apartment building, I was elated and smiling from ear-to-ear, too wrapped up to try to hide my joy. It's almost as great as when I got my license at sixteen! How sad is that?!

10

An Aside: Surviving Your Egyptian Co-Wife

A mong all the fascinating creatures nature affords us, perhaps none is so unique, nor so misunderstood, as the Egyptian co-wife.

Her clever camouflage—most often a warm smile and regularly timed laugh—makes her hard to see for what she truly is: a stealthy predator with tricks up her proverbial sleeve no foreigner would ever be able to detect or predict without proper training.

Without you even noticing it, she will plant herself in your home-life. You will find her carried into your home on the back of your (shared) spouse—her hair on his clothing, her lipstick (often a gaudy color) on his collar, her sickly-sweet perfume lingering on his person. Her ability to worm her way into your most intimate atmosphere is truly a skill not to be trifled with.

If your Egyptian co-wife is a homemaker, she's likely armed with ample time on her hands. Rich or poor, she probably has very little desire to better herself in extracurricular pursuits. When she has finished her share of the housework—because she almost never does anything without help—she bides her time watching Arab/Turkish dramas, replete with tactics she takes note of, adding them to her arsenal.

She relies mostly on her cleverly disguised "teases." Mention in her presence that you read some interesting tidbit regarding medicine, science, or nature—indeed display any proficiency in anything other than how to cook or clean a house—and watch how she will be on the prowl. A cackle here, a throwing of hands in the air there, a tossing of the hair, complete with a *"Ya doctora!"* or *"Ya sheikha!"* or a sarcastic *"Enti shatra!"*—'How clever you are!'—and everyone in the room will be hypnotized by her charm, unable to notice the gaping wound in your proverbial side, oozing and bleeding.

Under no circumstances whatsoever should you let her know she has offended you, or else be prepared for an onslaught of accusation that you're being "too sensitive" and "not fun." If you have the misfortune to have been seriously emotionally wounded by your Egyptian co-wife, be prepared for a long, slow, and painful death. You will receive no medicine, no salve, no relief, and never, not ever—not until the sun freezes over—an apology. You will be expected by all-and-sundry to march on.

The safest way of surviving your Egyptian co-wife is avoidance, avoidance, avoidance. If at all possible, avoid her presence like the plague that it is.

Family event? Take a rain-check. Holiday? Go visit friends elsewhere and crash their fun. Illness on her part? Send a plate of cookies and a nice card.

In the event you are forced into her presence, keep your wits about you. When you enter her lair, greet her with the customary greeting and bow your head in reverence. If she shows the inclination, take her hand in yours and kiss her cheeks, or give the air of kissing them, as many times as she initiates—be it one, two, three, or four.

After this greeting, sit down where she invites you, ask her how her family is, and how each of her children is, by name. Of course, you must ask how her health is. She will find any excuse to complain of pain here or an ache there, always with a gracious *"Alhamdulillah"* and a sigh. Make a sad face and wish her good health in the future.

By-and-by, she will offer you tea and/or coffee. Refuse adamantly. She will insist. Refuse again. Continue this game until the third insistence, and then finally accept her offer—or else be accused of being too hasty in accepting too soon or rude in rejecting her for the third time!

While waiting for the tea and other refreshments, she may ask about your family, siblings, mother, friends, etc. Never tell her more than you would tell a passing acquaintance, or else be prepared for all you say, good or bad, to find its way across town and back to your doorstep some twenty-four hours later.

Your health? Say nothing other than, "It's good, *alhamdulillah.*" If you mention anything ailing you, be prepared for the questions you're sure to be bombarded with, almost always culminating in a subtle inference as to the occupancy status of your uterus.

Before the meeting is finished, be sure you will be mocked and/or insulted. Prepare for it. Don't let your guard down for a moment. Don't let the tea or sweets tantalize you so that you make yourself unaware of your environment—you are, after all, in the very lair of the beast! Make no mistake: she'll ululate even as she dances on your grave.

When the insult comes—and come, it shall—smile with her. Laugh with her if you feel so inclined. Thank her for the tea and refreshments and leave her presence as soon as all decency permits. Assure her you will come back at a later time. Kiss her cheek again, shake her hand, say *"Salaam,"* and flee for your very life.

Were you to have been wounded by the attack, do not under any circumstances refuse to come to her lair again, for if you do, fire and brimstone will be yours for breakfast, lunch, and dinner. Every look, every greeting from your shared family will be of contempt. You will be asked, urged, and pressured to apologize to her for keeping away from her. If you protest and present your reasoning, be prepared for tears and gnashing of teeth from your mother-in-law over the fact that you—yes you!—have created disunity in the family.

Soon enough, your shared spouse will come to her aid and rebuke you, by God, for refusing to keep the bonds of kinship, as she is your sister in Islam. Be sure every saying of Prophet Muhammad regarding treatment of your fellow Muslim, of covering his faults, of making excuses for his ill conduct, etc. will be thrown in your face and will plague your thoughts constantly until you finally relent and agree to apologize to her for trying to protect yourself from her.

Above all else, never imagine things will improve with time. As my very own sister-in-law said, "We Egyptians, we love drama! It's the spice of life! Life would be so boring without it!"

11

The Shattered Thing

Sharqia Governorate, Egypt

Summer 2012

One afternoon a few days before Ramadan, Ameer came home looking worried—well, more worried than usual, anyway. I brought him a glass of water and took his *jilbab* from him when he removed it. It was scorching outside, and our ceiling fan in the *salon* didn't seem to be doing much to cool things off.

"What's wrong?" I asked. "You seem bothered by something."

"It's just money problems," he replied, wiping his face with the towel I handed him. "The shop is costing so much more to open than we imagined it would. And the rent for this place is so expensive," he said, waving his hand around to indicate the apartment.

I saw where the conversation was going. He had been

investing every spare dime in the new spice shop he'd opened in the *medina*, and more than once he'd lamented the cost of my modest apartment's rent.

"You own a home, Ameer. We are only renting this apartment because Shahida won't let me live on one of the floors of my own husband's building," I said simply, standing up to get Rumi, as she had awoken from her nap and was fussing.

"You're right. I know. Plus, if you both lived in the big house, the kids could all see me anytime they wanted. And we'd have total privacy. The stairwell door has a deadbolt so no one can come into the top floor unless you unlock it from the inside," he said.

We both sat pondering on this possibility for a while before he said he'd talk it over with his mom and get back to me.

"To be clear," I added, "I am not interested in living in the same house as Shahida. It's a separate apartment on a separate floor. If she feels like it would be imposing on her for me to live in the same building… let's not push it."

"No, no. Nonsense. You're my wife, too," he said, walking into the bedroom for his mid-day nap.

* * *

Two weeks later, we were moved in—but certainly not to a different floor. I was given my own room and bathroom and specifically forbidden from even entering the stairwell that led to the second floor, while she held reign over every inch of the building aside from my bedroom and bathroom.

Almost immediately, it was clear that things were not going to go as smoothly as we'd hoped. Rumi cried all the time—as infants often do—and I barely slept, what with all the noise in the house, day and night. Egypt is a noisy country anyway, but in Ramadan, it takes on a louder tone, with all-night parties and kids and adults alike laughing and yelling in the streets until 4 a.m. Being so sleep-deprived and trying to nurse a newborn while trying to wrangle two toddlers was exhausting, so I napped at any and every moment the baby did.

"Um Abdullah sits around all day, sleeping with her baby, while we do all the work!" I heard Shahida complaining to Ameer one day. "This is not even her house! It's not my house, or *Nayna's* house, or even your house: this is Khalid's house!"

Ameer just sat there sipping his coffee as Shahida and Mama Bushra continued to berate him in Arabic for my lack of investment in the running of the sheikh's house.

He sat me down afterward and explained that she was right: the house was not his to invite me to, it was his son's, and by extension, Shahida's. If she said no, the answer was no.

"So when will I have my own house, Ameer?" I asked. "I have given you two children now. Where is my house? Why do I have to produce children to *earn* a home?!"

"Daughters don't need a house, Kaighla. Sons do. Khalid was almost five years old before I started building this house for them. We had two daughters before he was born, but we didn't build the house until he was grown and healthy after we lost his baby brother, Abdullah, who was born dead, *Allah yarhamhu,* may he rest in peace."

Of course. I would be entitled to the safety and security of a home when and if I gave the sheikh a son. My daughters, until and unless they married, would be living in their father or brother's house as *guests,* only welcome at his pleasure.

The next day, as Shahida and Mama Bushra smiled on, he hired a few men to move all my kitchen appliances—including the infamous cabinets—out of storage and into the shed in his backyard.

"They said if you won't cook or clean with them, you aren't welcome to eat with them or to use their kitchen to cook your own food," he explained.

"You cannot be serious!" I cried. "How do they think this is okay? To make me cook in a shed?! And how am I supposed to get water for cooking or washing the dishes?"

"I guess you can use the garden hose?" he said, shrugging. "They're fasting and still cooking and cleaning, unlike you. You could make an effort. You had Rumi a month ago, not yesterday."

That was the end of the discussion.

* * *

One night, I had been trying to sleep, but to no avail, because as soon as Rumi fell asleep, some noise or other in the street woke her up, and the whole process had to start again. Then, as things outside began to wind down, the party came inside, and Ameer, Shahida, and Mama Bushra sat with the older kids in the *salon*, watching some Ramadan-special Turkish drama or other, laughing and hooting and hollering.

I decided against reason to ask them to please quiet down a bit, but I was laughed out of the room and told I needed to "relax."

After another two hours of that, enough was enough.

"Excuse me!" I shouted in English. "There are a small baby and a very tired mother trying to sleep, not to mention two other small kids, and you're being too loud! Can you please be quiet?!" I knew they couldn't understand what I was saying, but felt sure my facial expressions and gestures were effective in conveying my frustration.

Everyone in the room sat quietly for a moment, unsure what to say or do. Then Shahida broke the silence with her characteristic cackle. "*Ya* Um Abdullah! It's okay! You calm down," she laughed.

My blood was boiling. I was sleep-deprived. I was over-whelmed. I was at my wit's end. I turned to face her head-on.

"Can you shut the fuck up?!" I yelled before I realized the words were coming out of my mouth.

Needless to say, no one as much as said "*Salaam*" to me for days after that.

* * *

My only respite that Ramadan was walking in the evenings with Jennah. Intelligent and friendly, she carried herself with uncommon dignity and grace for so young a person. She also spoke fairly decent English and seemed to be the only one of Shahida's children who actually liked me. Sure, Khalid was kind and helpful, but Jennah seemed to sincerely care about me as a person, and more than once I overheard her defending me to her mother.

Of course, our little chats enraged Shahida, but Ameer persuaded her to let it go because hey, at least Jennah was practicing her English, right?

We'd talk about anything and everything, Jennah and I. It was nice to be able to almost have a flowing conversation in my own language with someone other than Ameer for the first time in months, and Jennah's bright personality was a breath of fresh air.

"Is it true that Baba didn't tell you about Mama when you married him?" she asked me one evening as we strolled down the street in front of Ameer's house after *Maghrib*, the street-lamps beginning to come to life above us.

I was stuck. I didn't want to talk badly about her father—something even my mother didn't do, although my father had offered her several hundred dollars if she would abort me when she found out she was pregnant at sixteen—but I was, once more, faced with the decision to either make the sheikh look bad, or make myself out to be the bad guy.

"Well, he wasn't completely honest, no," I said, trying to balance on my ethical tightrope. "But I knew he had been married to her previously, and I knew about you kids."

"Yes, I know. I know Baba lies, but I don't know why," she said. "I am sorry your life here is so difficult, *Tante*. I will *never* accept for my husband to have multiple wives!"

"Good thinking, honey," I laughed. "It's not a lifestyle I can recommend, personally."

Jennah was beautiful, inside and out, and always had an extra helping of compassion and fun. It was odd and concerning to me that my only friend then was a seventeen-year-old girl, the daughter of my mortal enemy, but it's what I had.

* * *

One morning, a few days later, I woke to someone banging pans and dishes around in the kitchen. Ameer had spent the previous night with Shahida, so I was alone in bed except for Rumi. Mama Bushra made breakfast for the kids during Ramadan so Shahida could sleep in, so I assumed she was just having a bad morning or something.

I got up and went to the bathroom to clean myself up a bit, hoping I could offer Mama Bushra some help in the kitchen. I was trying to get on her good side as of late.

I finished drying my face and walked out of the bathroom toward the kitchen, and out of the corner of my eye, I saw not Mama Bushra in the kitchen, but Shahida. She was standing in the sunlight, smiling as she flipped an egg omelet. She was wearing nothing but a red negligée—which barely covered the important bits—right there in the kitchen, at 7 a.m. on a Tuesday.

As I turned to go back to my room, she heard me walking and feigned surprise, then threw her matching robe on with a flourish.

"*Sabah al-khair*, Um Abdullah. I wake you? Sorry," she said, blushing.

Just then, Ameer walked out of the bathroom, drying his hair, and when he saw us both there—she in her sexy robe, and I in my perpetually ratty mom-with-a-newborn getup—his face flushed.

Just as I turned to walk away, I swear she actually smirked at me.

Later, when Ameer came to my room to check on us, I asked him about it.

"I swear by Allah, Kaighla, nothing happened last night. We don't even sleep in the same bedroom anymore," he said. "I don't know why she wore that downstairs, except.." and he trailed off.

"Except... she knew I'd wake up to her noise and come see her and feel jealous..." I said, realizing myself how clever her little scheme was.

* * *

One night, Ameer and I were sitting in the *majlis* together and he was cuddled close to me, kissing my neck. The light was off and the door was only slightly ajar, but if someone had really wanted to spy on us, it would have been easy using the light from the kitchen or hallway. My after-birth bleeding hadn't finished yet, but we were enjoying kissing one another.

They made a stink about us going in the *majlis* and closing the door behind us once before, saying it was inappropriate for us to spend time alone in a room other than my bedroom. We were like two teenagers, forced to sneak away to our bedroom if we wanted to spend any time alone in any capacity. No chilling in the *salon*, watching a movie like a normal couple, apparently. So, we left the door just barely open, enough to let a stream of light in from the hallway.

Mama Bushra interrupted our interlude when she barged in yelling something in Arabic about some cousin of hers who was coming to visit us. So later, when we were alone again for a moment in my bedroom, I asked him if he could maybe speak to Shahida.

"*Ya* Ameer, Shahida has an entire floor to herself. Can't you talk to her about just letting me have that *majlis* for my own uses? There's another living room, plus two more upstairs! You have two wives and two floors, so, technically, I should have my own floor," I said, exasperated that no one seemed to see my side of things.

"You're right, honey. I will talk to her, *insha'Allah*," he promised.

The next day, after *Maghrib*, I was sitting with Siham and the younger kids in the *majlis*, helping them with their English homework, when we overheard Ameer and Shahida arguing in the *salon*. My Arabic was still too weak to make myself clear, but I understood more than I spoke, and from what I could gather, she was not taking the new living arrangement as well as we'd hoped. We all tried to ignore their private conversation, but I knew Jennah and Khalid—as well as their middle daughters, Aalia and Barakah—were in the room with them.

Things got quieter for a moment as if they were trying to speak more privately. Just then, we heard hard skin-on-skin contact.

In a flash, all the kids were up, running into the *salon* to see what had happened. I managed to scramble to my feet and get into the *salon* just quickly enough to see Shahida holding her cheek and running up the stairs, and Ameer running after her.

The house was in an uproar, with all the small kids crying. Mama Bushra was screaming at the older kids to calm their siblings, and then she, too, ran upstairs after Shahida and Ameer. The ruckus woke up Rumi who started screaming, so I ran to my room to get her and make sure my kids and Juwariya were okay. They were scared, of course, but seemed otherwise unfazed by the scene.

For hours afterward, Ameer tried to get into Shahida's room. "*Ya* Khalid! Where's the screwdriver? No, bring me the other one, *ya ibn al-kalb!*" I heard him shouting.

When I asked Jennah what was happening upstairs, she dried her tears and tried to explain, stumbling on her English. "It's not safe for Mama to be in that room alone," she said. "We don't know what she may try to do to herself. Baba is trying to unlock the door from the outside."

By 1 a.m., most of the house had fallen asleep and Ameer still had not come to my room. It was my night with him, and I thought surely he would still come to sleep in our bedroom. I hadn't done anything wrong, after all, and I was sure we were on the same page about the *majlis*.

I grabbed Rumi, who had fallen asleep on me, walked to the bottom of the stairs, and called up to him, trying to keep my voice down. He came down the stairs, looking enraged, his clothes filthy with dust, and his hair disheveled.

"What?! What do you want, Kaighla?!" he yelled at me, *not* trying to keep his voice down.

I was confused about why he was yelling at me. "I'm just wondering if you're coming to bed anytime soon? Rumi's asleep and I'm almost there, so I wanted to check if you were coming?" I asked.

"No, Kaighla, I won't be!" he said, clearly annoyed with me. "As you can see, I am dealing with something! Now, go back to bed."

"Ameer… have you thought that maybe if Shahida ran into the room and locked the door, it's because she wants some privacy and doesn't want you to come in? You did slap her in the face, after all…" I replied.

His eyes changed then, and he bolted down the stairs and grabbed me by the shoulders, slamming me hard up against the cold metal door in the stairwell, just like he used to do in Dearborn when we had fights.

"You will shut your mouth and go to your bedroom right now or else I will do to you what I did to her, or worse," he said quietly in my face, his rage boiling with each seething word.

He was smashing Rumi between us, and she started wailing.

"You're hurting me! You're hurting the baby!" I cried. "I didn't

161

do anything wrong! Why are you punishing me for what she did, for what you did?!" I struggled in vain to push him away from me with my free hand.

He calmed down and backed away slowly, before turning and stomping back up the stairs.

"Go to bed!" he yelled.

I did go to bed then, and I cried myself to sleep.

The next morning, Shahida was gone. She had run away to her father's house, leaving her children, Mama Bushra, Ameer and I to clean up the mess she left in her wake.

* * *

A few days later, Ameer and Mama Bushra went to the village to try to repair things with Shahida, and the older kids went off to school for the day, leaving four small kids in my care, one of whom was a newborn.

Mama Bushra didn't exactly leave me with a list of household responsibilities, but I knew from watching her and Shahida what they did each day, so I got started as soon as I could. I really wanted to impress her and make her see that Shahida wasn't the only woman in the house who could keep things afloat.

But halfway through the day, the kids were fighting, Saji had peed all over the floor and herself, and the baby was vomiting every time I tried to nurse her. I had to decide between preparing the *Iftar* meal for after *Maghrib* or cleaning up the *salon* and hanging the laundry, so I focused my attention on the food.

When everyone came home later and saw that the *salon* had not even been swept, all hell broke loose. "Where is she and why doesn't she do her job?!" Mama Bushra yelled as she walked in through the courtyard.

I tried to calm down, reminding myself that she yelled about everything always, and her voice level wasn't ever an indication of her mood. But it was pointless; when she came into the kitchen, there was no denying she was angry.

"I'm sorry, *Nayna*," I said, genuinely feeling awful. "I really tried but the kids were too much." I wasn't sure she understood my Arabic, but she seemed to grasp that I was giving her an excuse. Frustrated, she yelled at Khalid to go to the shop and get his dad.

When Ameer arrived, she screamed at him, walking around the house and pointing at this and that, apparently criticizing my house-keeping skills.

"Why, why, why did you bring her in here and let her drive Um Khalid away?! Um Abdullah isn't even a woman! Aalia and Barakah are more capable than she is, and they're not even fourteen! What do American mothers even teach their daughters?!" she yelled at him as he walked in the door.

I sat in my bedroom, listening to the entire thing, feeling increasingly broken down and bad about myself. Why couldn't I be a normal woman? Why couldn't I keep the house spotless while multiple kids ran here and there? Egyptian women seemed to do it all, without fail, so why couldn't I?

An old familiar feeling began to rise up in me, the inner voice I heard so much as a girl, telling me, "You're not good enough." *He doesn't want you here and his mother doesn't either. You're a parasite. They wish you'd go away so Shahida could come back and be the real woman they all need in their lives,* I thought.

When he came into the room and found me crying, he had no kindness in his eyes. He demanded to know why I had allowed

163

the house to fall into such disrepair. What had I done all day? Why did I make Shahida leave if I didn't want to take her place?

"First of all," I said, choking on my tears, "I did not make her leave. *You* slapped her in the face, for dubious reasons I still don't understand, and then the next day, she was gone! How can I be blamed for that?" I asked, genuinely confused.

"If you had not made us come here, back to this awful country, none of this would have happened! It's because you insisted on being here and because you moved into her house, and then you demanded your own space in her house! That's why she left!" he said, his anger beginning to show through.

"And I'll tell you exactly why I slapped her," he added. "She called me a pussy-licker. She said I only show you kindness because you own me, because I love your... private parts!" he added.

"Yeah, well, you and I both know pussy-licking isn't your style," I quipped bitterly.

He scoffed. "Only men who don't respect themselves would ever do such a thing!"

"Oh, you won't give it, but you have no problem demanding it yourself!" I shouted. "No wonder your wives are never happy..."

I could tell from the way he smirked that I'd hit a nerve, but he didn't say anything, so I let it go.

"Ameer, it is not my fault that you didn't want to give your wife her rights," I said, trying to clean the *kohl* that was smearing around my eyes. "I just wish I never came here!" I cried.

"I wish you didn't either. You'll never be the woman Um Khalid is," he said pointedly.

Before I could respond, someone knocked on the door. It was Shahida, returned from her pilgrimage to her daddy's house, asking if everything was okay. It was late now, almost midnight, and she wanted to know if he was coming to bed. He got up to leave the room.

"You will go to her? When I am hurting like this, and you see it? You don't love me! I don't want to live! I cannot live like this anymore!" I screamed. "You tricked me into marrying you and then when I made us come here so *she* could have her rights, you walked all over me! I swear I will kill myself if you go to her tonight!" I cried.

"Yes, cry. Cry! Cry harder! Let your tears drown you for all I care! Eat yourself in your anger! Let your sadness kill you! I don't care!" he yelled, getting up to leave the room.

In a flash, I grabbed my computer charger, threw the ends around my neck and began to pull as tight as I could. The world began to get dark and Rumi, laying just a foot away from me on the bed, began to cry. But I pulled harder and harder, with all the strength I could manage, choking the air from my own lungs.

I could not see a way out. I could not escape him. I could not see that I would ever have a better life than the hell I was living in. My kitchen was in a shed and I had no privacy of my own, while she enjoyed an entire house for herself. I had no family to come and fight for my rights and every time he hurt her, it was somehow my fault for wanting some semblance of a normal life. I was hated and misunderstood by everyone I knew, from his family to strangers on the street. I was nothing but a parasite in their lives, a parasite they kept around in the hopes I'd produce the son Shahida had given up on producing. There was nowhere for me to run, now with three kids, and even if there had been, I didn't have the courage to leave, to tear my children from their father.

Ameer burst into the room right then, grabbed the computer

cord from my hands and pushed hard on my chest to make me let go. He threw it on the ground and held me as tight as he could, gripping my hands behind my back to stop me from clawing at him, and he was crying as hard as I cried.

"What is wrong with you?" he cried. "Don't you fear God?! Suicide is unforgivable!"

But I didn't care. I didn't fear Hell and I didn't crave heaven or salvation. I didn't even particularly want to die. I just didn't want to live my life anymore, and I saw no way out.

Rumi began to cry harder now, and he took her in his arms, trying to shush her. "She needs your milk, Kaighla! Please," he said, pushing her into my arms. I tried to nurse her, but she turned away from my breast like she wanted nothing to do with me, just like Sajidah had a few months after we got to Egypt. Eventually, I coaxed her into a latch, and she fed, her face red with exhaustion and fear. He kissed her head and then mine.

"I will go to her now because she has been gone many nights and it's her turn to be with me, okay," he said, not waiting for my approval. And just like that, he left.

My laptop charger lay on the ground busted, a testament to the events of the evening.

* * *

That night I dreamed I was drowning and could not find a foothold, the earth shrinking away from me with every wave.

When I woke up, I knew enough was enough. I needed to see a doctor, as soon as possible, and I wouldn't take "no" for an answer.

"No, I can't take you to that kind of doctor," he said plainly. "It would ruin my reputation to have a crazy wife. You are already

166

known as the crazy American, but if I took you to that type of doctor, I really would lose all the respect anyone still has for me here," he said.

He really was more concerned with his reputation than with the fact that his wife, the mother of his children, had tried to kill herself the night before.

"I will refuse to eat anything until you take me to the doctor," I said.

"It's Ramadan. Don't eat, I don't mind. If your milk dries up, I will buy formula for Rumi. And you're not that skinny, so you won't die," he said, laughing off my suicide attempt as if it were a joke between us.

And so I did not eat, not for several days. I drank water to keep up my milk supply, but I kept myself and the kids in my room, only leaving to cook food in my shed-kitchen and bring it back to the bedroom for them to eat. I didn't allow the kids to leave the room since Shahida and Mama Bushra had been complaining that my kids made messes that I "wouldn't clean up."

He came to the room one afternoon a few days later and it was clear what he wanted. He taught me when we first married that angels curse women who refuse to have sex with their husbands, according to a likely-fabricated saying by Prophet Muhammad, so I didn't try to resist, but I didn't welcome him either. As he moaned and rammed himself into me, I didn't react at all. I didn't touch him and didn't kiss him back. I just laid under him, like a corpse, with my eyes focused on the ceiling above me, unresponsive to his jerking climax.

Never once in our marriage had I been dispassionate in bed, or in life, so it was disturbing for Ameer. He finally took me seriously and agreed to take me to see a psychiatrist.

I could have died of starvation, or else successfully committed suicide, but as long as I willingly gave him my body and acted as if I liked it, he would have continued to ignore my suffering, even as I was slowly dying in every sense of the word.

* * *

The next morning, Ameer and I and Rumi went to Faqqous to see a psychiatrist someone had recommended to him when he asked around, discreetly. He didn't look at me the entire ride, choosing instead to focus on the Qur'an recitation we were listening to.

By the time we arrived, I was beginning to think this was a waste of time. But then the doctor called us into his office. Seeing Rumi, he smiled and asked how old she was. He didn't ask me about my mental health or what could be wrong but made polite, cheerful conversation.

"Little Rahmah seems healthy, *masha'Allah*," he said. "And tell me: were all your babies as sweet and easy as she is?"

"No," I answered. "The others were much more difficult." It was true. For all she'd been through in her little life, Rahmah truly had lived up to her name: she was the brilliant mercy in my life, the mercy I so desperately needed. She ate well, slept through the night, and was a generally pleasant baby, while both Dayo and Saji had given me a run for my money.

He stood up and asked me to stand on a scale he had in the room, and it was the first time since we arrived in Egypt that I had weighed myself. None of the obstetricians we visited seemed the least bit concerned about my weight. I couldn't believe it when he converted the number from kilograms to pounds. Any other time, I'd have celebrated being so thin, but now, I was malnourished and weak. There was nothing to celebrate.

He examined the marks on my neck then, touching me gently, like he was afraid I may break under the slightest pressure. "And how are you feeling otherwise. Beyond your physical health, I mean?" he asked, finally broaching the subject.

I started slowly, testing his English comprehension, unsure if I should dump the whole problem on him if he couldn't grasp my level of speaking, but I was shocked by how well he seemed to understand.

He began to ask probing questions about why I was in Egypt, and the floodgates fell open. Several times throughout my tale, he handed me the box of tissues, sure I would start to cry any minute, but I felt numb. I had given up on living, so there was nothing to cry about.

I told him everything, starting with the night I married Ameer and he began his campaign to kill my personality, bit-by-bit, all in the name of his twisted version of Islam, which was, at that time, the only Islam I'd ever known.

When I had finished telling the doctor what ailed me, he sat back in his chair for a long time, looking down at his desk, then the wall, then me, and briefly at Ameer.

Sheikh Ameer sat in the chair next to me, drumming his hands on his *jilbab*, looking at the floor, clearly wondering when he'd be able to tell his side of the story.

After what seemed like an eternity, the doctor finally sat forward in his chair. He looked into my face, smiled, and did something I never expected a man to do in Egypt: he grabbed my hand from across his desk and seemed almost like he would cry.

Ameer tensed in his seat, visibly shaken by the breach of

conduct the doctor displayed in his plain view.

The doctor let go of my hand and cleared his throat, then turned in his chair, squeaking, to face my husband full-on.

Ameer began to say something or other in Arabic, no doubt defending himself or making an excuse like he had so many other times before.

The doctor stopped him, mid-sentence. "No, I'm sorry to interrupt you, but we will speak in English, sheikh, if you don't mind, so that the sister can understand everything."

I felt afraid just then that he would take my hand, lead me out of the doctor's office and rail at me in the car home, but he sat back in his chair.

"I understand, sir," he said in his comparatively worse English. "I just have one question for you, though, doctor, before you speak."

The doctor nodded, inviting him to continue.

"Please, doctor, tell me: what is wrong with Um Abdullah? Is there some kind of medicine I can give her so she can stop being so sick and so crazy?"

The doctor, seeming half-amused and half-irritated, sat up straight in his chair and focused his eyes on Ameer.

"With my full respect for you, *ya* sheikh, I have to ask you: *what in God's name is wrong with you?*" he said in clear English, so I—the sister—could hear.

The sister was impressed.

"It is a simple question, Sheikh Ameer, so don't act so surprised and offended. How on earth can you come into my office and ask me what could be wrong with your wife when it's clear that you are the person who is deranged!"

At that, the sheikh's mouth fell open and he laughed in his uncomfortable way.

"I'm so sorry, doctor, but I really can't understand your meaning. We came here to see how we can help my wife, not me," he said, frustrated.

"Yes, and that is my priority, above all else. I am making it my personal mission to ensure that we do help your wife, and as soon as possible, but to do that, we must fix the problem," the doctor replied, "and you, sheikh… *you* are the problem in Um Abdullah's life."

Seeing Ameer squirm in his seat, the doctor went on. "How could you have done all that to this woman? How could you have brought her here to this place and neglected her and abused her as you have? I don't care about you having two wives. I don't even care to talk about how you intentionally deceived this woman, who was a new Muslim, into marrying you, using your religious authority to intimidate her *wali* into accepting you. That is over and done," he said, waving his hand as if to dust the past away.

"What I want to know is how you justify in your heart the many ways you have neglected this woman, she who has no one else to help her, she who has no family to fight for her rights? Do you have no fear of God?"

At this, Ameer's face turned red and it was clear he felt ashamed, if not sincerely remorseful.

"Yes, I am asking you," the doctor continued, "how you have continued like this for more than a year, leaving her without your care and comfort, without money, without help? And she was pregnant with your child, this beautiful baby we see here!"

Ameer started to speak in Arabic again, but again the doctor stopped him. "No, sheikh. No. English only. You did marry this woman who does not speak Arabic and you convinced her to love you and trust you, yes? Clearly, you have *some* English abilities. Please, answer my questions in English, then," he said sardonically.

When it was clear that Ameer was not permitted to justify himself in Arabic and lacked the vocabulary to explain his actions in English, he gave up.

The doctor looked at me again. "My dear sister, I must tell you that what this man has done to you is not okay in Islam and don't think because he is a sheikh he knows better than others. Only a very bad person neglects to care for those who depend on him, and you absolutely depend on this man."

He sat quietly again for a moment.

"Now, as far as what we can do to help the sister," he continued, turning now to Ameer, "I see two steps: first of all, you must—absolutely *must*—get your wife out of that house and away from your family, and it must be as soon as possible. I am confident that if you do not save her from this life you have brought her into, she will be dead within a matter of weeks."

He seemed to sit up straighter then, listening more intently. I began to feel like I couldn't hear his words clearly, the honking and shouting of the street coming in through the shutters. But it was the din of my blood rushing through my body that was loudest. I felt like I was underwater or else hovering above the scene and watching the conversation.

"And? You said there were two steps. What else?" Ameer asked.

"I can prescribe her some calming medication, very powerful, to take every few hours for the next several days until you can get her out of that situation. She would not be able to care for her baby or the other children, as she would be asleep or incoherent the entire day, just to stop her from having another episode. And she could not nurse little Rumi here because the medication isn't safe for babies," he added.

"No, of course, I don't want this," I spoke up. "I don't need medication. You said yourself there is nothing wrong with me."

"Yes, sister. You have laid out your entire mental health history for me well, and even considering your previous experiences with mental health professionals, your history, and your mental state now, I can promise you that what is causing you all this suffering is not in your head, and that's the good news," he said reassuringly.

"If we can get her out of this situation, I am very confident she will recover in no time. She is strong and resilient," he said, now looking at Ameer with softer eyes.

The sheikh looked at his watch as the mosque nearby called people to the *Isha* prayer. "Oh, you are in a hurry?" the doctor asked him.

"I'm sorry to offend you, but I do need to get back to town. My son is alone with my mother in our shop and I need to be there for the nightly Ramadan rush," he said. "I can't have her doing these things. She is scaring my other children and of course, I don't want her to suffer anymore. Please, can you write a prescription for some other drugs for her?"

The doctor was not amused. "No. As I have just tried to explain, aside from drugging her into oblivion, there is nothing I can do for your wife until you take her out of the toxic, dangerous situation you have placed her in."

And with that, we stood up, said "*Salaam,*" and went on our way.

I was terrified when we got into the car, sure he would berate me as he always did when I told anyone details about our home life, but he was kind and gentle and helped me into the car, stopping along the way to buy me a chocolate croissant and asking if I needed anything else.

When we arrived, he brought me into the bedroom and tucked me in, saying he needed to go close the shop for Khalid and Mama Bushra but promising to be back in an hour. I snuggled with Rumi and fell asleep, awakened momentarily when Ameer climbed into bed next to me a few hours later.

12

The Temporary Reprieve

Cairo, Egypt

Autumn 2012

J ust a few days after we met with the psychiatrist, I was
invited by a fellow convert I knew online to come and stay
at her place near Cairo. It was a welcome excursion, all
things considered. I left the other kids with Ameer and he drove
Rumi and me south.

Mariah and I had become friends a few months before when
we came across one another's blogs and had bonded over
our shared distaste for polygyny. Her husband had actually
waited a full seven years after their wedding to re-marry his
ex-wife—right when Mariah finally got pregnant with twins
after five years of miscarriages and fertility treatments.

Her twins were just a few months old then. She'd been able
to hire a nanny and maid to help her with the twins and the

house—a beautiful two-story apartment in an affluent suburb of Cairo. She seemed overall well-cared for, but generally dissatisfied and uncomfortable with her situation, so we spent hours sitting together, taking turns caring for our shared three babies and talking about the hardships and hilarities of life as a foreign, second wife.

After a few days, Mariah's husband was coming back in town, so I needed to either find somewhere else to stay or go back to the hell that was Ameer's house. Mercifully, just then, Sofia, a fellow blogger, invited me to stay at her place.

Sofia was Portuguese and had fled Lisbon when she was only seventeen years old. One night, she'd overheard her family discussing committing her to an insane asylum because she refused to abandon Islam. She was able to seek asylum in Egypt thanks to a friendship she'd developed online with two women, sisters from Cairo. When they relayed her pressing situation to their parents, they did the unthinkable and invited Sofia to come to live with them—she, a foreigner they didn't know from Eve, but who was clearly in need of rescuing.

It's hard to tell if their kindness was entirely selfless, though, since shortly after she fled to Egypt, the younger brother of her two friends came of age and began looking for a wife. Sofia became that wife, and it was the best decision she ever made, to hear her tell the story.

After more than three years of marriage, Sofia and her husband also suffered from infertility, like Mariah and her husband. I found it peculiar that I was overwhelmed with too much fertility while my friends so badly wanted babies.

Sofia and I had so much fun hanging out and watching movies in her small apartment in Ma'adi, an upper-middle-class neighborhood in Cairo. More than anything, we enjoyed sharing stories of the horrifying things our in-laws had done to us in their endeavor to make us more palatable to Egyptians. I found Sofia's warm presence to be such a welcome relief from the suffering of the previous year.

Eventually, though, I knew I had to find a more permanent living solution in Cairo if I wanted to avoid being sent back to my prison in rural Egypt, so we began looking in expat Facebook groups for English teaching positions. A few days later, an older American convert actually came to Sofia's home to interview me for a co-teaching position at an international academy in Fifth Settlement, a bourgeoisie neighborhood built in the middle of the desert on the outskirts of Cairo, made up of malls, gated communities, country clubs, and expensive international schools. Ameer came to help find us an apartment, and we tentatively agreed that he would spend three days a week in Cairo and four days in Sharqia.

Just weeks after attempting to take my own life, the kids and I were settled into our new apartment in Ma'adi Al-Zahra—a mere few miles from Sofia's apartment—and I was working at one of the most prestigious schools in the Middle East. All was looking up, just as the doctor had predicted.

* * *

Ring Road between Ma'adi and The Fifth Settlement is busy, and the traffic is congested, with smog rising above the streets and cars weaving dangerously near one another, the occasional motorcycle dodging minivans and trucks. Rumi always slept during the ride home, the bumping and jostling and horn-honking creating her own little Egyptian lullaby.

I'd made a few friends with some other teachers at school, but none I loved so much as Tina. A Greek, Tina fell hopelessly in love with an Egyptian man who came to her hometown as a travel agent fifteen years before, and they had never left one another's side since then. She was one of the few women I knew who converted for love, and then actually came to love Islam. Most others who convert for their *habibi*—sure and certain he's different, not like those other guys, and he *"really loves me"*—eventually realize it's not Islam they wanted at all. But Tina loved Islam and she loved life, and she enlivened the spirit of every person she came in contact with.

We lived around the same neighborhood, and we spent our rides home from school talking about the ways Egypt had made us crazy. But our favorite topic, and indeed the topic so many teachers loved talking about with me, was what life was like in what they called "the *balad.*" If only they knew what the real *balad* was like! Our little town was mild compared to that.

"I have first cousins who live out there, and I have never even visited them!" one teacher said to me one day in her heavy British accent. "I mean, it's bonkers! My God, how did you survive?!"

It was a theme, it seemed, that most of these Egyptian women could never imagine living in a place like our town in Sharqia, and yet, somehow, Ameer had expected me, a foreigner, to live like Shahida.

Before my time in Cairo, I'm embarrassed to admit that I truly never imagined there were educated, sophisticated women in all of Egypt. The women I met in our small town in Sharqia all strived to be incredible cooks and housekeepers, but never intellectuals. A good wife cooks and cleans well, and though it's important, typically, for girls and boys alike to complete high school, post-secondary education for a woman was usually seen as a luxury, at best, and a shameful waste of time and money, at worst.

But these women in Cairo were positively posh. They were stylish and smart and savvy, and I could not imagine a man doing to them what Ameer had done to me, or to Shahida for that matter.

Some of the Egyptian teachers scoffed at me for wearing hijab and praying in the break room between classes. They were raised to believe that hijab was for low-class, uneducated people from the *balad*, and they spoke of Islam as an unfortunate aspect of their heritage they'd like to ignore, at best. There were other teachers in the school, though, who really loved Islam and were eager to teach me. A few even joined Tina and me in her classroom to learn and memorize new Qur'an verses once a week.

When I wasn't co-teaching or helping the main class teacher with chores, I went down to the nursery to check on Rumi. I was hesitant to leave her with them, as the overworked, under-appreciated women I knew in our small town typically had no interest in actually caring for babies, happy instead to give them anything and everything to make them *just. shut. up. dammit.* But Rumi seemed happy and well-cared for there, and they always called or texted to tell me when she needed to nurse instead of just slipping her some formula.

There was a private room adjacent to the nursery for teachers to come breastfeed their babies, and it was my little oasis each day, sitting with the other nursing moms. Many of them had questions, too, about my life in rural Egypt, having heard about the crazy American girl working as a co-teacher who willingly lived in the *balad*.

What was more shocking than my village stories—like the

time Mama Bushra asked if I wanted a chicken for dinner, then killed it and plucked its feathers without disemboweling it or cutting off the head or feet, leaving the naked carcass on the kitchen counter for me to find—was my story about giving birth to Rumi.

It wasn't just the home-birth that shocked them—something which exceeded their wildest nightmares and seemed to them like a horrible, insane thing to have subjected myself to. No, it was the fact that I gave birth *vaginally* that shocked them first.

"Why on earth would you choose to push a baby out of yourself if you don't have to?! Modern science has made an easier, better way! Why stick to the ways of the past?" one mother asked me as we both sat in the nursing room with our babies.

I started to tell her about the mountain of scientific evidence that supports vaginal birth, but she seemed uninterested.

"Yeah, okay. Maybe. But at the end of the day, why subject yourself to that kind of hell if you don't have to? I loved scheduling my birth during a good time for my family, going to sleep comfortably, and then waking up with my baby in my arms! And," she added, quieter this time, in case anyone was walking by the thin door, "what about your husband? Don't you feel worried he won't enjoy being intimate with you anymore? Surely your body will not be the same… down there… after shoving a baby out of you."

I didn't think such a comment deserved an answer, so I let it go, but this mindset never got easier for me to handle.

My favorite part of the day was when I got a break between classes and Rumi was sleeping or otherwise not interested in nursing, so I had an hour to swim in the school's Olympic-sized indoor, heated swimming pool. They had a ladies-only session each day, and I couldn't believe my luck that it was scheduled during my break. It had been easily six years since I swam at all—since before I converted and began covering my entire body—so that time of enjoying myself in the water again was such a blessing to me. I took all my frustration and all my worries out, slapping my arms into the water, paddling back and forth, up and down the swim lane in my t-shirt and shorts.

On the days when Ameer was in town, he got the kids from the day-care across the street from our house and made an early dinner for us all, and it was the least he could do considering he laid around all day reading and relaxing while I worked at the school and Shahida worked in his shop in the village.

I started knitting again and set up a small prayer space in the spare bedroom, where I kept my Qur'an and my *hadith* books. I spent a little time each night reading a bit of this and a bit of that after *Isha* prayer, and it gave me solace. Tina also lent me a few great self-help books that I read a bit before bed, too.

All in all, I was so glad I was able to escape Ameer's family and that town, and I couldn't imagine a better set-up for us. We all—myself, the kids, and even the sheikh—seemed much happier and light-hearted. Slowly but surely, the light started to return to my eyes, and I began waking up each day with hope and ambition again.

* * *

Of course, things weren't always good in Cairo. Every time Ameer came to town for our cycle together, he seemed to forget whose house he was in. He ordered me around, acting angry and annoyed when I didn't serve him like royalty. By the second day, though, he usually remembered I was not her. I was the wife who worked full-time and had three kids to care for alone, while she worked part-time and had his mother and a slew of friends and sisters and other in-laws to help her. By about the third day, we'd have adjusted back into our more egalitarian lifestyle—just in time for him to leave and start all over again. It was exhausting, to say the least.

There was also the annoyance of him not being able to make money in Cairo, as no mosque was willing to hire him for private lessons when he was only in town a few days a week, but I tried to get over it. I also didn't understand how or why Shahida complained so much about working in the shop. If I had to work and he couldn't even provide more than twenty or thirty guineas to me per week, she should suffer, too, I thought.

Generally, I tried to think of Shahida as little as possible. I imagined him there in Sharqia with her, wishing he was with me—laughing, watching English movies together and having all the sex we wanted. I knew he only went there for his children, his mom, and his shop, and Shahida was a necessary evil.

But sometimes, when I was sitting in my little prayer room and reading my books, I had moments of deep thought. I came across a Qur'an verse on one such night that describes Heaven as a place wherein all our animosity will be dissolved and we will look at our former enemies as dear friends, and it made me think of her. I remembered the few times she'd been kind to me, and longed for those days.

Then, I came across a *hadith* one day that shook me to the core. Prophet Muhammad told his companions that a true believer will not keep up animosity for another Muslim by avoiding talking to him for more than three days, implying that someone who *does* nurse animosity isn't a real Muslim.

Three days, he said. It had been *three months* since I left her there to reclaim her home. Not once had we spoken, not even when I went with him to visit the family one weekend. When I approached her to say *"Salaam"* outside his shop, she turned about-face and fled. And I knew that I couldn't really blame her; she didn't trust me and believed I had intentionally come to Egypt to wreck her life, so it made sense she avoided me.

Good riddance, I said sometimes, until I came across such verses and *ahadith*, and my mind began to speak quietly to my heart, pushing me to try anything to reconcile with her, any way I could.

* * *

January 8th, 2013

> *I really don't know what happened. I have been working at the academy since August and everything was fine. I love my job and somehow the days Ameer wasn't here weren't all that bad, and I was able to manage things fine on my own. And then somehow—and I can't think when or why—things became too much.*
>
> *For one thing, I never see Sofia. She lives just a short taxi ride from here, but neither her husband nor Ameer will let us take taxis alone—for good reason, I suspect—and neither is available to shuttle us back and forth when I am not working. I feel almost as lonely and isolated here as I did in the* balad.
>
> *I miss spending time with my kids. I want to be the one raising them, not some random strangers. Saji actually prefers Fatima, the older lady who lives a few buildings*

from us. She came highly recommended as a sort of part-time nanny. On the days when Ameer is in Sharqia, she comes to sit with them in the morning, since I have to be at my bus stop two hours before their day-care opens. Seeing Sajidah's eyes light up when "Mama Fatima," as she calls her, comes in the morning... it just eats me up inside. That should be me she smiles at like that, but I'm never here.

I am tired of being the one to provide for the family, too. I have no reason to respect Ameer, as he has done so much to destroy the respect I once had for him. Within me, I feel a growing sense of bitterness and rage against him for coming here and living off of my hard work, contributing nothing financially beyond a few pounds here and there, and then going back home and making her work in the shop, too. If there is any hope of our marriage surviving, I have to be the housewife again. I have to depend on him for something or soon I won't have any respect for him at all.

Also, I feel guilty, knowing how everyone here and there is suffering because I am just not strong enough to make things work in Ameer's small town. All these children are missing out on time with their father and their siblings, all because I am just too selfish and weak to handle things there. That weighs heavy on me, day and night.

And under it all, there is the fear I have that God will not forgive me for breaking my relationship with Mama Bushra and Shahida. Sure, they're rude to me, but at the end of the day, they're my family as much as he is, and God forbids us from cutting off ties with our family. So long as I stay here, we will never be able to fix things between us, and I see that now. I will get comfortable in my world here and slowly forget any responsibility I have to them.

13

The Blame Game

Sharqia Governorate, Egypt

March 13th, 2014

I am happier. Happier than I was here before, at least. I get to spend my time with my kids again rather than working all day and seeing them for only a few hours at night. I am so grateful for the many ways my husband is trying to change. And I am grateful for this apartment.

It's beautifully designed with a large salon *in the front and a nice-sized bathroom. There are not one, but two patios! One is huge and sits in front of the apartment overlooking the road, just a few feet higher than the sidewalk. I sit out there every morning drinking my tea and listening to the boys at the high school across the street sing the Egyptian national anthem and do their exercises before school. It reminds me of my job in Cairo and gives me good memories. The back patio is where I dry the laundry and*

186

we sit in the evening, enjoying the sights and sounds of the neighbors laughing and talking in the grassy area behind the apartment bloc.

There are iron grates on all the doors and windows, for safety, but I don't feel unsafe here. I am right in the middle of town and I walk every morning to get our bread, fool, *and* tawmiyyah *from the stalls. I started wearing* niqab *again because of how the men here, unaccustomed to foreign women, stare at me. I guess that's one thing I miss about Cairo—men didn't stare as much.*

And there is so much green! Aside from the huge grassy knoll behind our apartment that all the buildings share, there are trees in my front yard that hang over the patio, giving shade and keeping the dust off of us. Dayo took my camera the other day and walked around the house taking pictures of all the beauty he saw.

But more than my surroundings, it's my thought processes that are making me happier. I finally pray on time, all the time, with very few exceptions. I read Qur'an every night before bed, then read the English translation so I can grasp what I'm reading.

I have chosen to be grateful for what I have. I know now that my thinking determines my circumstances, and I have Tina to thank for that shift. She lent me a few books in Cairo, including As a Man Thinketh *by James Allen, and* You Can Be Happy No Matter What *by Richard Carlson. More than ever, I understand that verse from the Qur'an that says God will never change someone's condition until they change what is within their hearts, so I focus more on changing my heart and less on changing my circumstances.*

I smile more, and that makes me happy, which makes me

187

smile more, which makes me happy. That's what wearing the niqab *is good for, too, beyond keeping me somewhat anonymous (until I speak, anyway...): men can't see my face, so I can smile more without fear. Smile at a man here and he'll go home and tell his mom to prepare the bridal chamber for you.*

I have also learned to apologize when I am wrong, something that my parents never taught me. It's the way of our family to scream, yell, fight, run away, come home when you've cooled off, and then... never speak of it again—ever—or else risk being blamed for "stirring the shit." No one says they're sorry, so no one ever gets the chance to sincerely forgive anyone else. That would require them to take an honest account of themselves, and no one in my family is capable of self-reflection. Not me, not anymore. When I am wrong, I say it, and I ask for forgiveness.

Another reason I am doing so well is that I actively plan my days around the prayers, so I feel much more productive with that natural structure in place. I plan my week, too, including what meals we'll eat so we are not constantly struggling to think of what to cook. I set aside time each day for reading, for taking classes online about spirituality, and for knitting or crocheting.

I have also kept up my blogging, too. I renamed my blog from "Struggles of an American Muslimah" to "The Amrikiyya in the Balad"—'The American Girl in the Village.' I try to write lighter, more positive posts these days after so much hate and backlash over the more honest, darker stuff I blogged when we first arrived in Egypt. I'm trying to focus more on the good parts of life here.

188

* * *

One weekend, we went with Ameer to the *balad* to visit his sister, Ihsan—my favorite of all his sisters. Her husband, Idris, had recently broken a hip in yet another car accident and was laid up in a bed in their sitting room. We all crowded around offering our condolences. Sajidah sat playing quietly on the floor next to us with her little cousin, while Rumi dozed in my arms, and the older kids ran in and out of the house and alley, kicking a soccer ball around and screaming.

"Saji getting old, *masha'Allah*," Idris said. "Soon she be big enough for the ceremony, *insha'Allah!*"

"Ceremony?" I asked, confused. Ameer hadn't given any of our children the customary *aqeeqah* ceremony to celebrate their births—thought he had provided one for each of the other children—but Sajidah was three years old at this point, so it hardly seemed likely he was referring to that.

"Ahem... the... ummm..." he said, struggling with the words and seeming shy and uncomfortable, which wasn't like him.

Mama Bushra cut him off, looked at me with a serious expression, held up two fingers in a downward "V" shape and used her other hand as scissors to snip the top off the V, laughing.

When my eyes gave away my horror, she and Idris burst into laughter.

"No. Never," I said adamantly. "My daughters will never be cut."

Mama Bushra was angry now and began shouting at me in Arabic. I understood about 60% of what people said to me in Arabic at this point, so Idris clarified.

"The *Hajja* say if you love Saji and Rumi, you want them to be clean for their husbands," he explained.

Mama Bushra carried on, and I heard the word "*sharmouta,*" (whore) in there somewhere.

"She says if you no cut them, they be too free like American girls, and this no *halal.* Not good for them," Idris said, tsk-tsking and wagging his finger.

I tried in my best Arabic to clarify my stance: that it's not one's clitoris which motivates one to be promiscuous, but one's mind... but it was to no avail. She never brought it up again, but female circumcision was just a normal part of life in rural Egypt. Never-mind that it was illegal in Egypt, or that it lacked any solid religious evidence to promote it; it was what good Muslim parents did for their daughters, they believed.

More than once people in rural Egypt told me that women were not designed by God to experience their own pleasure—sexual or otherwise—and that cutting a girl when she's eleven or twelve years old reminds her of her rightful place in this life: below her eventual husband, both in the world and in bed, allowing him to fill her with his energy and life-force as often and in as varied a way as he likes, regardless of her own pleasure or lack thereof.

Though Ameer had allowed the village doctor to circumcise all his other daughters—an unlicensed, traditional medicine woman working in a dirty house, using unsterilized scalpels and razor blades—he agreed not to force me to get our daughters circumcised, knowing full well the extent of fire and fury I'd unleash on him, and how quickly I'd raise international hell to take my children from him forever, *a la* "Not Without My Daughter."

One afternoon, Jennah and her friends came to my apartment,

excited to invite me to her sister Aalia's circumcision party. When girls are circumcised in rural Egypt, they are given a few days off from school so they can heal, and are then thrown a party by their female relatives to celebrate their official entrance into womanhood.

"Why on earth would you celebrate such a painful, awful thing?!" I asked, horrified.

"Well, I don't know, *Tante*," Jennah said, "but God loves it. It's cleaner and better. We celebrate because my sister is pleasing God and her future husband, and because now she is a woman."

I tried to remember everything I'd learned about respecting the culture I was living in, and so bit my tongue, but my face gave away my disgust and I was never invited to another such party.

* * *

May 2nd, 2013

> *God has answered my prayers and brought me relief, and her name is Rania.*
>
> *Thinking perhaps that I whine so much purely because I am lonely and need friends, Ameer introduced me to the wife of one of his colleagues.*
>
> *This woman is unlike any Egyptian woman I have ever met in my life. For one thing, she is authentic. She doesn't try too hard to impress me, like the village ladies, and she doesn't deride me, like some of the ladies here and in Cairo. She is patient with my terrible Arabic and is just as desperate to understand me as I am desperate to be*

understood. *She's also fun, and we sit and laugh together for hours.*

I know full well that she has only befriended me out of pity, and God bless her heart for it because if there was ever a time that I needed pity, it's now.

We hang out as often as we can, and our kids play together. She has a daughter a few years older than Dayo and the two of them play nicely. Her two young boys love chasing Dayo and playing soccer with him in the streets.

It began when Ameer took me to her house for Qur'an lessons. I decided to memorize Surah Al-Mulk, *as it is a protection for our souls in the grave, and I wanted a teacher this time—no more memorizing from a repeated soundtrack on my phone or computer.*

When I arrived at her house for my first lesson, it was well after Isha. *We sat under the lemon tree in her front yard on a rug, with the ceiling of stars above us, reciting Qur'an together by the light of an oil lamp. We lounged there, sipping mint tea and chatting afterward, and I felt better for days after that.*

As we started hanging out more often, I realized I really feel a particular kinship with her that is unlike anything I have felt in Egypt yet. Rania is a transplant from Mansoura, some three hours northwest of here, or an hour south of Alexandria. It's a much bigger city than this tiny shit-hole town, so she has known other foreigners and is more understanding of my differences.

I explained to her during one of the first visits she ever made to my house that I am not Egyptian, and this means that in my house, we go by my rules. That means if I offer you tea and you say no, I'm not going to keep offering, pushing you to just PLEASE drink some tea, because that's rude in my culture. She laughed and agreed to my terms. From that point on, we have followed Egypt's etiquettes in her house and America's in mine, and it has worked out fine.

But with Egypt being on the cusp of civil war—with visibly-practicing Muslims the main target—as well as perpetual problems in our marriage(s), I am in a dark place lately, despite the comfort this new friendship offers.

During one of my (repeated) visiting stints at Sofia's house in Cairo, after Ameer and I had sat with her and her husband for the tenth time, talking until late at night in the hopes of fixing things between us, I realized it was hopeless. He would never change. So I decided to focus on fixing me. I had the clear mind to sit down, open up PowerPoint and create a detailed list of what I need to do to be well; a daily battle plan, as it were, against the all-too-common depression I face here.

For a time—or several chunks of time—I have kept this plan in mind and stuck to it, like a sort of doctor's prescription for being overall "well." But I always end up slacking off, usually because of the universal fact that doing something preventative shows no obvious signs of benefit; it's only when you stop it that you notice detrimental effects of not doing the thing.

Ameer left for Canada last week and as hard as life is without him here, honestly his absence gives me such a sense of relief. Shahida and I even spend entire days together without so much as a bad look at one another. She's funny and can be warm and understanding, even. When he's not around, our animosity just evaporates, and we are two women trying to do our best to care for our children and keep our marriage intact in an absurd situation.

* * *

One afternoon in Ramadan that year, I was in the middle of baking a chicken in my oven when the gas tank ran out. Of course, Ameer hadn't bought me an extra contraband one like he did for them; the government kept a tight hold on how many gas tanks one family could own, and of course, as in all things, the sheikh's big house was the priority in his reckoning. The chicken and rice were all we had for food until Mama Bushra gave me more money in a few days, so I couldn't just throw it out, half-cooked as it was.

I called the only person I knew to call—Ameer's brother-in-law, Idris. I knew he and Ihsan were in town to celebrate the beginning of Ramadan. After I'd explained the situation as best I could, I overheard Shahida in the background.

"Go get her, Idris. How can we leave them without any *iftar* dinner? No, *khalas*, tell her we will come to get her and the kids, and Khalid will replace the gas-tank tomorrow morning. Tell her to bring clothes so they can sleep here," she said.

I was shocked Shahida was being so kind to me. I didn't expect it in the least, and I couldn't help but question her intentions. After all, only a year before, she'd been a key contributing factor to my suicide attempt.

When I arrived at her house, she acted like I was just another family member coming for dinner in Ramadan. My kids ran around the house laughing with their siblings while I sat with her in the kitchen peeling potatoes.

194

"Abu Khalid... far away... now. It's ... good, yes? *Fi Sakinah, ya'ani*," she said, trying to get her point across in English.

I understood exactly how she felt. Things *were* peaceful when he wasn't around. "*Sah. Fi sakinah,*" I said in my own embarrassing Arabic.

As we sat together doing normal feminine things in a normal feminine setting, I almost forgot what she was to me. The pettiness of our arguments seemed silly then, in that light. I wished we could maintain that level of kindness and respect with Ameer around, but I doubted it.

As time went on, I began to feel like I was ready to resolve myself to perseverance. I was ready to stop wallowing in my grief and rage over the loss of the life and marriage I believed I was entitled to. If I could endure my test in Egypt, I thought, I would come out purified, and—bonus!—God would give me better than what I had before, according to the Qur'an verse. I began praying *tahajjud*—extra prayers prayed in the middle of the night—in the hopes of drawing nearer to God and convincing Him to save me from my circumstances, or at least to help me accept them.

* * *

While Ameer was away during Ramadan, things between Um Khalid and I were much better, but relations devolved again a few weeks later.

Ameer's youngest sister, Aaminah, came to town to stay for a few weeks with her mother in Shahida's house. She was about to have yet another C-section, and she was not excited about it.

I went with her, Shahida, and Mama Bushra to the hospital—the same nasty, terrifying hospital I had refused to give birth in. Trying to comfort her, since she was crying, I asked Aaminah why they were forcing her to have another C-section. I understood from her answer that most doctors in Egypt say that VBAC (vaginal birth after cesarean) is out of the question, and considering their knowledge of health, I could understand that. But looking around at the filth of the facility, I worried maybe she would contract an infection.

Curious, I asked her to show me her scars from the two previous C-sections. Just as I suspected, they had cut her in half down the middle, from rib to pelvic bone, like a watermelon.

As I was looking at Aaminah's scar, I heard Shahida laugh behind me in her characteristic cackle. "Oh, *masha'Allah, ya* Um Abdullah! *Ya doctora! Ya sheikha! Enti shatra!*" she laughed. "God bless you, Um Abdullah! You're a doctor! You're a scholar! You're so clever!" she'd said.

I didn't laugh back with her this time. I didn't joke at my own expense like I usually did when she flippantly insulted me for being intelligent. This time, I looked at her hard, with my eyes narrowed. She seemed uncomfortable but still chuckled under her breath as she left the room.

Something rose up in me that day that only grew more powerful, and I was no longer willing or able to deal with any of her bullshit—or Mama Bushra's, for that matter.

* * *

Some weeks passed, and Ramadan ended. Ameer came back into town, and all adjusted back to the way it always had been—almost.

Just before he left for Canada, the Egyptian military ousted President Mohamed Morsi in a *coup d'état.* The country was in an uproar by the time Ameer arrived home.

Like many conservative Muslims in Egypt, Ameer was an active participant in The Muslim Brotherhood—the political group which Morsi belonged to before his election as President in 2012. In fact, Ameer had a massive pro-Morsi sticker placed on the side of our red mini-van during the run-up to the election—a sticker which nearly cost him his life many years later.

It wasn't just Morsi's politics that Ameer supported, though; Mohamed Morsi was also from Sharqia, so he was a hometown hero for many of the people in our state.

When the Rabaa Massacre happened on August 14th—wherein Egyptian security forces brutally murdered more than eight hundred pro-Morsi protesters as they sat in around Rabaa al-Adawiya Mosque, and the smaller group near Cairo University, in Giza—Ameer and his friends were fired-up. It was "one of the world's largest killings of demonstrators in a single day in recent history," according to Human Rights Watch.[1]

One morning, shortly after Rabaa, Ameer and several men from the surrounding area loaded up in two minibusses and headed north to Cairo to protest in support of their President. Mama Bushra wailed, Shahida begged, and I cried, but nothing would stop him from going.

That day, the three of us realized, with startling clarity, how very futile our fighting had been. While Ameer and his friends were away in Cairo, we three sat together in the *majlis*, waiting to hear news of his death—something we felt was certain in

---

[1] "Egypt: Rab'a Killings Likely Crimes against Humanity. No Justice a Year Later for Series of Deadly Mass Attacks on Protesters." Human Rights Watch. August 12, 2014. https://www.hrw.org/news/2014/08/12/egypt-raba-killings-likely-crimes-against-humanity

that hostile, violent atmosphere Egypt was trapped in that year. We prayed together, we cried together, and we vowed not to let our silly jealousies ever get between us again, knowing full well that if something were to happen to Ameer—indeed, when he would surely die—we would only have each other.

Thankfully, he did not die, and he was not harmed, but the same could not be said for everyone in his group. A few days, a few weeks passed by, and we fell into our same hostilities.

* * *

I was feeling sick and light-headed for several weeks, and Shahida started bothering me with incessant inquiries as to whether or not I was pregnant again, something I felt strongly was none of her business, and I said as much, as kindly as I could. Every cough, every complaint of nausea, and she was smiling wryly and asking if I was "with baby" again.

When I found out that I was, indeed, "with baby" again, I made it very clear to Ameer that I didn't want him to tell her or his mother, because, truth be told, whatever he told his mom, Shahida was informed of within moments.

I was not ready to act excited. I was not ready to pretend that this fourth baby to grace my womb was somehow welcome. Such sentiments are not acceptable in polite company anywhere, but certainly not in Egypt where every pregnancy heralds the possible arrival of another blessed male child.

Of course, she found out within days and of course, she acted thrilled for me.

"Good! You give him more son! *Khalas* for me!" she said in her broken English, laughing like she always did. I only ever saw that woman laughing sardonically, or else angrily. She never seemed genuinely happy about anything, ever, and used sarcasm to shield herself from her own reality.

One afternoon a few weeks later, Shahida called my phone several times, but I ignored her calls. I knew she was looking for Ameer since she'd already called his phone repeatedly before finally calling me. He'd left his phone at my apartment and gone to the mosque for *Dhuhr* prayer.

I was too hot and too nauseated to even try to deal with her, so I asked Dayo to answer my phone and tell her that Baba was at the mosque and would call her back soon. But when Dayo asked why I wasn't answering the phone myself, I made the mistake of being honest with my five-year-old.

"Because Mama doesn't really feel like talking to your auntie Shahida right now, honey," I said.

Dayo answered the phone, and when she asked where Baba was, he told her he was in the *masjid*. Then, I heard her ask where his Mama was.

"Is everything okay? Why isn't Mama answering? " she asked in Arabic.

To my horror and repeated knife-to-throat imitations, Dayo said in his perfect Arabic, matter-of-factly, "Because Mama doesn't want to talk to you, *Tante* Shahida."

I could hear her gasp and then try to cover it with a laugh, but when she asked him a second time, perhaps thinking she misunderstood him the first time, he gave her the same answer.

For days and days, the family refused to speak to me or to even send Khalid to bring us things we needed when Ameer was too busy and I had no cash. I was effectively cut off.

* * *

I enjoyed the peace and the silence for a bit, but Egypt requires a man, and since Ameer was perpetually busy with her or them—or, for God's sake, anyone but me or my children—I needed Khalid's help. So I took myself to the family house and I sat in the *salon*, that old place of horrors, smiling in Mama Bushra's face.

But she was not interested in making nice, and she made it known. "Um Khalid is sleeping right now, and good for her and you, because otherwise, I would not allow you in this house. How dare you insult us!" she yelled.

"*Nayna*, please. She is not my family. She's my husband's wife, not my sister," I said in my broken Arabic, "but you are not her. You are my mother-in-law. I love you. Please. Me and the kids need Khalid to help us, *ya Nayna*," I appealed.

But she wasn't having it. "Listen to me carefully, Um Abdullah, and hear me clearly. I know you don't understand Arabic, but try to understand me," she said in her rapid-fire way. "*You are not my daughter.* I helped raise Shahida. I have loved her for her whole life. I planned for my son to marry her when he was still a small boy. I refused to allow him to marry any of the other girls he fancied—all for her."

I sat listening, waiting for her point. None of this was news to me, after all.

"Her kids are like *my children*, not my grandchildren. I raised them when my son and she were in America. I love them more than I could ever, ever love your kids. And you will never be to me what she is to me!" she yelled.

There it was, out in the open. She didn't love us like she loved Shahida and her kids. We *were* second-rate, at best, just like I thought. I was holding back tears now, all the secret fears I had now all come to light at once.

"And let me ask you this, too," she said, shaking her finger at me. "How dare you get pregnant when I specifically told you not to?!"

Now I had really had enough. "It wasn't my idea, and it's not something I am happy about, *ya Nayna*, but Ameer demanded that we try again for a son!" I cried.

"You stupid girl! How dare you shout at me?!" she yelled.

Jennah came into the room then, aroused from her own afternoon nap. "*Ya Teita*, please calm down. You'll hurt yourself," she said, trying to calm her grandmother.

"You be quiet and mind your business, *ya bint al-kalb*," Mama Bushra cursed, calling her own granddaughter a "daughter of a bitch."

"You had better hope that baby you're pregnant with now really is a boy, Um Abdullah. You owe my family something for all you have taken from us," she said, scoffing, as she poured herself another cup of coffee.

With that, I stood up slowly and grabbed my hijab, leaving the house in silence. I somehow kept back the tears as I walked down the scalding, bubbling road, waiting for a *tuk-tuk* to come along. I had left the kids there with her, including Rumi, and I knew she would send them home when she got tired of them. I managed to wait until I got home before I burst into tears.

* * *

September 9th, 2013

> *Ameer has officially given up on trying to be fair with the time, but it's worse than before. Now, rather than*

simply refusing to apologize for being late all the time and neglecting our family, he has resorted to gaslighting me about when he comes and goes.

Last week, he came in several hours after Isha, even though the kids were waiting for him all evening. He'd promised them candies from the shop two nights before and they were waiting. Just a bit after they finally fell asleep, he came in the door as if nothing happened.

I reminded him of his promise and he swore he hadn't promised them anything. I remembered the conversation well, and clearly, the kids remembered, too.

I began thinking it was time to start recording our conversations just to prove I wasn't lying or crazy but quickly banished the idea. I mean... that's exactly what a crazy person would do, right?

Then, a few nights later, he came home at eleven o'clock, again, but tried to say he'd gone to her house at the same time the night before. I clearly recalled him calling me at eight that night and telling me he was laying in bed, at her house, about to fall asleep—and his voice was drowsy, so I knew he was telling the truth.

"It must be the pregnancy making you forgetful, Kaighla," he said when I reminded him.

So I taped a piece of paper to the back of the front door and began writing down—in pen—the time he came to my house in the evening, as well as when he left the next morning.

The first time he tried to gaslight me after that, I went and showed him the paper. He looked at me like I was crazy, and said I was making things up.

Physical proof, right there, for him to see, and he still

denies responsibility! He is at my house so rarely, and he pays so little attention when he is here, that he didn't even notice the paper hanging there for several days before I pointed it out to him.

* * *

One cool Autumn evening, I was relaxing on the couch, trying to get past a particularly tough wave of nausea. Saji was watching cartoons on our new-to-us little TV set, Rumi was sleeping in her crib, and Dayo was playing in the dining room. He had been making a tent, putting a sheet on top of two plastic chairs. Suddenly, I heard the chairs crashing to the floor and Dayo screaming.

At first, I thought he had simply toppled over again, as he often did when he was playing. His reaction to pain was always so dramatic, so it was hard to know when his cries were serious. But when he didn't calm down right away, I turned to see him on the floor writhing in pain.

"*Habibi.* Dayo. Please, honey. Calm down. Tell mommy what hurts," I said.

"My arrrmmm!!!!" he screamed.

I took one look at his left elbow and knew it was badly broken. Instead of an "L" shape, his bent arm looked more like a broken "Z".

I immediately got dressed and started trying to call Ameer, but realized I had no credit. I also had exactly one single guinea, and that was not enough money to get to the hospital, let alone to buy credit for my phone. I tried collect-calling him, but he wasn't picking up or calling back, so I tried Jennah, thinking maybe Ameer was back from the wedding they'd gone to in the *balad*.

A few minutes later, Jennah called back.

"*Habibti,* is Baba home? Or *Teita?*" I asked.

"No, *Tante,* I'm sorry. He's still in the *balad* with *Teita* and Mama. But what's wrong? Why is Abdullah screaming? What happened?" she asked.

"He has fallen and I think he's broken his arm," I explained. "Could you grab a *tuk-tuk* and pick us up? I don't have any money."

"Oh, no! I am so sorry, *Tante.* I have to stay here because the kids are at tutoring, and Khalid is at the shop. I have to stay at the house. *Teita* says we have to keep the gate locked at all times and she has the only key, so I have to be here to open the gate for them from the inside," she said.

Dayo was still screaming at the top of his lungs, and by this point, Saji was crying, too, because she was scared. Rumi was whining because she wanted me to get her out of her crib, having been awoken by the ruckus.

I texted the only other person I could think of to help me: my friend Rania. She sent her husband, Sheikh Kareem, to take us to the hospital.

The whole time I waited for him to arrive with a *tuk-tuk*, I was pacing on the front patio, seething with rage. I couldn't stop mulling over, again and again, how much I hated Ameer for putting us in that situation with no money, no way to contact him, and no one to help me, leaving me to wait on a friend's husband to come help us.

I had already spent the entire day angry with him because of his being unfair and irresponsible with his money. I had needed to go to the doctor a few weeks prior because I was in serious pain, but he'd said he didn't have the money to take me. Lo and behold, just a day later I saw that he'd bought Khalid a brand-new phone.

I was boiling with sick bitterness by the time Sheikh Kareem arrived. We all piled into the *tuk-tuk* and went to his house to drop off Saji with Rania, before going to the hospital.

When we arrived, the nurses rushed us into an exam room and without a word to me, they popped Dayo in his bad arm with a shot of what I could only assume was pain-reliever. Then they took him to the X-ray room in the back while Rumi and I waited in the exam room.

I could hear him screaming and trying to tell them how much his arm hurt because they had to wiggle him this way and that to get a good picture. I broke down in tears before they even finished the X-ray. Just listening to my son—flesh of my flesh and bone of my bone—screaming like... it that made my insides hurt.

Just then, Mama Bushra came running into the room, sweaty and out-of-breath. I was surprisingly overjoyed inside when she arrived; at least I wouldn't be alone. She said Ameer should be there any minute, as he was supposed to be right behind her coming back from the wedding.

When they brought him back into the exam room, Dayo was lying on a cold metal table—a rolling table like they use in a morgue, not at all a proper gurney. They'd cut his shirt off in an attempt to get a better look at his damaged shoulder blade, which was apparently knocked out of the socket when he landed on his elbow. There was no sheet between him and the cold metal, and nothing covering him, either. He was crying now, less hysterical than before, but constant tears poured from his little eyes.

Mama Bushra stood next to me as I caressed him, and she cried with me. It was one of the very few times I had ever experienced mercy from her, and it was surprising considering our most recent encounter.

Finally, Ameer arrived, and I let loose my fury. He tried to hug me, but I shouted in his face, crying, ordering him not to touch me.

"*Habibti*, please. People are watching. Calm down, please," he insisted quietly, but I yelled louder.

"You did this to him! You left us with nothing and no one to help us!" I yelled. "What if this was Saji, your precious princess? Would you care more then because it's your child?!"

Ameer ignored me at that point and began talking animatedly with the doctors. He explained to me then that we were going to a doctor's house who could set the bones in Dayo's elbow and shoulder to heal correctly.

When we arrived at his house, the doctor took one look at the X-ray and made a grave expression before delivering some commands in Arabic to Ameer and Sheikh Kareem, as well as a few other men who'd come with us to help. Without warning, they grabbed Dayo and held him down so the doctor could shove his shoulder back into its socket. The sounds that emanated from my little boy were unbearable, and I buckled over in tears.

When they finished, the doctor turned to Ameer and explained the extent of his injuries, in English. "His shoulder is back in the socket, so it should be fine, though he'll be sore for several weeks. But he will need surgery to set the elbow, and it has to be as soon as possible. Even a few days would be too much time. The bones could begin healing incorrectly, which means we'd need to re-break them," he said, stroking Dayo's head as he laid against Ameer's chest, darting his eyes around wildly in fear and crying profusely.

"Okay, so can we schedule it for tomorrow?" I asked him.

"I'm so sorry, Um Abdullah, but I am going out of town tomorrow morning, at *Fajr*. My mother is sick in the *balad* and I have to go be with her," he said. "But I could suggest a few other doctors in town who could operate on Abdullah at the hospital."

"Wait, *this* hospital? The one in town? The hospital we just came from," I asked, shuddering.

Ameer nudged me in the side and began speaking to the doctor in Arabic before ushering me outside so we could talk in private.

"Ameer, we can't do his surgery in that hospital," I said. "It's not safe."

"*Insha'Allah khair*, Kaighla," he said, seeming annoyed with me. "It's what we can afford, okay?"

I was livid. "Why?" I shouted. "So you will buy Khalid a new phone, and you'll buy your mom anything she wants, whenever she wants it, but when I or my children have a literal medical emergency, the money is gone?!"

"You will keep your voice down, Kaighla," he said in a threatening voice. "They can hear you, as can everyone on the block, I'm sure."

Once again, I knew my outburst painted me out to be the crazy, pampered, impatient foreigner everyone in our town believed I was—lacking any modicum of propriety and being clearly uninterested in how my public and private behavior could impact my husband's honor.

Afterward, they put a cast on Dayo's elbow—something I tried to argue against, considering that when I broke my ankle, they had to wait a day for the swelling to go down before casting it. Ameer said that's not how things were done in rural Egypt, though, and Dayo's break needed a cast to protect it from further damage.

* * *

Dayo barely slept in our room that night, and cried all night, off and on. By the time the sun rose, it was clear I was right about the cast: his fingers were blue and as big as sausages, the cast having cut off his circulation. The Ibuprofen we gave him wasn't helping with the pain at all.

By now, I was at my breaking point. Sleep-deprived, pregnant, and traumatized one too many times by the Egyptian medical system, I was at my wit's end. We went back to the hospital as soon as possible that morning and made them remove the cast, which they did with a saw that sparked across the exposed wires that lay on the floor, mere feet away from a puddle of water.

They began to talk again about doing the surgery there, in that nasty hospital, in two days, and that was it for me. No way was I about to let my son be knocked out and cut open in that disease-ridden, germ-infested hellhole. I asked, begged, *demanded,* that Ameer find the money for a cleaner, safer hospital in Faqqous.

"The money is gone, *habibti.* You know we don't have the money even for this surgery, let alone a more expensive one," he said. "The shop just isn't as profitable as we had hoped it would be."

Right then, I decided we were going back to America. At least there, my children could get good medical care in sanitary conditions—and it would likely be free or very cheap, considering our financial situation. There, I could give birth to our new baby without fear of what would be done to my body without my permission or consent.

When we left the hospital and went to Mama Bushra's house, I demanded to talk to my husband alone.

"We're leaving, Ameer. I am contacting family and friends, and reaching out to the embassy for help. We can't stay here. He needs this surgery right now, and it can't be in that hospital," I said.

"Fine, Kaighla. Find the money and go. Get out of my life forever," he responded, and that was the extent of our discussion. His eyes were ringed with dark circles, like mine, and he looked easily ten years older than he really was.

Knowing how important it was that we get the surgery as soon as possible, I called the embassy in Cairo the next morning and spoke with the vice consul.

"There are two options, Ms. White," she said. "You could come to Cairo and search for a surgeon willing to operate on your son for this set amount we're authorized to give to American citizens in duress abroad. But honestly? Good luck. It's not much money."

"Well, what's the other option then?" I asked.

"We can send you home—with a loan. It's high-interest, and you won't be permitted to travel outside the country until you pay it off completely," she explained. "I know it's a serious thing for Muslims to deal in interest, but those are your options."

After we spent a day in Cairo asking around at several doctor's offices and hospitals, finding that she'd been right about the money, I agreed to accept the loan. They called it a "Repatriation Loan."

Before he sent us through security at the airport, Ameer cried over the kids and begged me to protect them. Then he reminded me of his place in my life—even across the ocean that would soon separate us.

"This is not a divorce. I am not divorcing you. I will not. Ever. You are my wife," he said, intending not to comfort me, but to assert his rightful ownership of me. "You are choosing to go there against my will, and I cannot send you money, so you will be alone and dependent on your family, who never cared for you before. And you must remember to be faithful to me," he added, looking into my eyes gravely.

"Good luck. May we be reunited," he continued, kissing me on the forehead before I walked with the kids through the security line.

Another year, another airport, leaving behind another man whose child I carry, unsure when or if I will ever see him again, I thought, as we walked through the security gate.

14

The Withdrawing

Central Illinois

December 5th, 2013

Sitting at the laundromat in the same apartment complex I lived in when I was in elementary school, I can hear someone's zipper clanging around in the dryer across the building, a rhythmic ka-ching, thump. ka-ching, thump. ka-ching, thump.

Of course, the place is cleaned up and updated. The machines are newer, and there are flat screen TVs hanging in each of the corners. But all I see is seven-year-old me chasing around my best friend, Misty, slipping on dryer sheets and getting scolded by the ladies from the apartment complex who all knew us by name.

As I'm walking to the car, a man hands me a tiny sock, thinking I must have dropped it from my basket. I smile and thank him. Going back in, a lady opens the door for me and seems genuinely surprised when I, hijab and all, thank her in clear English—with a Midwestern twang, to boot.

We drive down the road—familiar drive, familiar sights and sounds. But as my mom's house comes up in the distance, far left, my stomach sinks.

This can't be real. This isn't the house I know. This isn't the land I ran from. Where are the barns? The house looks so naked and lonely out there by itself, with nothing to guard it against biting winds. The pasture is overgrown and the siding is coming off. The chimney is crumbled, lying in pieces on the ground nearby.

I came back to this house in my mind every day for two years and sat on the front porch, drinking sweet iced tea and talking with my mom as she smoked. But my memory is so much kinder than this cold, hard reality.

I glance at myself in the rearview mirror. Yep. Still no hair sticking out of my hijab. I'm still me, or the version of me I have known these four years. But somehow, I feel more whole. The pieces of me that I thought God wanted me to keep severed are coming back together here.

I am a girl from the Midwest. I am homegrown, raised on meat-n-taters. I just happen to cover myself and pray with my face on the ground. I don't need to be like you—not like you Arabs, not like you other Midwesterners.

All of me matters. All of me has been along for the ride. Ignored, sometimes neglected, but along nonetheless. I am all of me. And it feels good.

* * *

For the first few months back in my hometown, the prevalent feeling I had, aside from being cold, was one of relief. There was a time I was very, very sure I would never be in my own country again, let alone in my hometown. It was surreal. Even the trees seemed to welcome me. I always felt like nature itself didn't want me in Egypt.

The moment she found out we were coming back to America, my sister, AJ, flew into action to make a place for us in her life. She had a roommate at the time, but within days of Dayo's accident, she had moved her out to make room for us. She even took a second job, just so she could afford to pay all the bills alone, knowing that in my state—both physically and mentally—I couldn't be expected to find a job, try as I certainly did; no one in our small town wanted to hire a Muslim, and certainly not an obviously pregnant one.

There were the reunions with friends and family, of course, and I was pleased to find out that the small, Muslim community—made up of primarily Pakistani and Indian doctors and engineers, of course—in the next town over had moved out of their basement gatherings and come up with enough funding to convert an old church into a mosque. I attended the mosque and introduced myself to the ladies there, who were, as Muslims almost always were, suspicious of me because I was an American convert. But they eventually warmed up to me and helped us a ton. When I explained the situation we were in, they not only bought us groceries until the food stamps started up, but they brought us used winter shoes and such for the kids.

But after some time, things began to go sour in Illinois. In hindsight, it's clear I was suffering through reverse-culture shock. I remember learning about this phenomenon in Bible college when our Missions professor told us stories of his hard adjustments back home after living several years in the Congo. I'd struggled to re-adjust to life back home after my time in India, but never like I did then.

English didn't come naturally to me anymore, and I struggled to interact with my own countrymen in a way that didn't feel contrived. I also found myself feeling truly appalled by aspects of my family members' lives that were commonplace in our culture. Men made me nervous, in general, and young men especially. I felt offended if a man smiled at me, sure he was planning to find a way to flirt with me, like the majority of men in Egypt had. It was as if I had gone not just to another country, but back in time, to the 1950s, and found myself unable to acclimate to life in the 21st century.

Of course, my choice of clothing didn't help things. In our tiny town—population four thousand primarily white, Christian people, the majority of which had probably never met a Muslim in their lives—I stood out like a sore thumb. My roomy, always-black *abayas* and oversized scarves in dull, drab colors—coupled with my well-trained resting bitch face when in the presence of men—didn't really scream, "Hey, fellow Americans! I'm friendly!"

Though I was in my own country—in my own hometown, even!—I felt more alien than ever, and it hurt.

* * *

February 2nd, 2014

> *I had a nightmare.*
> *She was taller and larger than me. She didn't cover her*

214

scraggly blonde hair, and she seemed less intelligent and less attractive, on the whole. But I tried to be nice and friendly, as best I could.

We were walking somewhere together, arm-in-arm, undisturbed by the glaring of people who knew one or both of us. I understood who she was in relation to me and she understood who I was, likewise, but neither of us seemed overanxious about it. Things seemed like they were going swimmingly.

Then without notice, I saw myself in a fit of anger, screaming at Ameer. I had seen pictures of them together on his Facebook page. There was snow in the background and I realized he must have married her not when he said he had, but now, in America, during the time that I have been living without him. He must have come here and married her and hid it from me while the kids and I were struggling without him.

I saw us in the mosque in Dearborn, in his office, but it was here, in Illinois. I was crying and screaming at him. He was calm, assuring me he loves me, assuring me there was nothing missing from our marriage, and him marrying her had nothing to do with not loving me. He asked me what I wanted, but I couldn't decide.

"There is no easy, painless way to get out of this marriage, not for anyone involved," he said.

"The painless thing would have been if I never, ever met you!" I shouted.

He held me near him and told me I was the love of his life. He said he could not imagine a happy life without me.

At that moment, I remembered our beautiful daughters. I knew I couldn't choose a life without them existing in it,

even if I could go back in time and avoid him. I heard Dayo
in the distance yelling at his sisters. And then I woke up.

* * *

I got out of bed, dressed, helped the kids dress themselves, and got started on breakfast. But as I went about my day, the dream kept knocking on my heart, beckoning me to ponder on it further.

Sometime around lunch, it hit me: *I was the girl with the scraggly, short blond hair.*

I was taller and fatter than Shahida. By rural Egyptian standards, I seemed undoubtedly inferior, and definitely less intelligent. I had invaded her life, stolen her husband, and taken up residence in her home. Once, long ago, we'd walked hand-in-hand through Faqqous, shopping for curtains, and she didn't mind the stares or the odd questions.

And right then, I couldn't hate Shahida anymore. All the many ways she hurt me, all the many times she acted in a way unbefitting a Muslim woman—all of them seemed justified then.

I understood finally that I was asking for war when I showed up in her country, in her town, in her home, expecting a warm reception. Yes, my intentions were pure; yes, my heart was clean. But none of my good intentions were keeping her warm at night when he was away, or calming her spirit when the neighbors gossiped about how Um Khalid couldn't keep her husband pleased, so he had to go and find a pretty young American girl.

For only a moment in a dream, I felt the betrayal and sadness she must have been experiencing for years, and it was so very real. I felt the deep desire to run far away from him and never look back, all being counteracted by the equally deep need to cling to him and wrap my arms around the family we created together and do everything I could to save it—a constant tug of war between part of me and the rest of me.

Without constant mindfulness and intervention, it is the nature of hurt to breed more hurt; oppressed ones become the best oppressors. But I wasn't sure I wanted to be free of the hatred I felt for her. If I let the flames of that hatred die out, I knew I would witness beautiful things growing in its place, feeding on the embers of that old hate. Without hatred, I knew I would begin to love Shahida because love is my default setting.

My hatred for her protected me from the vulnerability that came from seeing her as my equal. After all, if we were equal, I thought, what would set me apart for Ameer—both my judge and jury in the court case perpetually deciding just how valuable I was?

* * *

February 19th, 2014

> *Green walls in the quaint downtown café. Soft light from the lamp on my table. Peculiar Brazilian music in the background. Semi-sweet Darjeeling tea harkens me back to the last time I held a male child.*
>
> *Quiet stirrings in my heart. What joy awaits me! I'll be the mother of his son! I'll have the right now to have my own home—Bayt Ismayil.*

Is this the 14th century? Who have I become? Yet strangely it's a peaceful feeling, one of belonging with the billions of quietly longing mothers-to-be around the world, past and present. The Lord is giving me a boy—a protector when I am old and helpless!

And then I think of Dayo, my son. I already have a son, after all. I am Um Dayo. This younger boy will never have the honor of being my kunya *giver. My Dayo is my joy. Ekundayo. Always joy mixed with a helping of sorrow, flowing into and out from one another.*

And I think of my sweet, sweet girls. They're the only reminders in some seasons that there was ever any beauty in me to have been the life-source and wellspring of such life, emanating in their deep brown eyes. They're my reminders that beauty is in the mess, not afterward.

While the birth of this boy will bring us a roof and four walls, my girls will be my windows, showing me the beauty in this world.

Finding out I was finally pregnant with Sheikh Ameer's son was perhaps the best news of my life up to that point. Everything I needed, everything out of my reach, would come nearer to me now that I carried his male offspring in my womb.

When he told Mama Bushra the good news, she cried tears of joy and ran around to all her friends and neighbors announcing the news, in much the same way as she had gossiped about me when I "disobeyed her" and got myself pregnant a few short months earlier. Apparently, she'd meant it: producing a male changes everything.

Just as she'd requested, I was giving her a grandson, and now she spoke to me with kindness whenever she found Ameer on the phone with me. Rather than degrading me for leaving him there and "breaking the family," she chatted away happily, asking about all the kids briefly before asking for more information on her unborn grandson's health.

I knew right then what I would name him: Ismayil, after Prophet Ibrahim's first son. Ameer was Ibrahim, the prophet who cried out to God for a son for all those years. I was Hajar, the handmaiden-*cum*-wife who'd given him the blessed male, and then was discarded in the desert with her prize, left there to serve God's higher purpose for humanity.

We would not be forgotten now. Ismayil would save his sisters and his mother, having given us a promised place in Ameer's family dynasty, just by being created of a stronger Y-chromosome.

* * *

At first, my sister, AJ, was so thrilled to have us there, and my mom and my other sister, Emily, came to visit us pretty often. But as time went on, my resistance to adapting to my own culture and circumstances began to grate on everyone's nerves. It wasn't just my inability to adapt, really, that was making things so hard between us, it was my refusal to allow everyone to go about their own lives as usual.

One night in early spring, I woke to hushed voices in the hallway outside our room. AJ had brought home a guy. As I listened, I realized it was one of my old church friends, and it was clear he was drunk from his mumbling and giggling. Eventually, they quieted down and went to sleep in her bedroom, but by the time I woke up the next morning, I was enraged. When she came out of her room, I was ready.

"How dare you bring a man in this house with me and my kids?! You know that is entirely inappropriate for us!" I whisper-yelled at her in the hallway between our rooms.

"Calm down. It's Billy. You know him. He's a good guy," she tried to say, but I was crying in my anger now.

"You knew he was drunk and there is nothing to separate me and my kids from your drunk, horny friend, aside from this flimsy particle-board door!" I cried, louder now.

She stood there in shock, unsure of how to respond.

AJ had gone above and beyond the call of duty of any sister, and there I was berating her for having a guest in her own home, purely because he was a man.

I was so upset with her that I called one of the older Pakistani women from the mosque in town and asked her to please come and pick up the kids and me because I didn't feel safe in AJ's apartment any longer. She arrived half an hour later in her tiny car with her son, who was close in age with me, in the driver's seat. When I got into the backseat, loading all my kids and their car seats in, she seemed annoyed.

"What is the problem, sister? Why you called me like that? Like there's some emergency? I brought my son with me because I didn't feel safe!" she shouted at me.

I burst into tears and explained the situation, expecting her to warm up and see that I needed compassion and a kind ear.

"Listen to me, sister!" she shouted at me. "You must stop this crying and this carrying on! Be strong for your kids! Look, you are terrifying them! I have never seen a grown woman cry like you are! Get over it! We have all been abused by our men in one way or another! It's the life of women! Just move on and accept things! Good God! Stop being so weak!"

Shocked by her shouting, I mumbled something in affirmation

of her horrible insults, then grabbed the kids and went back into AJ's house.

* * *

From that day, things were not the same between AJ and me. We never spoke to one another, even when I tried, and she stayed in her room most of the time to avoid us all, including the kids.

I never went back to that mosque, feeling sure the Pakistani sister would have told the other ladies about the event. I had instead been getting rides to the larger, more diverse mosque in the college town forty-five minutes' drive from our apartment. Made up predominantly of college-aged students who were either currently enrolled in one of the several colleges in town or were alumni who still supported them, that mosque was much more welcoming and better-suited to support members in need.

They had by this point begun looking for a van for us because I was struggling to get to my doctor's appointments, let alone to apply for jobs around town. AJ went with me to pick up the van and sign the papers and things seemed to be improving between us.

But then one day, AJ came home in a bad mood. She'd had a particularly rough day at her second job, and I'd had a particularly hard day with the kids and with fighting with Ameer on the phone non-stop. I had done very little work around the house because I was so depressed and overwhelmed.

She took one look at the garbage can in the bathroom and, seeing that I had not put in a new bag yet, and the kids had thrown dirty diapers and all variety of trash inside, she lost it. She came to my room holding the freshly emptied garbage can

221

in one hand and a grocery bag in the other.

"You puuutttt the baaaaag in the caaaaan! It's not that hard! JUSTPUTAFUCKINGBAGINTHEFUCKINGCAN!" she yelled.

One night a few days later, things finally came to a head. Mom refused to help me with the kids, AJ still wasn't speaking to me, and Emily hadn't been by the apartment in weeks. To make matters worse, we were rapidly running out of money, and I was only getting larger and more obviously pregnant, so finding a job was becoming increasingly unlikely.

I couldn't take it anymore. The feeling that I was a worthless parasite to everyone in my life, both there and in Egypt; the culture shock; the trauma I'd endured—it was too much to bear.

I decided I would drive the van through the guardrail on the bridge into the icy river below. I left the kids alone in the warm apartment, happily watching "Frozen" for the tenth time in two days, then texted my mom and both my sisters and told them the kids were alone and I couldn't go on living any longer.

But as I came nearer and nearer to the bridge, I changed my mind. I realized I wanted to live, just not in that situation, and I knew I couldn't leave my babies like that. So, I turned around and headed to the hospital, unsure of how they could help me but sure I couldn't go home.

When they put me in an exam room, I was both appalled and pleased to find that my nurse was a girl I had gone to middle school with. She acted perfectly normal, like it was a common occurrence for her to see an old classmate, seven months pregnant, claiming she was ready to commit suicide. Just another Thursday night in the ER, right?

When I explained my situation and how hopeless it felt, she listened quietly and asked if there was anything she could get me.

"Actually, a Qur'an would be nice, if the hospital has one," I replied.

"Just a minute and let me check," she said. But when she came back a few moments later, it was clear she hadn't had success finding a Qur'an in the Catholic hospital.

"Well, you'd certainly think that with the number of Muslims in this small town, we'd have at least one copy, but it seems we don't! I am sincerely sorry," she said, touching my knee before she left to do her rounds.

A few minutes later, someone knocked on the door, and in walked a young nurse with a warm smile, pushing a rolling computer ahead of him. "I heard you needed a Qur'an, and I am so sorry that we don't have one. But I found Qur'an.com and thought you may like to read it from the computer," he said. "Please, accept my genuine apology. I hope it gives you the peace you so desperately need tonight."

With all my heart, I wanted to hug him. To have been treated with such kindness in such a cold place where most stared and jeered at me... it filled my heart with hope.

When they finally released me to go home, I was told that the front desk had called the police to go check on the kids when I told the receptionist that I'd left them home alone. They'd found both my mom and AJ at home, both having apparently arrived there just five minutes after I left, so the kids were never truly in danger. Nonetheless, because I had left them alone, she said I could expect a visit from the Department of Children's Services in the coming days.

"You can go now, but you must report to the local free mental health clinic in the morning to begin a relationship with a therapist," my old schoolmate said, handing me my discharge papers.

I walked in the door at 2 a.m. and found my mom asleep on the couch with Rumi sleeping next to her and the other two kids passed out on the floor under their blankets, the credits rolling for "Frozen," yet again. I woke my mom and thanked her, sending her on her way without an explanation, assuring her we'd speak about everything tomorrow. She seemed relieved I had come home safely, and she hugged me tightly, but it was clear from her face she was getting tired of helping us.

When I went to the mental health clinic the next day, I sat in a room with an older female therapist and tried to explain my alien life to her. After an hour, she popped off some vague diagnosis of "Adjustment Disorder," which is psych-talk for "I'm normally fine, but when I face a crisis situation that has no deadline or end in sight, I can't cope and feel depressed, anxious, suicidal, etc. But get me out of the crisis situation and I'm fine again, almost like nothing ever happened." Then they sent me on my way without even scheduling another appointment or telling me what to do to help myself.

Sure as Hell, when I pulled into the driveway, there was a black car parked outside. An attractive young woman in a sharp pencil skirt and heels walked out of the apartment and began heading to the car just as I was getting out of the van. When she saw me, she smiled warmly and came to introduce herself.

"I'm sure you were expecting me, but please don't be worried. I already spoke with your sister, and she answered all the questions we had. I can see that you are a wonderful mother who just reached her breaking point," she said, patting me on the arm. "I am so sorry for the situation you're in, and I hope the therapy you're attending will help you."

I thanked her and went in to find the kids bathed and happy

as if nothing had ever happened.

"I gave them a bath so it'd look like they have a loving family," AJ said, jokingly. She didn't speak to me again after that, though.

* * *

March 15th, 2014

I feel heavy, like making it through a single hour is too much to ask. Ever since that night with the van, I've been seeing a therapist twice a week, and I feel like it's doing more harm than good, dredging up a bunch of disturbing feelings I am totally unable to cope with. Thankfully, mom found me a much better therapist than the hack I saw the first time at the free clinic. Mom's been paying for it out of pocket because this therapist doesn't accept Illinois Medicare.

These days, I just cannot bring myself to pray for relief. It's not that I doubt that God has the power to remove this burden from me. But I can not—absolutely can not—beg His assistance in my situation, which kinda sucks because the only way I will get out of this alive is with His help, and He wants me to ask Him.

I see God as this big sheikh with a full beard who sits in His office stroking said beard and frowning at me, shaking His head in disappointment. I just believe that God doesn't support my decisions. I have a deep resounding belief in my heart that if I had listened to God, I would never have left Egypt. I would have stayed and persevered for the sake of my family. I would have let them sell the land to pay for Dayo's surgery and worry about safety in birth and such when the time comes.

Of course, I am not saying God wanted me to stay in Egypt and suffer and die of depression. No, I think God wanted me to find a way to be well in Egypt. I am afraid God wanted me to forgive Shahida and Mama Bushra for the thousandth time because "a true believer makes a thousand excuses for his brother in Islam," according to the hadith.

I am afraid God wanted me to focus on my children and my soul and be thankful like all the other sisters living in less-than-desirable circumstances in oppressive and corrupt Muslim-majority countries who don't just give up. I am afraid to beg Him to bring my husband here because I'm afraid His response would be, "Nope. You chose to leave. Suffer without him awhile and learn your lesson: you need a husband, so you'd better be grateful when you have one."

Even if Ameer and I were somehow reunited, how much of what we once had will be left between us? I know one thing: it will never be like it was before Egypt. I cannot forget how he didn't protect me there. I cannot forget the times he chose to please his family against all admonitions to fear God and care for me. I cannot see him without seeing the man who made me cry so many tears so often for so long. Only in rare moments can I catch a glimpse of beautiful memories from a long, long time ago and it's those memories that keep me hanging on.

15

The New Hope

Central Illinois

June 2014

Death invited me home. It felt less like a light at the end of a tunnel and more like a warm glow filling the space around me. I felt completely at peace. But in that space of peace and light, I felt a firm resolution well up within me: *"No, I think I don't want to die right now,"* it said, and with that, I began to wake up.

Throughout the emergency C-section, I remember talking, but I wasn't choosing my words, and I heard my own voice three seconds after I felt my mouth producing the sounds. It was surreal and disconcerting. I felt the doctors rocking my body back and forth, hard, apparently trying to get the baby out. I heard people say that he wasn't breathing.

A very long time later, at least in my mind, my son was passed near my line of vision and taken away very quickly. When they pushed me back into the delivery room, my legs were still numb, and I felt light-headed. A kind nurse came in and explained to me that my baby was very, very sick.

Ismayil had been given a chest X-ray right after birth because he came out blue, floppy, and not breathing. They found his lungs full of meconium and had to place a breathing tube down his throat. She explained that he was being rushed to the Children's Hospital some thirty minutes away because he needed to be in their highly-specialized NICU.

I was confused and scared and could not understand why I was not allowed to hold him or see him. She kept explaining that he was very sick, and they were trying to stabilize him before taking him to the other hospital. Then, a neonatologist came in and elaborated: my baby had only a 2/10 on the Apgar test. He used the words "life support."

My heart sank into my stomach and I sobbed. "I want to go with him. Please. I need to be with him," I cried, begging them.

The nurse just smiled gently and stroked my head, "Sweetie, I know that. I know you do. But listen, you lost a lot of blood in the surgery, okay? He's too sick to stay, but you're too sick to go."

I began to get angry and told them they had no legal right to stop me from going. But I was met with more kind, concerned refusal, so finally I gave up.

They brought Ismayil in so I could see him before he was taken to the other hospital. He was in a long, narrow plastic box with arm holes near his head so I could touch his face and body. It hurt so, so much not to be able to take him to my chest and kiss him and smell his head and nurse him. Then, just like that, he was gone, far away from me. I spent the night passing between sleep and tears, AJ at my side.

* * *

The next morning, I sent AJ home to relieve my mom of the kids. She'd been with them more than twenty-four hours by this point, and I knew she had very little patience for them. Also, some deep part of me felt like somehow, my mom would be a comforting presence.

When she arrived, though, I saw that I was mistaken. She was shook-up, not understanding all that had happened. The short time she was at the hospital, she provided comfort in her own way, but I remembered why I had chosen not to have her with me after my labor and delivery with Dayo: she is not level-headed when she's scared.

The doctors came around that morning and explained what had gone wrong: my son had such wide shoulders that he could not even begin to descend into my pelvis. The umbilical cord was wrapped many times around his neck, as well, so he would never have come out vaginally, period.

What's worse, the situation inside my uterus was ghastly. My placenta was the worst anyone in the room had seen. It was old and calcified. Plus, his umbilical cord had begun to shred, and the amniotic fluid was more like sludge than fluid.

Hearing these things broke my heart with guilt.

All my research—as well as my own experience with both Dayo and Saji's artificially induced births, based on predictions about their "large weights," both of which proved to be highly exaggerated—told me doctors hyped up these potential complications to scare women into inductions because of the larger checks they received, and because of their hospital policy—rarely because induction was truly necessary. My own healing home-birth with Rumi also assured me that my body would naturally go into labor in its own time if I allowed it to, so I waited. For forty-one full weeks, I waited.

Seeing then how my sincere but misguided choice not to accept an induction had truly endangered both my baby's life and my own—it was just one more ten-ton weight that landed on my tired shoulders.

Next, the doctors elaborated on just how bad my own health was: I had lost two-and-a-half liters of blood—a quarter of my entire blood volume. They explained that while trying to wrestle him out of the incision, they accidentally hit an artery and I began bleeding out, thus my loss of consciousness and belief I was dying. They reacted in a timely manner and were able to save me, but only barely.

I cried and cried while listening to them. I could not have imagined a more traumatic birth experience. After feeling so empowered after my home-birth with Rumi, this delivery traumatized me and made me fear birth altogether. I was (literally) scarred for life.

Seeing my emotional response, the surgeon smiled and began, "It may be the last thing you want to think about right now, but I want to assure you that should you ever choose to have more children, there is no reason to worry. You're an excellent candidate for vaginal birth after a C-section. I've sewn the internal incision using a strong, double-layer method that makes VBAC very safe, so long as you wait two years from now. Everything is going to be fine, ok?"

"Why didn't you just tie her tubes when you were in there?!" my mother suddenly shouted at the doctor.

I felt sad and angry that she reacted like that. She was

always so emotional in her reactions to things, and she lacked foresight and patience. "I don't want any more children, mom," I explained. "But I'm not even thirty. I can't make such a lasting, invasive choice right now, okay? Also, don't forget I have a husband who has a say in this, too, and he's not here to give his opinion."

Before she could respond, one of the nurses came in and said that they needed me to try to go to the bathroom, as they had taken out the catheter and needed to be sure everything was in working order. Two nurses and my mom helped me sit up in bed and try to walk to the bathroom.

By the time I got to the toilet, I was too weak to move and I was pale as a ghost. As I sat down, I realized I couldn't hear anything. It sounded like I was underwater and then my vision began to go black around the outer rims of my sight. I pulled on the emergency cord next to the toilet, and one of the nurses burst through the bathroom door and yelled for someone to bring a wheelchair and an ammonia stick.

"You're about to pass out, Kaighla. I need you to calm down and just breathe deeply," she said, passing the ammonia stick under my nose.

They wheeled me back to bed and the doctors came in a few minutes later after deliberating in the hallway.

"Ms. White, it seems you are going to need a blood transfusion," one doctor explained. "Your Hemoglobin is only at a six-and-a-half on the scale. A healthy, normal Hemoglobin level hovers around fourteen, and we need you at least at a nine before you can leave the hospital."

I accepted the transfusion and a few hours later, I had two units of someone else's blood pumping through my veins, which was an odd sensation, on the whole.

While I sat in my hospital bed trying to learn to breathe again after the invasive surgery and trying to balance rest and movement, as well as pumping my breasts to try to make my milk come in, my baby was thirty miles away, getting better and better, *alhamdulillah*. Ismayil had the breathing tube removed the same night he arrived at the NICU and was by then breathing on his own with a cannula in his nose, providing him room oxygen. He had torn out both the cardio line going into his belly button and his feeding tube. He was strong, clearly, and he wanted out!

Once during my three-day stay in the hospital, AJ went to the Children's Hospital to get pictures of Izzy and a blanket that had been around him so I could smell it and see him while pumping, to help us bond and encourage my milk to come in. She also took a blanket to him I had kept in my gown so he could be wrapped in it and swaddled in my scent.

Although my Hemoglobin levels were only at a seven after the transfusion, I was released from the hospital once I was able to walk on my own without passing out, as long as I was holding onto a railing and moving very slowly. A very good friend from my Bible college days drove me to the Children's Hospital so I could be with Ismayil.

I was wheeled into his room and saw him there in his clear plastic bed, and I began to cry. The nurses were touched when they realized I hadn't been able to hold him yet. They closed the curtains so I could be free to nurse him without worry of compromising my modesty, and they kindly removed the crucifix from the Catholic hospital room to make me more comfortable. Thus we began our relationship, Izzy and I, four days late.

Only a day later, he was discharged, and AJ came to pick us

up and take us home.

* * *

It had been a very difficult recovery time, two weeks in, for so many reasons. My other three children had contracted whooping cough from AJ and her friend. Though it was scary listening to them coughing, it wasn't all that dangerous for them. It was life-threatening for Izzy, though, so he and I had to be kept as far from the kids as possible. They were given an intense antibiotic which seemed to be working, albeit slowly.

We also discovered that the older kids had lice. Without treating and combing their hair every few days, stripping and washing bedding and walking a quarter mile to the laundromat in the apartment complex every single day—something which would have been impossible with my energy levels—it was just not feasible for me to eradicate it alone.

Family and friends had understandably stepped away from us to avoid getting either of these ailments, at exactly the time I needed people to step closer and help, but I understood their hesitation.

I expected more from my mom, though. "I'm old," she said, but she was only forty- five. "I'm tired from working in the office all day," she said, but AJ worked a full-time job, too, as well as a second, part-time job, and she still managed to help me with the kids and the house daily. "I still have two kids at home, Kaighla" she said, but Garrett was fourteen (so clearly not helpless) while Emily technically lived with her father. "The dogs need me," she said. *The dogs needed her, so she couldn't help care for her grandchildren.* It was absurd.

One day I was completely unable to move or get out of the

bed on my own. I was sure my incision was infected, and I was still too anemic to walk from one room to the next without feeling faint. I had to be constantly vigilant in trying to keep the sick kids in the living room away from the baby, and it was all starting to wear on me.

I called my mom and begged her to come help me.

"Not tonight, honey. I don't feel like it," she said, all nonchalant like I had invited her to play a game of poker.

"But mom, I really need help and you know AJ has work tonight. Please, mom, I need your help," I begged.

"I can't. Not tonight. I'm sorry. You'll be fine," she said pointedly, and with that, she hung up the phone.

I began to hyperventilate and that turned into a full-blown panic attack. When AJ came home an hour later, I was still not okay, sitting stock-still in bed, barely acknowledging Izzy's screams.

"Why didn't you call someone, Kaighla?" she asked, sincerely concerned for me and the kids. She picked Izzy up off the bed and shushed him, bouncing him gently as she stood next to the bed. "Why didn't you call mom to come help you?"

"I did! I did call mom and I begged her to come help but she said no, that she doesn't feel like it!" I cried.

With that, AJ stood up, gave Izzy back to me, grabbed her keys and said she was going to deal with mom. Two hours later, she came in, tears on her cheeks, enraged like I had never seen her before. She wouldn't tell me what happened, but my mother decided after their conversation that she wanted nothing to do with Ariel, or me and my children.

* * *

234

July 28th, 2014

I gotta say: no one throws a party like my family. I can't believe, still, how invested they are in my kids and I feeling at-home here.

Ramadan was awful this year, mostly because Izzy is so young and all the kids were super sick. Like always, I was not looking forward to 'Eid. It's usually a holiday everyone else (non-converts, I mean) seems to enjoy so much, but me and my kids just sort of cope with, which makes the prohibition on celebrating Christmas and birthdays that much harder.

Not this year! They went all out!

Emily went with me and the kids to the big mosque. We prayed the 'Eid prayer while she sat in the back of the room with Izzy, and then we all enjoyed the barbecue and fair they had set up in the back parking lot of the mosque.

By the time we got home, we were happily exhausted and our bellies were full. As I put my key in the door, I thought I heard AJ inside, whispering to someone, but she'd told me she had plans with her best friend.

As I stepped into the house, AJ popped out from behind the couch. "Salami and Bacon!" she yelled, playfully mocking our greeting of "Asalaamu alaykum." She and her friend had snuck over while we were at the mosque and decorated the entire apartment with streamers and balloons. They even bought the kids a bunch of presents and wrapped them in colorful wrapping paper.

The kids—who were, just moments before, too tired to even walk inside themselves and demanded Emily and I carry them in—suddenly had a burst of energy and ran around screaming and laughing.

Seriously, it was the best 'Eid ever, which is crazy since my family isn't even Muslim. I know so many converts who can't even tell their family they are Muslim, so I know how blessed we are to have them.

After the horrible events of the summer—including mom deciding she doesn't want anything to do with us—we needed that celebration so badly, man. I am so grateful to God for my family.

* * *

I knew Ameer was hiding something from me. I could feel it. He had been acting secretive and finding any excuse to end our calls as quickly as possible. I was tired, sick, nursing a newborn, caring for three sick kids under five, and I was losing my patience.

"Ameer, stop. Just tell me what's really happening," I said finally. "Please stop acting like everything is okay and be honest with me."

He breathed deeply for a second, exhaling the air in a loud sigh. Then I heard him excuse himself from the people he had been sitting with and walk into another room.

"Okay, Um Abdullah, calm down," he said. "I will tell you. But please control yourself. okay? Yes, I have not been telling you everything, but for good reason. You were so sick with Izzy's delivery and all that happened before that. I couldn't bear to hurt you."

I tried to calm myself but wanted him to hurry up and get to the point.

"What on earth is going on? Did you marry someone?!"I asked, feeling frantic.

He actually laughed, and he sounded so light-hearted that I almost forgot he was in the middle of revealing yet another secret he'd hidden from me.

"No, Kaighla. No. Of course not," he said.

"Ok… so what is it then?" I asked.

"Shahida is pregnant. She's due in a few months. But I swear to you, I had no idea until a few months ago. She hid it from me," he said, talking louder to cover my crying.

I crumpled onto the floor, wishing with all my might that I could sink into the carpet, to be anywhere except right there in that room with that truth sucking the oxygen out of me. He'd kept me consistently pregnant for years based solely on the lie that Shahida wasn't capable of getting pregnant again. She herself heavily implied that she had been given a tubal ligation after her last birth.

"You lied to me! Again! You said you weren't even touching her! You said… you said you were as lonely as I was, and that you were suffering without me!" I screamed.

"*Habibti*, Kaighla. Please be calm. You will hurt yourself and you'll hurt the kids if they see you like this. Please, calm down. I didn't lie to you. I really had no idea, and when I found out, you had only just checked into the hospital because you wanted to kill yourself! What should I have done?!"

I cried more and called him a liar more times than I could count, and his voice grew darker and fiercer.

"Stop yelling at me. Stop crying. I know what I told you. Yes, I lied. Of course, I was sleeping with her. She's my wife and it's my right to enjoy sex with her whenever I want, and I will continue to do so whenever I want," he said.

When I cried even harder because of his cruelty, he got truly vicious.

"Yes, *cry*. Yes, eat yourself with your tears, Kaighla. It won't change anything," he said, snarling, his voice vindictive and hollow.

"I will never trust you again. You're a very bad man!" I cried, trying to mask my sorrow with anger.

He sighed in exasperation then. "I don't know what to say, Um Abdullah. This is the reality," he said, his voice calmer and softer now. "Now please, try to get some rest, and please let your sister help you with the kids."

And with that, he hung up the phone.

* * *

AJ came home from work in a bad mood for the fourth day in a row, and it became more and more obvious to me: she was tired of having us there—tired of having to adjust her life in her own home to keep me and my kids comfortable; tired of the crying baby, day and night; and tired of my crying day and night, and of my constant inability to keep my shit together.

I began looking for another living arrangement. I still didn't have a job, but I was able by then to stand and walk without assistance. I thought surely there had to be a home or an organization somewhere, anywhere, that helped struggling Muslim mothers whose husbands had abandoned them.

When I found out about a Muslim women's shelter in Texas, I could barely contain my excitement. I called and spoke with the man who set up the entire shelter situation—one for men and another for women. He was a kind, understanding fellow convert who had seen plenty of women who had suffered as I had.

"Our home is humble, and everyone has to contribute in one way or another, but you and your children will be safe, and we have many opportunities for our sisters in the community," he assured me. One such opportunity was a job placement program, as well as free or very cheap childcare for working mothers, he said.

I spent several days thinking about it, pondering on it, and even talking it over with both of my sisters before finally deciding this could be our chance.

AJ had changed her entire life to make room for us, and it had been nearly a year at this point. She had worked two jobs to provide for us while I struggled to find work. Enough was enough. It was clear if there was any hope of salvaging our once-close relationship, it was time for me and the kids to go.

We loaded up the kids and all our suitcases into the van and drove eight hundred miles. Emily and I took turns driving the van, while AJ and her boyfriend followed us in her car to be sure we all arrived safely.

16

The Ordeal

Dallas–Fort Worth, Texas

Autumn 2014

The motel TV played in the background as I sat in the bathroom and cried my heart out. I had been waiting all day for a moment of peace and solitude to finally get those tears out, but when you're living in a motel room with four little people, those moments don't come often.

I had taken the kids with me to yet another mosque that day and tried to explain my situation, hoping someone could help us. At the large, beautifully-furnished new *masjid*, I was ushered into a small meeting room with a long table in the middle with around fifteen people—mostly older, immigrant men—sitting and sipping their coffee. The person at the far end of the table motioned for me to sit down, so I did.

"Why are you here, so far from home, and with four kids—one

of them less than four months old? And where is your husband? You do have a husband, right?" he asked, clearly suspicious of me already.

By the time I finished sharing the basic skeleton of the story of how I ended up before them, begging for help, half the faces in the room looked sad for me, but the other half looked skeptical. One of the skeptical faces broke the silence.

"So, sister, you're telling us that your husband—a sheikh from *Al-Azhar*, no less—tricked you into marrying him, took you to his small town in Egypt, neglected and abused you in various ways, allowed you to come back to America to give birth, and now knows that you and his kids are living in a motel? And he doesn't send you money or try to help you in any way?" The suspicion in his voice was palpable.

I sighed deeply and tried to hold back the tears.

"Yes, that is what I am saying, brother. He has sent a few hundred dollars in the past year, but that's hardly enough. He has his mother, six kids, and his other, pregnant wife to support there, and he doesn't make enough money for even them," I responded.

They whispered to one another in a smattering of Arabic and Urdu before one of the two women in the room full of men turned to me and smiled. "Please, sister, wait for us in the hall. We will deliberate here on what best to do to help you," she said.

As I sat in the hall, waiting and hoping they would just help us in any way at all, I reflected on what we'd gone through in the previous weeks. How, indeed, had I gotten into that situation?

* * *

When we arrived at the women's shelter, it was a letdown, to say the least. When the brother who ran the Muslim women's home said the house was "humble," I didn't think he meant run-down. He also didn't mention there were dogs in the house, and my children were terrified of dogs.

I was glad my sisters and AJ's boyfriend had elected to keep the kids at the motel while I went to check things out. I didn't want them to see what I had just made them bring me to.

After the tour, an older woman, who was the caretaker of the house, told me how all the women there had to work at the local stadium selling candy bars for twelve hours or more every weekend and throughout the week sometimes, were not given regular breaks, and didn't receive any of the proceeds from their work. She said it was part of the "everyone contributes" catch he told me about.

"But surely they'll find other work for you," she said. "They can't expect you to work at the stadium concession stand while you have all the kids."

"Things were great," I lied, smiling at my sisters when I went back to meet them at their motel. "Thanks for driving us, you guys," I said, hoping I had been convincing enough. They hugged me and began driving north, back to Illinois.

When the kids and I arrived at the Muslim women's shelter, we took all of our stuff into the largest room, which had several bunk beds and a tiny twin mattress in it. It was the only room large enough for the five of us.

"Why does the new girl get the best room in the house?" I overheard someone complain in the hallway. "She marches in here like she owns the place…"

I didn't sleep that night. I felt unsafe and unsure of my surroundings, and all my inner alarm bells were going off. So the next morning, I grabbed the kids, along with all of our bags, and loaded everything back into the van to find another option. Going back home wasn't a possibility, so we had to find another place to live and begin establishing a life.

I remembered that I knew someone nearby, an old friend I had known for years. She was a convert, too, and was also married to an Egyptian, so I reached out to her, and she was happy to help.

The first mosque she took me to turned us away without fanfare. "We have tons of women who play like victims, and who act Muslim and give us a sob story and, in the end, they're all liars and druggies. Why should we believe you? Can anyone corroborate your story?" they asked me.

I wept there, right in the *masjid* office, for the helplessness I felt. *Of course,* I didn't have anyone to corroborate my story. Like any good narcissist, the sheikh had successfully cut me off from all my friends and family and convinced me to hide our private lives from everyone I knew. Even AJ didn't know the full truth of my life.

For a few weeks, we stayed with another convert we met through my friend. Heather was a brand-new Muslim with a small daughter from a previous marriage, now freshly wed to a Yemeni abroad who was waiting on his papers. We worked together to feed all our kids and shared our own stories of conversion and suffering at the hands of the Muslim community. She was kind, selfless, and broken in her own ways. Our friendship was a kind of balm for us both.

But that living arrangement could not go on forever. Heather's husband's papers could have come through any day, so I knew we'd have to be out soon so she could get her home ready for him. It was hard for two adults and five children being crammed into her tiny two-bedroom apartment, and it often felt like we were standing on top of one another. Plus, her young daughter, unaccustomed to sharing her space and toys, could not adjust to having so many other kids in her life at all hours, so there were daily arguments between the kids, which caused friction between Heather and I. Just a few weeks after she'd welcomed us, it was time for us to leave again, so off we went.

On the bright side, I had found employment through Heather's mosque. I was able to secure a job with one of the older women in attendance who was an author and a self-help guru. She was trying to get more publicity for her books and courses, so she hired me to build a website for her.

When I explained our housing situation to my new employer, she immediately got to work trying to help us. She talked to some of the people in her own circles and secured a long-stay motel room, which she paid for week-by-week, until we could find another way.

Long after I finished creating her website and editing her videos for her self-help course, she still paid me my wages, giving me little odd jobs here and there so I could feel like I was earning my keep, dignity intact. But it just wasn't enough, so we were forced to keep seeking help at mosques around the area.

* * *

My reminiscing was interrupted by the sister with the kind face opening the boardroom and asking me to come back in.

"Thank you, sister, for telling us your story. We think we have a solution for you," one of the brothers said. "But first, we must ask you a hard question," he said.

Bracing myself, I invited him to continue.

"Can you tell us why you have not divorced your husband? If he's really so bad as you say he is, surely you would have divorced him by now," he said.

My mouth fell open. How many times had Ameer and men like him lectured me about how a good Muslim woman doesn't divorce her husband, no matter what, and remains patient with him, seeking her reward in Paradise?

"Because he is a good father and because I still love him, somehow," I said, choking on my tears. Someone slid a box of tissues my way.

"Well, sister, all we can say is that a woman in your situation needs a husband," he said.

There it was, the same horrible advice I had been given all those years ago when I was a single mom with Dayo, working at the school in Chicago: "You have a big problem, sister. Only a man can solve this for you."

"If you were willing to divorce him, we would be happy to arrange a marriage with a better man," a kind sister assured me, touching my hand to comfort me.

Shocked, I dried my tears and thanked them. "I cannot divorce my husband just because we are in a hard situation. Thank you for your time," I said.

Before I left, they handed me a check for $100 and sent me on my way.

I sat in my van that night crying like I had never cried before while the kids slept in the back. My dignity was gone. These people had forced me to lay bare my entire story, asking for intimate details of my life, and in the end, all they gave me was $100 for food and gas, and suggested I was in some way deserving of my hardships because I hadn't just divorced my husband, like such a thing was simple.

After we arrived at the motel and I got the kids to bed, and after I cried again in the bathroom, I had a spark of clarity and knew what had to be done.

The next morning, I called Ameer. "Please, bring us home. We have nowhere safe to live here, and no one will hire me since I wear hijab and have had almost no job experience the past six years," I begged.

"*Alhamdulillah,* you finally see you were wrong to leave Egypt. Come home, *habibti,*" he said, smiling into the phone.

Within two weeks, he'd sold Mama Bushra's ancestral home in the *balad* to pay off the Repatriation Loan so we could get our passports back, and I'd sold my van to get the money for the tickets back to Egypt. We had nowhere else to run, so I fled back to my personal hell, which was, nonetheless, better than homelessness in America.

17

The Return

Sharqia Governorate, Egypt

December 19th, 2014

It's sunrise and I'm sitting on our balcony, overlooking the vineyards and the orange groves. Our new apartment is on the edge of town, as far away from Shahida and Mama Bushra as we could possibly be. But we're only two streets over from the apartment we lived in before, the one across the street from the boys' high school. Now, Ihsan and Idris and the kids have moved from the balad *and are living in that apartment, and it's so nice to sit and visit with her more often.*

Ameer closed the tiny shop in the medina *while we were in America, and then opened another in the big mall next to his mosque. It's pretty far from both Shahida and me, so we've worked out a system where we're not allowed to visit him in the shop unless it's our day with him, and it seems*

247

to be working out thus far.

There's no water in our apartment today, again. The internet often doesn't work, per normal Egypt, and the construction guys knocked our satellite dish off the roof. So here I sit, journaling. As much as I whine about my life in Egypt—about how hard things are here, I mean—if I didn't live in a place where the water, the electricity, the internet, and the satellite often fail me, I'd not resort to journaling—something I find immensely helpful—and I'd be far less mindful in general.

The time we spent on the beach at Al-Arish when the kids and I first got back to Egypt was so important for us, as a family and as a couple. It was odd, though, coming back together after everything we have been through, after all this time. Sleeping with him was a strange experience. On the one hand, it had been a year since a man even so much as touched me, so I was hungry with need. But I couldn't just forget all the lies, all the bullshit lies, he fed me during the year we were away. Letting him sleep with me felt just like that: letting *him sleep with me, something he doesn't deserve but I need too bad to turn down.*

The look on his face when the kids and I finally came into the airport in Cairo was something I will never forget, and for a moment, the ice around my heart melted for him. He bent down and all the kids ran into his arms. He was starting to cry already, and when I handed him Izzy, the tears poured from his eyes. He held him and kissed his forehead, whispering the athan *in his ear, a rite he should have fulfilled at birth. Finally, he took me in his arms and gave me a brief peck on the cheek.*

Sitting in the beach house those two weeks and looking

out across the Mediterranean sea below us, I would open all the windows—even though it's winter and the wind was cold—just to smell the salty air and let my worries and all the pain I felt this past year wash away. We talked a lot, too, about the pain, the separation, the homelessness, and he promised me things will be different this time, that he will be fair, that he learned his lesson while we were away.

That lasted a month. But I am trying not to let it get me down. I am working harder on letting go of what I can't change.

It helps that our apartment truly is beautiful, despite the unfortunate modern Egyptian color palette. There's a striped yellow and red pattern on one wall in the salon, *right as you walk in, making that wall look like clown pants, and all the other walls are a different color with contrasting patterns. But at least the space is very open! There are two living room areas and we designated one as a* majlis *and eating area, and the other as a* salon, *as well as my office. The kitchen is one of the smallest I've ever had, but it's laid out nicely. They actually kept all my things in my old shed-kitchen at Ameer's house, sure I would come back some day, so I still have all the same furniture and those damned kitchen cabinets that caused us so much hardship.*

The apartment building is perfectly situated, too, facing northeast, so we get so much sun that we have to close the shutters by 10 a.m., even in winter, or the salon *will be hot all day.*

The Bedouin who live on the edge of town bring their cattle and sheep to graze on the sparse grass and trees, much to the chagrin of the community at large. They are always young girls, looking not much older than sixteen, all of them with their faces covered, shouting at their animals in a strange Arabic dialect I've never heard before. The kids love watching the animals coming into town and walking below our second-floor apartment, munching on things.

I enjoy my little world here in my little apartment. I am basically self-sufficient, taking walks with the kids to Ihsan's house whenever I feel like it, or else going by tuk-tuk *to Rania's house to sip mint tea and laugh about old times that used to make us cry.*

When I'm cooking or cleaning, I listen to my music—I finally gave up on my obsession with music being haraam *months ago—or otherwise, I listen to interesting, inspiring podcasts. Let her be the perfect wife he needs to present to the community; I'm happy to be his obscure, problematic second wife, in my own little corner in my own little world.*

* * *

One bright morning, Dayo and I were walking in the *medina* to get some *tawmiyyah* and hummus from the corner stall when I saw a flash of brown hair. Thinking for a moment it was one of the Coptic girls in town who wore an *abaya* without wearing hijab, I paused to look more closely.

There, standing in the middle of that tiny Egyptian town, was an authentic millennial hipster—complete with heavy, black-rimmed glasses and a long, baggy, button-up shirt and jeggings, like she'd just stepped out of 1987.

I stood in rapt amazement for so long that Dayo started

tugging on my clothes to get me to keep walking. Maybe she was a European of some flavor, maybe a Canadian, but there was at least a small chance she spoke English. When you live abroad for so long, there comes a point that the only standard you have for friendship is the ability to speak the same language, and at least a moderate sense of cultural appreciation between you, if possible.

"*Ya* Kaighla!" Ameer called to me in the kitchen as he sat at the dinner table a few nights later. "You'll never guess who came to my shop today looking for 'reeeel honey'!"

I knew who he was referring to without having to ask, and without the assistance of his exaggerated word usage.

"She's married to a Coptic guy that lives just a few blocks from the store," he said, gobbling stew as I sat down to eat.

"Where's she from?" I asked, trying to seem casual. It felt like a friend was about to set me up with a blind date and I, homely and desperate, tried to seem nonchalant.

"Somewhere in the States, but I don't really know for sure where," he said. "I think her husband said she's from the south. Georgia, maybe? Anyway, they live here now."

I couldn't believe what I was hearing. "Are you sure they're not just here to meet his family?" I asked.

"No, no. He came into the shop a few minutes later with his parents and they told me he and his wife are staying for at least a year while he waits for his residency papers," he said.

"Oh, tell me you got her number!" I asked, not even trying to hide my excitement then.

"I mean… I didn't get *her* number, of course. But yes, I got his. I've told him to bring her by the shop again tomorrow night."

I shrieked with joy and kissed him on the cheek. For a moment, I didn't hate him. For a fleeting moment, I remembered loving him and appreciated that he had thought of me.

"But why not tonight?" I whined.

"Because it's not your night with me. But come tomorrow afternoon by *tuk-tuk,* or I can have Khalid drive you after *Maghrib,*" he replied.

That had to have been the longest twenty-four hours I'd experienced in some time. The next night when Khalid showed up, honking his horn, I had created an entire world in my mind, with her at the center. Sure, I loved my friends in Cairo, but none of them were American; none of them knew the movie references or the songs I remembered, and they weren't there, in that tiny town, mere blocks from my apartment.

* * *

The mall was bustling when we arrived. Khalid handed Izzy to his Baba and grabbed two chairs to place in the courtyard for the two *Amrikiyaat* to sit and chat. Had we been Egyptian, we'd have simply invited one another over to our homes and hosted a huge meal to set the stage for friendship and secure our image in one another's minds. But our husbands were both reticent to leave us alone together—two independent American women of two different faiths.

When I saw her walk into the mall with her husband, she was wearing just as fabulous a getup as the first time I saw her. I wondered what it must be like to have that kind of confidence, to dress like that in a place like rural Egypt. Aside from not wearing hijab, she just stood out in every way, and though she didn't seem to be enjoying it, she didn't seem bothered by the stares and whispers at all.

I stood up and walked toward her, offering her my hand which she shook briefly before throwing her arms around me in a hug, like we were old friends, just casually meeting up in that hellhole town for some chai.

After some brief pleasantries—wherein I learned her name was Rachel, and she was from Mississippi but had shed her southern accent as hastily as I had shed my Midwestern twang—we got down to the real question: *what on earth were we both doing there?!*

"When I met my husband, we were both working at a vet hospital in Amman," she told me. "I wanted to get some volunteer hours in to build up my resume for vet school and he was just finishing up his degree."

They fell in love in the heat of a Jordanian Summer. When it was over, he had to return to Egypt. Newly graduated and ready for real life to begin, he asked her to marry him, and she decided to follow him to Egypt.

"We want to go to the States soon so I can finish my degree and he can start a practice of his own, but those pesky papers..." she said and we both chuckled.

A whole year she would be there in that town, just as frustrated as I was, although she spoke fairly decent Arabic and mine, though better, was still atrocious. I didn't know whether to be sad for her to be there or relieved for myself to have someone to share the pain.

After that, Rachel and I were together as much as possible. I would ask Ameer to keep the kids, and he'd happily take them all over, doing this and that. I'd load myself into a *tuk-tuk* to ride over to her house, just a few blocks from the mall, right next to the unfinished Coptic church on the corner. Several times a week, we'd sit in my house, or in her comparatively posh *salon*, sipping tea and building an odd sort of friendship.

Rachel had a rambunctious *baladi* puppy and a moody, antisocial cat. When I took Izzy with me, he would squeal with delight as her dog jumped and barked and made a general ruckus. It felt so nice to have a friend again, though, truth be told, I knew in our "real lives" back home, Rachel would never have chosen me as a friend. She was an Ivy League grad—intelligent, suave, and confident, though a bit awkward—while I was from white-trash, backyard America and my education consisted of three semesters of Bible college.

Strange and confused, I had lived so far away from my own world for so long that I struggled to seem "natural" in any context. But she welcomed me nonetheless, and we enjoyed our time with one another, a brief reprieve from the oddities of our daily lives. At least together, there was no need for niceties and faking it. We understood and appreciated the struggle the other was suffering. There was a "Namaste, babe" feeling between us: *the goddess in me recognizes and respects the goddess in you—and shit, I feel your struggle, girlfriend.*

18

The Spark

Egypt

Spring 2015

My new friend, Rachel, had a job—the same job she had in Amman that paid to cover her volunteer time at the vet hospital—as an outsourced worker for some web company based in California. They were paying her pennies to do the work they would have had to pay someone living in the USA minimum wage to do. But this was Egypt and the dollar stretched far. While her husband studied for his certification to be able to practice in Mississippi, Rachel worked a full-time job while also trying to develop a relationship with her husband's elderly parents who lived downstairs and invaded her privacy at their leisure.

"You know," she said one day, mouth full of cake, "I could get you a job if you want. They always need people, and you and I are kinda the perfect fit for them. I mean, we're American, so we understand the work environment and are fluent in English, but we're living here, so we're super cheap and we have no legal recourse to do anything about it."

If there was ever a choir-of-angels-singing-Hallelujah moment in my entire life, that was it. My own money? My own way to provide for myself and my kids? The ability to buy what I liked without having to beg Ameer, even as he lavished all his money on Shahida? I couldn't even imagine what it would be like to live in such luxury.

A week later, I was proud to be an outsourced worker. Like Rachel, I made $3.53 an hour, which was a veritable fortune in rural Egypt. Soon, I was able to afford to buy the stuff my kids and I needed, and even some of the things we liked.

Better than all this, AJ decided on a whim to fulfill her promise and come to visit us. She planned a ten-day whirlwind tour of Egypt so we could finally see all the touristy things that make Egypt attractive for everyone but the poverty-stricken who live there. Plus, she was bringing me a new laptop and a few thousand dollars to buy myself all the comforts of home I was living without.

* * *

The morning AJ arrived, I had been trying to make Ameer get ready for hours, but he kept saying we had more time.

A full two hours after her flight landed, we parked the van at the airport. I ran ahead of him and the kids, breaking all codes of conduct for a Muslim woman in a Muslim-majority country. I began looking around the crowded baggage area for her, but I couldn't find her anywhere. I knew she had neither reception nor Wifi in the airport, so I began to feel panicked.

Just then, I heard someone shout my name from just outside the baggage claim.

"You took long enough!" AJ yelled, drawing the attention of every Egyptian in the vicinity. I ran to her and apologized profusely, just before Ameer and the kids met us and he took her bags from her.

"I almost got right back on the plane," she laughed as she hugged the kids and kissed their foreheads, one-by-one.

"I'm sorry, dude… Egyptians, amirite?" I said, and we both laughed.

After a night at a hotel in Giza, right next to the Pyramids, we began our big adventure. We planned to visit the Pyramids the next day, then take a plane to Luxor so we could visit the Valley of the Kings and the temples around there. Finally, we'd spend a few days in Hurghada, enjoying the beach and submarining. Before she was to leave, we planned to take her home to our little town in Sharqia so she could see the "real" Egypt.

The trip was wonderful, but Ameer and I couldn't seem to get along. At a mall in Cairo, before we left on our cross-country adventure, AJ decided she wanted to buy some new shoes for Rumi since she had grown out of her old ones and had only one pair. AJ saw a pair she loved, but they were super expensive imported Sketcher's or some such American brand, nonetheless made in China.

"No, no. I won't let you buy those for her. It's *haraam* to waste that kind of money," Ameer scolded her, trying to seem both serious and care-free.

"Listen, bro. It's my money, not yours, and I came to Egypt to spend it on my sister and my nieces and nephews, sooo…" she said, in that way she does, leaving the sentence open-ended, lingering there for effect.

"Okay, but I insist. Please. Let's buy her something simpler. You know her feet will grow out of these very soon, so it's pointless, anyway," he responded, clearly annoyed at her for arguing with him at all, let alone in public—something he was not accustomed to, not even back in Brooklyn.

I felt so embarrassed he was treating AJ like this—my sister who had housed and fed us for more than a year and who now spent thousands of her own money to come visit us and take us on a nice vacation.

"*Ya* sheikh, leave her alone," I spoke up. "She's right. It's her money. Let her spend it how she wants. You know '*haraam*' doesn't apply to her anyway," I insisted.

His face changed to that one I'd known all those years before, the "you had better make me look good in public or else..." expression.

"What? Don't look at me like that. It's her money and she wants to buy our daughter nice shoes," I said, a little louder than I meant to.

He did not speak to me for the rest of the night.

"Do not talk to me like that in front of the people, *ya* Um Abdullah," he scolded me in the car on the way to the pyramids the next morning. "You know that people have great respect for me and when my own wife can't respect me, it's not right."

The people respect you because they have no idea who you really are, I thought to myself.

This sort of fight went on the entire trip, from Giza to Luxor to Hurghada. Every time AJ tried to spend money on us, he would argue with her, and it went way beyond normal Arab modesty. He was genuinely upset with her for spending so much, and it was starting to bother me.

Things were especially tense among the three of us in Luxor. So one night, when the kids and Ameer were sleeping, AJ and I snuck out of our hotel rooms and had dinner and dessert at an Italian restaurant on the resort grounds. When we came back to the hotel room, Ameer was enraged.

"Why did you sneak out like that without telling me?" he asked me after AJ had gone back to her room.

"Ameer, you were asleep, and the kids were, too. Why should I have woken you? I left you a note and took my phone with me. I don't see why you're so upset," I said.

"Clearly, spending time with your sister and with Rachel have affected your mind. Don't forget: you're a Muslim woman, and you can't just go places without my permission, and certainly not here in Egypt, where you really could be in real danger," he explained.

It had been a long day of walking around the Hatshepsut Temple, as well as the Temple of Karnak. I was tired, and I didn't want to argue.

"*Hadr, habibi*," I said. It was the common way children spoke to their elders, and fathers to their kids when they wanted to be sweet. It meant something like, "Your wish is my command, my love."

The last few days before she was going to fly home, AJ came home to our town in Sharqia so she could see what our life was like, day-to-day. We spent some time alone together in my apartment while the kids hung out with Ameer and his family in the shop. It was the first time since we lived together the year before that we had a chance to really talk, and I needed it so much.

One night, while helping me clean up my room, she found Ameer's outfit for the Friday *khutba*, the *Azhar*-issued Santa

Clause-style hat and heavy black coat he wore on top of his *jilbab* every Friday. She put it on and danced around using her arm beneath the coat to mimic his giant, protruding belly. We laughed and laughed, and it was such a relief to be with someone so familiar and so close after so long trapped among people who looked at me like I was a complete moron. This fun would have been deemed sacrilegious by any Egyptian friend. Mocking the sheikh's uniform for prayer? *Haraam*.

The night before she left, as we sat on the balcony together. AJ got suddenly serious. "You know I love you and the kids, and although things weren't too great when you guys lived with me before, I need you to know that you are always welcome to return," she said, placing her teacup on the balcony railing.

Sensing my own tension, she continued. "I see how things are here. I see how he treats you and I see how it hurts you. The kids see it too. I know you've both tried to be on your best behavior while I've been here, but it's still clear," she said.

I sat sipping my own hot tea, looking at the stars jutting out over the vineyard to the southeast. A *tuk-tuk* flew by on the road below us, blasting something or other from Puff Daddy, and a couple of teenage man-boys laughed and tried to sing along. I took in a deep breath of cold, earthy air.

"I know. I do. I know you mean it," I said, trying to avoid her eyes.

"Kaighla, this is not you," she said, tears clouding her voice. Since the day she came into my world with her fiery hair and her blue eyes, confirming the name I wanted mom to give her so badly—Ariel, after the ginger, underwater Disney princess—I had seen her cry only a handful of times.

"I miss my sister. I have not seen the real you in so many years and it's killing me, man. Those kids don't even know the real you, and they are missing out on your incredibly amazing self," she said. "Underneath all... this," she said, gesturing to my excessive layers, "you are a strong, independent woman, and I can't handle watching you submit yourself, all of yourself, to that 'man,'" she said, holding up universal air-quote fingers.

"I would never tell you what to do with your life, you know that—even when you ask me to, I won't. This is your choice. But I have watched this man, almost from the moment you married him, work to kill my big sister. I have watched the way he destroyed your unique, fucked-up personality. At first, it scared me, then it made me angry, and now it makes me sad."

We sat together in silence then, the dark sky and the bright stars keeping us company.

The next morning, we drove her to the airport in Cairo. At the entrance to the security area at the airport, she hugged me and got her wallet out of her carry-on.

"Buy something you want, anything you want that he refuses to buy for you. Buy stuff for the kids, too. Whatever. But it's yours, not his," she said, pressing more money into my hand. She'd already transferred a thousand dollars to my account before we left Sharqia.

I cried when she walked through the gate, both because I would miss her and because I felt ashamed that my little sister had, once again, come to save me from a man I'd given myself to far too completely.

* * *

After we dropped AJ off at the airport, we planned to stop at the Carrefour Supermarket next to our old apartment in Ma'adi Al-Zahra on the way home so I could buy a dishwasher. Along the way, we stopped at an ATM, and as I was closing my door to go inside and get the money out of the bank, Ameer grabbed my hand.

"Hey, please take all of it out," he said, nonchalantly.

"Why? I only need to take out half... I would really like to save the rest for emergencies," I answered.

He sat looking at me for a moment, as if he was trying to decide if he wanted to answer me.

"Why, Ameer?" I asked, pressing him.

"I need you to pay your rent this month. You know I lost a lot of money in the shop by being away these two weeks and I had to pay the kids' tuition for school, so I don't have enough for your rent this month," he said with a calm face.

It all made sense now. Now I knew why he had been so angry with her for spending all that money: he knew full well that whatever she didn't spend, she would give me, and he had planned all along to take this money from me.

I didn't respond and walked away to the ATM. When I returned to the car, I didn't speak to him. When we walked through Carrefour and I bought the dishwasher and other creature comforts, I didn't speak to him. When we arrived home, I didn't speak to him, beyond asking him to bring the kids to my house and go home to his wife.

The next morning, he came to get me so I could buy groceries with my own money, too, and that was the last straw. I was finished.

I opened my wallet and handed him a full eight hundred Egyptian pounds, the equivalent of my *mahr*—$100.

"Sister," they had told me back when I was discussing marriage with him, "the best Muslim wife expects very little in *mahr* if she truly cares for her fiancé. The Muslim women of the Prophet's time only asked for their intended to teach them Qur'an!"

I had sold myself to him for $100.

"This is not for my rent money," I said as I handed him the money, serious as death. "I demand *khula*, and this is the money you gave me when we married. We are finished."

He looked down at the money and up at me as I was standing outside the car, next to the grocery store. A look of terror flashed across his face, just for an instant.

"I am serious," I said. "You cannot manage two wives, as you've proven these four years. And you will not choose, so I have chosen for you. Go to her and be the husband she has deserved all this time. But we are done," I said, and I made sure he knew I meant it.

He took a gulp of air and strengthened his jaw, swatting a fly away from his face. "No, Kaighla. No. We are *not* finished, and may God give you what you deserve for trying to break our family apart. You know God hates divorce, *ya* Um Abdullah," he said.

"Please, spare me your lectures, *ya* sheikh, and give me my annulment like you are supposed to when a woman gives you back her *mahr*," I said, impatiently.

"No. I do not grant you *khula*," he said sternly, looking into my face, shielding the light from his eyes with one hand. "I will take this money and pay your rent."

With that, he drove away, leaving me in the *medina*. I bought my groceries and took a *tuk-tuk* home.

19

The Awakening

Sharqia Governorate, Egypt

Summer 2015

Ameer had not been allowed into my home for almost two weeks. The day he left me on the street in the *medina*, I texted him, telling him in no uncertain terms that he was not welcome in my home any longer. Somehow, I'd managed to stick to my guns and not let him in.

"So you will keep my kids from me?" he asked over the phone.

"No, of course not," I replied. "You are most welcome to send Khalid to get them, or you could come and pick them up yourself outside. Just honk like you always do and I'll send them down. Then send them back home when you're done with them."

Finally, after ten days or so, he realized I wasn't bluffing and decided to do something about it.

"Listen, Um Abdullah. I am coming to the house tonight with

Sheikh Kareem and Rania Um Omar, as well as my other sheikh friend and his wife," he announced. "We have to talk."

I silently acquiesced, if only to get the chance to make my case.

When they arrived that night, and everyone had their tea and was situated in the *majlis*, the discussion got started.

"Tell us, *ya* Um Abdullah: what is the problem, exactly? We won't interrupt you, and then when you're done, we will give Sheikh Ameer a chance to make his points. *Mashy?*" Sheikh Kareem asked, calmly.

His voice and his presence were soothing. The night that Dayo broke his arm, it was Sheikh Kareem who came to the house to take us to the hospital. His gentle demeanor was reassuring during one of the scariest moments of my life, so I welcomed his intervention in our divorce proceedings, and inwardly wondered why we hadn't consulted with him earlier.

In fits of tears and periods of calm, I explained all that Ameer had done to me, from the moment I met him on the matrimonial website to that very moment—right there, in our rented apartment. I told them about the tricks, the outright lies, the broken promises, the gaslighting, the abuse—all of it.

I had been speaking in a mix of English and Arabic, and both Rania and Sheikh Hassan had to translate several points. They listened, though, and it seemed like they understood. They looked visibly disturbed at times, and at other times, seemingly unconvinced of the more worrisome details I relayed. After nearly an hour, I had exhausted myself.

By this point, Ameer was up and pacing the front room, just a few feet away from us in the *majlis*. He cleared his throat in the annoying way he always did, and he came to sit down next to his friends on the couch.

"Thank you, Um Abdullah," Sheikh Hassan said in English. He was far less familiar with the situation than Sheikh Kareem was, and his wife less familiar with my personality—and my honesty—than Um Omar was, and she looked disturbed.

"*Ya* sheikh, would you like to give your perspective?" asked Sheikh Kareem.

Ameer sat staring off into the distance and rubbing his beard, fidgeting uncomfortably. "I have nothing to say about what she told you. But I love my family, I love my kids, I love Um Abdullah, and I don't want us to divorce," he said, plainly.

The two sheikhs looked at one another and then at the floor, unsure of where to go from there.

"Excuse me," Rania suddenly spoke up in English. "I am sorry to interrupt, Sheikh Kareem," she said, addressing her husband, "but I need a moment to speak, please."

Sheikh Kareem nodded in kind agreement, and Um Omar began speaking, quietly and calmly at first, but with time she switched back to Arabic and her voice grew louder, more emotional.

"*Haraam alayk, ya sheikh,*" she said, leaning forward in her seat. From behind her *niqab*, her fury was palpable. The fire burning in her eyes conveyed, along with her voice, the passion she felt. "Shame on you. I have seen, all these years, the way you treat Um Abdullah. She doesn't have friends or family here. I told her many times, 'Just be patient.' I want to think good about you, as my brother and my sheikh, but *khalas*. Enough," she said in English, calming down now. With that, she sat back in her chair and signaled she had finished her rant.

Ameer stared at her, shocked at the woman—patient, modest, and kind as she normally was—now sitting before him, shaking in her tiny frame, her words dripping with passionate accusation.

"*Mashy*. Thank you for your opinion, *ya* Um Omar. I really appreciate it," he said calmly.

Like always, there was no apology, no admission of guilt.

"Okay, we've listened to you both, Um Abdullah. I don't think there's anything you have left to say, right?" Sheikh Hassan asked rhetorically.

"No," I answered anyway.

All sat in silence and stillness for a moment, listening to the ceiling fans humming away. Finally, Sheikh Kareem spoke up. "Um Abdullah, can you not give him one last chance?" he asked warmly.

I sat for a moment pondering, asking myself if there was even a slight chance he would ever change. The idea of having to serve him and give him my body when he didn't have the slightest intention of honoring or protecting me was too much.

"Yes, but I will not do a single thing for him," I said, suddenly.

With that, every face in the room looked up, surprised to hear me say anything other than a firm "No."

"No problem!" piped up Sheikh Hassan, sitting forward in his seat. "You don't have to give him anything, anything at all."

"He will not touch me. He is not welcome in my bed," I said, my voice shaking with determination. I hoped I had been clear enough that he understood exactly what I was implying.

"Sister, you don't have to give him any of his rights during this month. Nothing. Just allow him to come back. Get back to normal as much as possible. That's all we're asking from you," said Sheikh Kareem, and Um Omar translated for me.

Did I have hope he would change? Not really. But they refused to issue the *khula*—wife-initiated divorce—without me giving it one last chance.

Before they left, Sheikh Hassan turned to me and said, in all seriousness, "Um Abdullah, you are doing the right thing, *wallahi*. Did you know that if you two were to have *khula*, you could never, ever marry him again?"

Seeing the shock on my face, Sheikh Kareem stepped into his shoes and motioned to Rania to do the same thing.

"Yes, he is right, Um Abdullah," Ameer said. "If it's just *talaq*—just regular divorce—we can make up. Maybe God will fix our hearts and fix things between us. If you insist on *khula*, on an annulment, that's it. We can't ever remarry," he said, gently. "Please, give me this last chance."

That was a bald-faced lie, and all three of the educated, trusted Muslim clerics in the room went along with it, knowing it wasn't true—all to keep me married to him. But I didn't know that then.

* * *

A week after our meeting with the sheikhs, Ameer moved us into an apartment we found across town that was closer to Rania and further from Shahida and Ameer's sister, and from the shop.

We almost never had reliable water in the previous apartment, since the landlord refused to replace the water pump, but the new place had ample water. And it was grandiose, in a word: there were three bedrooms, two bathrooms, two big living areas, and a nice-sized kitchen. There were balconies off of every room, including the kitchen, and an enormous room-sized balcony on the front of the house. It was so hot that we put one of the kids' mattresses out on the balcony and would relax out there all evening and into the night.

I finally acquiesced to sleeping with Ameer, mostly because I was in need, too. Twenty seconds in, his erection was gone—*completely gone*. That was not a new thing, necessarily, but it was getting worse with each month. He had gained a hundred pounds since we first came to Egypt because he sat around so much, being waited on hand-and-foot. As I got thinner and sicker, he got fatter and sicker.

I got out of bed and walked into the bathroom, turning on an ice-cold shower. I stood under the frigid stream, washing him off of me, screaming into my hands to release the tension my body had built up. I wasn't sure how much more I could take.

Throughout all the suffering Ameer subjected me to over the years, we had maintained, at the very least, a moderately happy sex life. To see even that tiny aspect of marriage going down the drain was the final grain of sand that tipped the scales toward divorce. I'd be damned if I was going to allow him to do all he'd done to me and then not even try to keep me happy in bed, to boot.

* * *

One afternoon during our last-ditch month, Ameer came by my house on Shahida's day and sat relaxing in the coolness of the *salon*, enjoying a brief respite from the heat of the day. A few minutes after he settled in on the couch, his phone started ringing. I was in the kitchen making some tea for myself, largely ignoring him because he shouldn't have been in my house anyway, not on her day. I heard him silence his phone once, twice, three times.

Finally, the fourth time his phone rang, he answered. He coarsely mumbled into the phone something about being in the mosque, as if he was trying to be quiet because he was in the prayer hall. I was sure I must have misheard. But then, he said it again, and I heard it clear as day: *"Wallahi, ya Um Khalid, fil masjid."* "I swear to God, Um Khalid, I'm in the mosque," he said.

My mind raced across the years, checking in with all the many times he didn't come home on time because he was "in the *masjid*," or "in the *balad*," or "busy with the brothers."

I can't explain why it was that day I realized what a foul liar he was—after all, he had been lying to me for years, and I knew about it. But to see him lie to her in such a bold, shameless way, made it clear to me that I was not, in fact, the problem. I was not the cumbersome, impossible woman he made me out to be. It wasn't my incessant requests and needs and whining that made him lie to me out of necessity.

Moreover, I saw with stark clarity that Shahida was not the enemy. Ameer had lied to everyone, had turned us all against one another to protect himself from us, and I was just one of the many people in his life he had no qualms about deceiving.

"There are two situations, my brothers, when it's acceptable for a Muslim to lie," he said once in a *khutba* at Friday prayers. "If you're trying to reconcile two warring parties and decide to make each side seem more willing and positive and warm toward one another than they truly are, by talking to them separately and exaggerating their love for one another. The other time is when you need to please your spouse."

So, she asks if she looks fat, and you tell her she's the most gorgeous woman on earth, for example. She thinks since she had babies, her body has gone to shit, so you make her feel better. That's what that *hadith* meant. But not for Sheikh Ameer. No, he used that *hadith* to justify all the lies he drowned his wives in.

Every time he didn't want to be found out, he lied. When he didn't want to be held accountable, he lied. When he felt himself being pushed into a corner, he lied. And he was convinced God was okay with it.

Needless to say, by the end of the month, it was clear Ameer had no intention to change anything, and I was done. When I approached him at the end of the month and insisted he divorce me, he didn't even argue. He knew as well as I did that it was time.

* * *

I always imagined the day one divorced would be ugly and full of crying and gnashing of teeth, but in fact, it was a beautiful day. June 1st, 2015, we drove to Cairo to file the divorce papers, so we left the kids with Mama Bushra. It was one of only three times during our lives in Egypt that we actually had alone time somewhere outside, so it felt bittersweet.

We held hands walking the streets to the divorce office, and we just looked into one another's eyes over dinner afterward, in no rush to get home. It was a calm understanding we shared that day, something totally unexpected, as if we were agreed that *we had a good run, kid.*

Equally unexpected was the way it felt to be sitting in the exact room we had sat in together three years before when we got married in Egypt: one waiting room with a café, full of couples and families.

More than half the couples in the room were Egyptian men and white women of various nationalities, and more than a few of the women were clearly twenty years older than their intended. The day we came to get married, I felt an affinity to

271

them, a sort of camaraderie with these foreign women who had made the plunge I had made, too. But on this day, I felt nothing but a sick, twisted pity for them. Each of them truly believed their *habibi* loved them. They honestly believed these Egyptian boys—rich and poor alike, who had been born and bred to produce heirs to the family throne—had somehow thrown away their parents' hopes and dreams all for love of a foreign, non-Muslim woman without any connections beyond money and perhaps immigration papers.

I didn't even register the divorced couples in the room the day we got married. But on this day, I sat in that room and noticed the broken-hearted Egyptian women sitting alone while their soon-to-be ex-husbands argued with officials in the adjacent rooms. These women were facing a veritable death sentence, anticipating a life alone forever, or otherwise without their children if they were lucky enough to find a husband later—remarriage for divorced women being a rare thing, by and large.

I knew my chances were much better. I felt confident that I would not be alone forever, and I knew no one could ever take my kids from me. I didn't worry for a minute that I would be shamed and ostracized by my community, because my community was back home in America where divorce was a normal part of life, and where a lasting marriage was rarer than a divorce.

When they called us back, we saw the same men who had stamped our marriage certificate three years before, the same men who had been smoking and drinking tea all day, gawking and judging us. Of course, it didn't help that when we got legally married in Egypt, I was already eight months pregnant with our second child.

The day we divorced, we were ushered from room to room for stamp after stamp, and each time the conversation went like this:

*Official: *Incomprehensible Arabic**
  Ameer: *"He says you should reconsider. Think about the kids. Don't break up your family. Fear Allah."*
  Me: *"That's nice of him. Tell him to mind his business and stamp the paper."*

And on-and-on it went, in office after office. They assumed that it was my fault we were divorcing, that I had it in my power to change things if only I were a better wife, and that he was the one wanting to be done with me, rather than the other way around.

Finally, after an hour, we were sat down in the final office. The middle-aged, balding official behind the desk handed me a paper covered in Arabic writing and asked me to sign it.

"I don't know what it says," I said. "I need to understand it before I sign it."

Annoyed with me, he asked Ameer to translate for me.

"It just says I don't owe you anything and once we sign these papers, you have been granted one *talaq*," he said.

"*Khula,* you mean," I corrected him. "I gave you back my *mahr*. This is *khula*, not *talaq*. I have a one-month *iddah* period, not three."

The official behind the desk listened as his assistant translated, whispering into his ear. When he understood the dilemma, he told Ameer to translate for him.

"He says a *khula* is a long, complicated process, and you're a foreigner, so a contested divorce would be hard for you. If you want to be divorced quickly, he says, just sign the paper and let me grant you one *talaq*."

I was at an impasse. I had no idea if Ameer was faithfully translating the official's words, but I had no one else to turn to. I believed him, too. If I tried to fight him, I knew I'd gain nothing and perhaps lose my children. If I accepted his offer of one *talaq*—meaning we could reconcile twice more before Islamically we were required to walk away forever—I could be done with it there, that day, and spend only three months in the interim period, rather than months or years in divorce court in a foreign country.

I agreed to the *talaq*, albeit reluctantly, and only if he gave me back the *mahr* I had given him that day outside the grocery store. He handed me the money, and they gave us the papers that guaranteed that within three months, I was free to remarry, should I choose to. We were legally divorced right at that moment. Ameer could have walked right back into the same office and married someone else that same day, assuming he had all the many steps done beforehand, but I would have to wait to be sure I wasn't carrying yet another of his children before seeking a new spouse.

As we walked down the street, hand-in-hand, now officially, legally divorced but still in the *iddah* period—or waiting period, during which a couple is still religiously married, and they're supposed to continue living together in the hopes they'll somehow reconcile—the thought struck me how for once the Egyptian government had done something in a much more logical and overall better way than back home.

It's so easy to get married in America, but divorce is typically expensive and takes months or even years. But in Egypt, marriage is a multi-step, multi-day affair, while a divorce is complete within a day, assuming it's not contested. That's how it should be: you should be forced to really ponder deeply if you want to marry someone before being allowed to take the plunge, and you should be able to easily leave if you need to.

On the way home, I sat close to Ameer in the front seat, enjoying his warmth for the last time in my life. The feelings rushing through me were not at all what I expected them to be, and I half-regretted the decision to be over and done with it. The thought struck me that if only we'd had more dates like that day, we could have found our way back to one another.

But alas, the distance between us could not have been closed with some date nights. No, he consistently put miles and miles between us, building an ever-higher wall with each lie, each broken promise, each choice to gaslight me and call me crazy for reacting in the same way any woman would, and each willful decision to suppress every aspect of my true self.

That night, he took me to my nice, new apartment and volunteered to keep the kids at his house so I could have the night alone. I curled up in bed and allowed myself to cry for the grief and heartbreak I felt. I cried for all he had done to me and all that I had done to myself in allowing him to break me. I cried for our children who were innocent and didn't understand why their Baba wasn't living in our house anymore, even half-time, or why they had to go to their *Teita*'s house to see him.

The next morning, I got up and made a "divorce boot-camp" plan to get myself through that hardship, and it was on that day that I actively sat down to meditate for the first time in my life—beginning the number one habit that would get me through the coming months of hardship as a single, foreign mother of four in a place like rural Egypt.

* * *

Rania came to visit me in the middle of the day, something unexpected in Ramadan, especially in summer. Ameer and I had divorced just a week before, and I felt fragile and isolated, so she was a welcome sight. When I opened the door, she hurried in without greeting me, which was also odd.

When she removed her *niqab*, I saw that she was in tears, so I thought something had happened to her or one of the kids. After she made herself comfortable and sat fanning herself with a book, I coerced her to tell me what was going on.

"*Habibti*, tell me the truth," she said in her broken English. "Am I… the reason… the cause… of your divorce? *Wallahi?*"

I was confused and asked her to repeat her question again in Arabic and English so I could be sure I understood.

"It's the sheikh," she cried, "Sheikh Ameer. He tell everyone in town that I'm the reason you divorce him, that I say for you 'Kaighla, divorce Sheikh Ameer!'"

Lord knows how many late-night conversations we had wherein she begged me *not* to leave him.

"You'll never find a husband, *habibti*," she used to warn me.

Our friend Shadia would interject often, "*Haraam, ya* Um Abdullah! You so young, so pretty! Alone forever! No, no. No divorce him. *Habibti*, please. No divorce."

No, those women tried, again and again, to convince me to be patient, to be hopeful, to prepare myself for the reality that that was my marriage, that was my life, and that was my home now, so I had better adjust sooner rather than later.

Through tears, she explained in a smattering of English and Arabic: Ameer was so infuriated by her choice to speak against him, even in a private setting, that he spread the rumor to the other sheikhs in town that Rania Um Omar, Sheikh Kareem's heretofore honorable wife, had caused our unfortunate divorce.

Sheikh Kareem caught wind of it, of course, and was incensed. Not wanting to stoke the flames by reacting publicly, he went directly to Ameer to find out what had happened, and if there had been some sort of misunderstanding.

"No, there hasn't been any misunderstanding. Your wife convinced my wife to demand divorce. That's it. Shame on her," he'd said to Sheikh Kareem.

Ameer and Kareem had been friends for nearly two decades. Kareem was, in fact, in a position of authority over Ameer, but he never used that as an opportunity to hold it over Ameer. Twenty years of friendship, gone—just like that.

Ameer's image was more important to him than anything else. Even the Qur'anic injunction to avoid shaming an honorable woman hadn't stopped Sheikh Ameer from lying about Rania, all to distract people from his own shameful acts.

"I cannot believe this, *habibti*," I said, stroking her arm. "You are not responsible, of course. You did everything you could to protect us from this."

Though she cried, it was not her image she worried for and it wasn't even her husband's image—something no one would have blamed her for working to protect. No, her dignity was unaffected by Ameer's horrible actions against her. She carried herself with grace and restraint in the face of a level of drama she had not experienced prior to that situation. Rania cried that day because she truly feared she had inadvertently aided in the path to divorce, and she was afraid of God holding her accountable. She was concerned first and foremost for her eternal soul, and then for the well-being of myself and my kids.

We sat in silence for some time until she got a call from her husband telling her he was downstairs. She hugged me tight and assured me everything would be okay.

My friend, Rania, could have distanced herself from me then. I would have understood if she hadn't wanted to give people any more opportunity to gossip about her. But still, she invited me for dinner; still, she came to my home for tea; still, we laughed and cried and tried to understand one another in our broken shared languages, and still, she stood by me when I needed help with this or that.

* * *

Just two weeks after our divorce, Ameer went to Alberta, Canada for a mosque position that he hoped would establish him as a resident. He did try to coerce me once more to go with him before he left, though.

It was a hot afternoon the day before Ramadan and the kids were at his sister's house hanging with their cousins. He had come to my apartment and let himself in. He found me working in my office, so he made some tea, then sat in the *salon* under the ceiling fan. He doffed his *jilbab* and hung it on the back of the couch, relaxing in his white t-shirt and cotton pants, as he often did.

"*Ya* Um Abdullah," he called, "could you please come to the *salon*? I need to talk with you."

I sighed and closed my laptop, unsure of what else there was to discuss. Yes, we still had another two months of *iddah* period to be technically still religiously married, but he knew full well that reconciliation was out of the question.

"When does your flight leave?" I asked as I sat down, wanting to get straight to the point. I saw that he'd made me a cup of tea, as well, but it was too hot to drink, so I left it on the glass coffee table to cool off.

"In two days. I fly first to Toronto to take care of some things and then on to Alberta to spend Ramadan at that *masjid* that I worked at a few years ago. *Insha'Allah* they will hire me on after Ramadan."

"Mmmhmm, okay," I said, taking a sip of my own tea, now cooled off under the whipping fans, trying to seem polite and aloof at the same time.

For a moment we sat in silence, the only noise coming from the beating fans and the occasional dog fight outside. Usually, the street would be full of people at this time of day, but everyone was resting in preparation for the month of fasting. There were no boys screaming and jumping and kicking each other for fun, and there weren't many *tuk-tuks* that came by that part of town very often, though we sometimes heard their music booming a few streets over.

"Listen, *ya* Um Abdullah..." he said, seriously.

"Let me cut you off there," I said, stopping him with a hand in the air as I leaned forward to place my cup of tea back on the table. "There is nothing to talk about. You are going alone—or taking Um Khalid with you if you like. Either way, I am staying here with our kids and Dayo. *Khalas*. We are divorced."

He sat for a moment weighing his thoughts.

"And do you imagine anything on earth could motivate me to marry the man who destroyed a good woman's reputation—my best friend!—breaking his own best friend's heart—all in the pursuit of saving his own ego?!" I asked.

Ameer didn't even respond to that comment, skipping over it as if he hadn't heard me. "First of all, Dayo is *my son*. It's not 'our kids and Dayo,'" he said. "I have raised him since he could barely walk, and I changed his stinky diapers. I am the only father he has ever known."

"Touché," I replied calmly, looking up at the fan, pondering what would happen if it fell between us now, as it shook violently in its orbit around the thin pole that kept it attached to the ceiling.

"Please reconsider. I know things have been hard here. I know. But please. Canada will be different. We can have a life there together again. We can. It will be just you and I," he pleaded.

"And what of Um Khalid, hmm? Just gonna abandon Shahida and your children here again? I guess since she gave you yet another daughter, you have no use for her?" I asked.

"I think you have learned these four years that she doesn't need me, and I do not need her, least of all for a son. She gave me Khalid, you gave me Ismayil," he said, pulling his shirt away from his sticky skin.

"And as far as the kids..." he let the silence hang in the air. "I do worry about Khalid growing up without me, but I know they will be fine. They need my money more than anything."

I didn't respond there. It was my incessant harassment that brought us there in the first place, all based on my thoroughly American ideas of what a father is supposed to be, and I had been proven wrong—very, very wrong.

"And anyway, you have successfully turned at least half my kids against me, so..." he casually dropped off.

Yes. Of course. Bad, bad, evil Um Abdullah, turning the sheikh's own offspring against him.

"Hmmm, yeah. Yes, that was all me. It's not like they saw you slap their mother across the face, and threaten her, and make her cry, and ignore her, and break your promises to her for the past four years. Yeah, it's me. It's all my fault they hate you," I spouted off.

I had been faced with the decision again and again in those years to either deceive people into believing my husband deserved the respect and honor people gave him—while allowing them to believe I had intentionally chosen to break up a family—or else tell the truth about what he had done to me in tricking me into that marriage and neglecting me so thoroughly. It was always Ameer's honor or mine. Never both. I did try to protect our kids from the truth about him, but kids are sharp and they pay close attention.

He was enraged now, in his silent burning kind of way. There was no shouting or beating. No, his *modus operandi* had always been to gaslight me to the point that I wasn't entirely sure I even existed as a separate entity from him, and he didn't stray from this well-worn path.

As the argument got more heated, before I knew it I was crying and screaming and slamming things around, making myself into the monster he always accused me of being: the crazy American who made Sheikh Ameer's life hell.

He put his *jilbab* back on and told me he would have Khalid bring the kids home later after *Maghrib*, and he left. I couldn't have known it then, but that was the last time he ever walked out of my apartment.

I threw myself onto my bed and wailed like I had so many times in the years previous. I felt trapped in a horrible, torturous place in my head, unsure how to escape the crushing pain and betrayal I felt.

"You. Must. Do. Something. About. This. Pain!" my heart was screaming at me. *"This pain is too much, it's too heavy, and the only way to be rid of it is to be violent and passionate, weeping and*

breaking everything you can."

But just then, another thought came to me, clear as a bell, in my own voice, but almost too quiet to hear inside: *"You don't actually have to do anything, Kaighla. You could just sit with this pain and let it wash over you. It will subside. Nothing lasts forever, not even pain."*

Immediately, I stopped weeping, and it was as if the clouds hanging over me suddenly moved away down the horizon before dissipating completely. I could choose what to do with that pain; I could choose to not let it overwhelm me; I could choose to not allow it to control me and force me to do things I would regret; I could sit still and allow it to hurt as much as it wanted to, and then watch it dissolve.

And so I did. I closed my eyes and I began focusing on my breath, just like I had been every day for the previous two weeks of my fledgling meditation practice. The pain came in waves, and heartbreaking memories came flooding over the plains of my mind, but just as quickly, they ebbed again, and I could feel the sun warming me.

I knew that was the way forward. Meditation placed a tiny moment in space/time between the horrible, daily triggers I experienced in that confusing, unnerving place, and my own reactions, reminding me that I was the boss of me, and I could choose how to react. From that point forward, I was hooked.

* * *

Rania invited me to the mosque where she was memorizing Qur'an with her teacher and several other women. She'd explained the directions pretty well, and I felt much more confident in my Arabic than I was before.

282

The younger kids were visiting Mama Bushra's house, so Dayo and I left the house just before *Maghrib* prayer so that we'd arrive before it started to get dark. There weren't as many *tuk-tuk*s around our new neighborhood, so it was hard to be picky. One was already full, with a woman and several bags of groceries nearly spilling out of every corner of the buggy. Another was apparently headed home for the day, because he shook his head when he passed us, and then kept driving.

Finally, one with two teenage boys pulled over. Immediately, I felt nervous because Ameer taught me never to trust drivers that age, but then there were two of them and usually that meant you were safer, he said. So, Dayo and I hopped in and told them the mosque we needed to get to, across town. They laughed at my accent and my shitty grammar but seemed to understand where we wanted to go.

It should have taken just a few minutes to get there, but ten minutes later, we realized we were on the wrong side of town, neither close to home nor close to the *masjid* we needed to visit. I kept asking them where we were going and emphasizing where we needed to be, but they kept laughing and asking me to repeat myself. Dayo was fluent in Arabic and spoke without an accent, but they disregarded his pleas because he was so young. As my blood pressure mounted, Dayo started to whimper next to me.

Finally, I decided it was time for us to get out of that *tuk-tuk*. I asked them to stop, but they kept laughing and drove even faster.

Somehow, by the grace of God, the wheels got stuck in a sandy pit, and Dayo and I were able to climb out. I demanded my money back, but the boys just kept trying to rock their vehicle out of the sand, ignoring me.

283

As Dayo and I started walking in what I believed was the right direction, I saw a man around Ameer's age getting into his car. I had no idea where we were or if I should trust him, but I had to take a leap of faith.

"Excuse me, sir!" I called in Arabic, "Could you please help us? Those boys won't return our money and they won't take us where we need to go."

He seemed truly concerned for us and began heading in their direction, insisting that Dayo and I wait next to his car, which was parked just outside his large, gated home. We could hear him shouting from a block away, and he was using fighting words, so I began to worry. Dayo was terrified at this point, clutching my *abaya* with all his might and crying quietly.

When the man came back toward the car, he apologized profusely and offered me the money he'd managed to get back. "Where can I take you, sister?" he asked. "Please, don't worry. I know your husband, the sheikh, and you can trust me."

Considering I didn't have any credit on my phone and had left all but those few guineas for the *tuk-tuk* ride at home, I felt like it was the safest bet, so Dayo and I climbed into his car.

Thankfully, we pulled up to the mosque just in time for the *Maghrib* prayer to start. I thanked our savior-friend for his help and went inside with Dayo, but the fear of being kidnapped was a daily occurrence from that point forward. The Bedouin on the outskirts of town had already kidnapped the son of a wealthy politician living in town, hoping to generate a hefty ransom, so we knew it was a real possibility.

* * *

That Ramadan, the kids and I developed a post-*Maghrib* ritual.

Even though I wasn't fasting—because I was still nursing Izzy—we all waited until *Maghrib* to eat dinner, so that the kids could get into the habit of at least delaying their dinner a bit. After we ate dinner, we'd turn on the Ramadan lights—Christmas lights my sister brought to us in the spring—and start reading stories about Prophet Muhammad and his companions. Then I'd put them to bed, despite the festivities outside. It was my great fortune that they were too young for "but everyone else is outside playing, Mama, why can't I?!" arguments.

Once I was sure they were asleep, I'd sit down in my favorite chair and make almost constant *du'a* to God, pleading with Him—Allah, who calls Himself *Al-Fattah*, "The Opener." God was my locksmith. I knew there was no way I would ever escape that situation without God opening doors for me. I imagined Him ahead of me, chopping down a path through the dense woods that surrounded me with a scythe, making a way forward for me to my destiny—which was, beyond a shadow of a doubt, not in that tiny Egyptian town.

I cried. I pleaded. I implored. I did not stop calling out to God, night and day. I didn't know what I wanted, aside from getting out of Sharqia. All I cared about was getting away from those people and my dark past in that town.

20

The Open Door

Alexandria, Egypt

Summer 2015

"But that's literally half of the money I have..." I said, opening my wallet wider.

Abu Reem was standing in the kitchen counting the cash I handed him to give to the crane operator. A vein bulged in his neck. "Sister! This is the cost! *Authu billah!*" he shouted.

Everyone in the room seemed to cringe and physically distance themselves from him. This was the same man who had broken Sara's heart—the sister that I met in Detroit in 2011 before we came to Egypt, the same convert who told me all about how much she hated her life in Egypt, largely because of her husband's philandering.

"*Mashy,*" she said, calmly. "Okay, I will take Um Abdullah next door to get things situated." She grabbed me by the hand and nearly dragged me to my new apartment next door.

They'd moved back to Egypt in 2013, just before I went to live with AJ after Dayo's accident. Now, they were moving out of Egypt, but not going back to Michigan. His Egyptian wife and their kids still lived in her hometown a few hours from Alexandria, and they would stay there while he, Sara, and their children went elsewhere. I found it odd that they didn't disclose where they were going, beyond a vague reference to eastern Europe, but didn't want to add more pressure on her.

"All you need to do is pay the rent via PayPal once a month and things will be fine," she assured me. I had been to that very apartment several times in the previous four years, and every time it was a strange, semi-sweet experience. She was very hospitable, but her children treated her and one another with such a level of cruelty that I no longer questioned her initial assertion that religion had made Abu Reem an even angrier man than he was before. *Someone* taught those seven children to treat one another like garbage, after all, and Sara seemed completely incapable of such evil.

The apartment itself was clean and spacious once, but they had now cut it down the middle to rent out to two different tenants in their absence. It was on the eleventh floor of a high-rise, in a lower-class area in Alexandria, but just a short *tuk-tuk* ride from the *corniche* and shopping area, so it was a good catch.

Only a few days after Ramadan ended, I had received her call. They were leaving Egypt and renting out their loft, and would I like to rent an apartment? she asked. "I know you're not in love with living on this high floor, but it's better than your little town, right?" she laughed.

Right. It certainly was.

I began immediately preparing things, trying to keep my plans a secret. Eventually, I told Rania and Shadia and made them swear not to tell their husbands. I didn't want word to get to Mama Bushra before I could tell her myself.

The day I did sit down to tell her we were moving to Alexandria, she was in shock.

"But how can you go?" she asked in Arabic, the tears already beginning to flow. "What about Izzy? What about the kids? We love them, *ya* Um Abdullah!" she cried.

I sat quietly and smiled, taking her hand in mine. "*Ya Nayna*, we love you too. I know you're worried about the kids. But we will be in a very safe area. I make enough money, and Ameer still sends some, too. Don't worry. We'll be fine." I assured her.

"But don't you worry about life there? What if something happens? Izzy has been so sick all the time!" she said, this time almost pleading with me.

Before she left, she held me for a long time and kissed my forehead. It was odd how much things had improved between us after the divorce. It almost felt like divorcing her son brought a bit of distance between us that conversely enabled us to draw nearer to one another; no longer forced to interact, it was sincere when we did choose to spend time together because we *chose* to.

* * *

Just before they finally departed, Sara invited all her foreign friends to her home for a going away party. "This way you'll meet some of them, too," she said as we were getting tea and biscuits ready for everyone, placing dates and baklava on trays in the middle of the room.

There were women from all over the world in that room,

and as some left, more came. Sara had been an important member of that women-only world for many years by then. Several of them she'd met back when she lived in Mansoura, and they'd maintained their friendships across the distance when she and her children lived in Michigan. Several of the women she'd known in Mansoura had moved to Alexandria during her absence, and she had developed new friendships in Alex, too. Her husband had business dealings with their husbands, too, leaving the women alone with each other for hours.

All of them were polite, some hardly spoke English, and many came with their entire brood of children, filling the apartment with twice as many kids as women. At one point, several of the kids escaped her half of the apartment into my new half, which was still dusty and full of sharp objects from the construction of the kitchen in what used to be a bedroom.

"Kaighla!" I heard Sara calling as she came toward me with a friend trailing behind her. "This is Khadijah. We only just met a few weeks ago, but she's a convert who's new to the area, too, so I thought you guys could maybe hang out?"

Just then, one kid came running back into her half of the flat, hands covered in dust. Sara took him to the sink to wash off. "Do you think we should maybe look for his mother..." her words trailed off as she looked around the melee of women.

"Oh, they should not be there! It's very dangerous!" another sister chimed in, hastily slipping her shoes on to grab her offspring from said danger.

"Nah, I'm sure they're fine," Khadijah said casually, taking a bite of baklava.

"I like the way you think," I laughed.

By the time everyone cleared out, I had made a few new friends, and Khadijah was foremost among them.

* * *

British, black, and much taller than most of the men around, she was also nearly five months pregnant with her third child. She was previously divorced, and her new husband was a French African who insisted she cover her face. She often came to my apartment absolutely drenched in sweat from walking to drop her kids off at school.

"I literally cannot breathe," she'd lament when she got inside and began stripping off her outer layers. "I'm pregnant, clearly," she laughed, rubbing her mini-bump, "and I feel like it's insanity to force me to cover like this!"

Her husband had sworn to divorce her, pregnant or not, if she dared remove the *niqab*.

Much as we like to tell the non-Muslim public that we wear all those layers to please God, and not because we're being forced by our husbands, I've met many women in Khadijah's shoes over the years. It happened so often, in fact, that those platitudes began to feel like a farce.

"I wouldn't wear hijab if my husband didn't force me," one sister had said during my time in Cairo. "But I see it as pleasing God by pleasing my husband, so I'm grateful he insists on it."

Ameer had used that same rhetoric to break me down over the years. "Please your husband and you're pleasing God; anger your husband and you've angered God," he'd said. I later learned that this mindset had its roots not in Islam, but in toxic Judeo-Christian patriarchy, inherited from the colonialism that had destroyed so many African and Middle Eastern countries. It had leaked into the collective male psyche, planting in the fertile soil of oppressed hearts that when God said he had placed men as "*qawwam*" over women (historically interpreted as "guardians"

290

or "protectors"), He meant that men were to control women—to basically own them.

It's a tale as old as time: men who are oppressed often find relief in oppressing the women in their care.

"I mean I hate *niqab*, but I'm not trying to divorce again," Khadijah said. "But then I guess you're handling things okay, innit? Divorce wouldn't be too bad, right?" she asked, gesturing at my kids running through the apartment like hellions.

In truth, I was not handling things okay—not at all. I was a complete disaster, in fact.

I spent my days trying to take care of the kids while also working for the same American company Rachel had got me a job with back in our small town in Sharqia, making $3.53 an hour. That was more than enough money in rural Egypt, but the cost of living was higher in Alexandria, so I still relied on Ameer's monthly child support payment—as well as my scant alimony, since I was still breastfeeding our son. I struggled to manage my time and energy—trying to raise four kids alone, keep the house clean, keep them fed, and work full-time. Plus, I was still living in fight-or-flight mode, thanks to the trauma I had endured at Ameer's hands, so I never felt calm or relaxed.

* * *

Seemingly out of nowhere, I received an interesting Facebook message from an American sister in mid-August.

Asalaamu alaykum, *sister,*

I know you don't know me, but my name is Sasha and I have some questions about a man I think you knew once—Sheikh

Ameer. He recently contacted me on a Muslim marriage site. He lives across the border from me in Toronto (I'm in Ohio) and before I move forward, I wanted to get your perspective. Is he a good guy? Why did you divorce him?

I couldn't believe my eyes. *Ameer was living in Toronto? And already looking for a new wife?!* I shouldn't have been surprised, knowing him, but I felt sure he learned his lesson. He had still not given up asking me to come to Canada, and all the while he was courting at least her, and most certainly other women.

As proof that her story was true, she sent me a few pictures of them together—nothing inappropriate, of course, but enough to prove that if she wasn't his wife, he was okay now with kissing and fondling *haraam* women, something I felt was still beyond him.

The photos were so achingly familiar. The sheikh with his new wife, sitting in a car, taking pictures of their wedding rings; kissing at a restaurant; holding hands walking in a park—all pictures we used to take before things went sour.

I wasted no time in telling her to run, as fast as she could, in the other direction.

"No, he isn't a good guy, and no, you can't trust a single word he says. He did so much wrong to me and plenty of other women, and he will do the same to you," I told her.

"I wish I wasn't already married to him…" she said.

So, she hadn't been totally upfront about the situation. Still, she had a right to the truth.

"Many things about him rub me the wrong way, and I feel concerned, for sure," she said.

"Yes, you're right to be concerned," I told her. "Trust those red flags. You should run."

* * *

The kids were in Sharqia visiting their *Teita* and siblings for a few days when Rania called me in a panic one afternoon. "*Habibti*, Kaighla!" she said. "You know Ismayil is in hospital here?!"

"What?!" I asked, feeling frantic. "What are you talking about? What's going on? No one has called to tell me he was sick."

"Yes! Just now, I take Omar to have shot and I hear *Hajja* Um Ameer yelling at the doctors. I looked in and saw Izzy with her. He very sick. Coughing, looking so sad," she continued.

I thanked her for calling and immediately arranged for Khalid to meet Dayo and me at the halfway point, then started preparing to take a taxi to the bus stop. On the way there, I called Ameer and berated him. I knew exactly why they hadn't told me about Izzy being sick: because Ameer forbade them. He didn't even apologize, saying it was better for Izzy and everyone if I didn't come and "make a scene."

When we finally arrived at the hospital in Sharqia, I flew to Izzy's side and kissed him, ignoring Mama Bushra as she tried to pry him away from me.

"Why didn't you tell me he was sick, *ya Nayna*?!" I demanded. "He's my son! My baby! I should have known!"

"*Wallahi, ya* Um Abdullah, I'm sorry. I am. Ameer told me not to tell you. He thought you would worry too much," she explained.

After things had calmed down and Izzy was sleeping, Mama Bushra cornered me and demanded to know why I refused to marry her son again.

"Please *Nayna*, it's been a long day, okay?" I said, trying to finish the conversation before it got started.

"Um Abdullah, *khalas*! We know he was bad to you here. But he's there now, in Canada, so close to your home! He needs you!" she said.

"I can't. I just can't, okay?" I said, trying to persuade her to leave it alone. But she wasn't having it.

"But why?! How can you do this to the kids, and to him? He is there without a wife! *Haraam alayki!*" she cried.

I brushed Izzy's hair with my fingers absently and tried to ignore her, but she wasn't giving up. Finally, I had enough.

"I cannot and never will marry him again, *Nayna*. And actually, he already has a wife there, so you don't need to worry about the sheikh," I said, in clear, simple Arabic.

She sat nonplussed, clearly not believing me. "Never. He would never. He has no money to send us! How could he have a wife?" she said, confidently. "You just don't care about what's good for the children or him!"

"Okay. You don't believe me, *Nayna*? Here," I said, taking my phone out of my purse, shakily. "Look. You see that picture? Who is that woman? Why is your son, Sheikh Ameer, kissing that woman if she isn't his wife? Huh?" I yelled back, thrusting the phone into her hands.

A nurse popped her head in the room to check on us, having heard me yelling at the old woman, but just as quickly ducked out when Mama Bushra shot her a glance.

She looked long and hard, shuffling through the three or four pictures Sasha had sent to me as proof.

"Yes. Yes, Ameer has another new wife, *again*, and he is intentionally hiding it from you and Um Khalid, *again*," I said.

"*Mashy*, Um Abdullah. Thank you, *habibti*," she said calmly, squeezing my hand in hers and turning to leave the room, the kids trailing behind her.

A few weeks later, Sasha divorced him.

In the future, he'd forbid his family from speaking to me, telling them that I didn't want to talk to them, and ordering me not to try to contact them. He wouldn't even let our kids talk to their *Teita* or siblings on the phone because he was afraid they'd spill the beans that he continued marrying women even after Sasha, and continued hiding them from Shahida and Mama Bushra.

21

The Second Iteration

Alexandria, Egypt

Autumn 2015

My three-month *iddah* period finished in early September—making Ameer and I really, really divorced. Just a few weeks later, Um Ubayd, one of the ladies in my building, came to talk with me. A German national, she was married to an Egyptian, and she and her husband were close friends with Sara and her husband. Um Ubayd and I had met, albeit briefly, at the going-away party.

Um Ubayd's husband had been approached that morning by a Qur'an teacher in the mosque at the Friday prayers.

"He asked my husband if he knew whether 'the white woman with all the kids' who lives in our building is ready to re-marry yet," she explained, laughing along with me.

"Ummm, what?" I asked, again shocked, just as I was after my conversion, that there could be men in this world who would seriously consider a woman for marriage that they had never spoken to, based solely on her appearance or nationality.

Though I was technically "available," I was not exactly gung-ho to get married right away, and I certainly wasn't interested in marrying another Egyptian. I saw first-hand, to my great disappointment, how deceit—in matters both big and small—seemed to be the bedrock of the society.

"No. No, I am not interested," I said calmly.

Um Ubayd nodded in acceptance, but just a few days later, she invited me to her home for tea. As I walked in, I saw there were three Egyptian women sitting on the couch opposite us. Two looked to be about my age or younger and the third was easily older than my own mother.

"*Asalaamu alaykum, ya* Um Abdullah," the older one said, as if we were great friends.

"This is Um Muhammad, and her daughters," Um Ubayd said in her heavy German accent. The entire conversation happened in a smattering of English and Arabic, but it didn't take long for me to discern what was happening.

"She says her son, Sheikh Muhammad, would be honored if you would come to their home for tea," Um Ubayd translated for me.

Sheikh Muhammad, the aforementioned son, was the same man who asked my friend's husband about me. Not taking one "no" for an answer, he sent his mother and sisters as emissaries to request my presence.

"But there is something you should know," his mother said. "My son will not abide his wife going out without *niqab*."

"Ah, then no, again," I said, plainly. "I am not interested. I wore the *niqab* when I first came to Egypt, and I am not interested in

297

wearing it again."

They politely accepted my response, finished their tea, and went on their way, and I never heard from them again. But it seemed *niqab* would not leave me be.

Several weeks later, an English-speaking French sister I barely knew approached me and said, after some pleasantries, that I was wrong not to cover my face.

"But God doesn't expect this of me, so why would I do it?" I asked.

"Sister, as a foreign woman, we already stand out, and by not covering in the way that the women around us are, we make ourselves stand out even more, creating *fitnah* in the street," this stranger said to me, presuming she had a right to give me her opinion about my choice of dress.

There was that word, *fitnah*, again—that word used to suppress Muslim women from Melbourne to Mecca since the beginning.

"Don't smile too much or you're creating *fitnah* in the hearts of the brothers," they told us.

"Don't walk in too suggestive a way, being careful not to let your hips sway too much. You don't want to make *fitnah* for the brothers," they said.

Where, I wondered, *are the men and women concerned with the fitnah men were making in female lives—sexual and otherwise?*

* * *

I had never been single. Ever since I was old enough to feel attracted to boys rather than annoyed by them, I had been in a revolving series of relationships, of varying levels of seriousness. When I was just twelve or thirteen, I filled journals with page-after-page of gag-inducing tales of my obsession with boys, each declaring he was "the one for me," only to be followed by yet another boy just a few days later. Sometimes, the stories even overlapped.

Of course, the sensical, self-compassionate thing to do that fall would have been to focus on trying to heal from all I had suffered, to give my heart time to heal. But being a single mother of four children under the age of seven, trying to work full-time and care for my kids alone—without any family support, and surrounded by women who were all just as busy with their own brood—and living in a foreign country that was male-centric, to boot... well, it made the prospect of staying single on principle increasingly far-fetched.

On top of all this, I was surrounded by a culture that sent me two very different and conflicting messages, and all argued their side was the right way.

When Ameer's father died, Mama Bushra was young and beautiful, but she refused to marry, and many people I spoke with seemed to think a widow or divorcee intentionally choosing to remain single was an honorable thing—no doubt, at least in part, because of the aversion most Egyptian men seemed to have toward raising another man's children, or letting another man raise his.

But then there was the other side of the argument, the same side that I'd been duped into accepting when I married Ameer all those years ago: "a Muslim woman needs a husband, period," they said. To intentionally withhold marriage from oneself was sinful.

"We're not like Christians, sister," one older Muslim woman told me once. "We know that celibacy is unnatural. You're just begging for trouble if you choose to remain single unless you have a really good reason."

Not more than two weeks after the Sheikh Muhammad incident, another brother came forward, but in a much sneakier way.

"He wants you as a secret second wife?!" Khadijah asked, shocked.

"Yeah…" I replied. "And he says I should be grateful that he is proposing to me at all me since 'no one else will be willing to raise your ex-husband's kids,' he said."

"Ah haaaaa, is it so, then? Well, *masha'Allah*, we should all be so grateful these men are so selfless in their pursuit of a wife, yes?" she laughed with me.

I had not even actively been seeking a husband and these men were coming out of the woodwork. And why then? How did they even know I was available? Sure, word spread that the new girl in the building was divorced, but not a single offer came my way until just after my *iddah* period was officially over. The power of gossip in Egypt was truly mind-blowing.

I'd been on a lifelong, desperate search to find a man who would love me enough to fill the massive hole left in my heart from both of the men who had been my fathers. I had been without any male affection for several months by this point, and I'd been handling everything for my kids alone. I was lonely, and life as a single mom in Egypt was proving to be even harder than I'd imagined it would be.

As Khadijah and I were walking down the road one day after we had dropped our kids off at their daycare centers, I spotted a brother I'd seen around the area several times. I found him extremely attractive, but he never seemed to notice me, good Muslim man that he was. On this afternoon, though, he glanced up for a second and saw me staring at me, shamelessly, and smirked a bit before looking back at the ground and walking past me. Without meaning to, I turned all the way around and watched him walking away.

"Girl!" Khadijah whisper-yelled at me. "We have *got* to get you married soon! You're gawking at blokes on the street for God's sake!" she laughed.

A few short weeks after my divorce, long before we moved to Alexandria, a woman I'd known for years, a close friend and fellow convert from New Zealand, broke our friendship off abruptly.

She and her Egyptian husband—as well as her young daughter from a previous relationship, and their son—were living in a ghetto in Johannesburg, South Africa. We'd met online somehow, and become fast friends. It broke my heart to hear how often her husband would beat her. He actually beat her nearly to death on several occasions for such offenses as not dusting effectively.

After my divorce, she decided she didn't respect me anymore, and all because I confessed that at twenty-seven years old, I had no intention of remaining alone forever. She hung up on me and then sent me a simple message on Facebook.

"You're going to give up your children for the chance to fuck someone, and I don't respect you for it," she'd said, and then blocked me.

That exchange ended a friendship that had lasted for years.

Contrary to what she said, I was not willing to give up my children—not at all—but I did want a husband. I wanted my children to be loved and protected, and I was not in any shape to be both their mother and their father.

I wasn't interested in trying to navigate the sticky waters of husband-finding in Alexandria—considering the sample I'd been shown—so against my better judgment, I joined another Muslim matrimonial site.

* * *

Many of the men I met online were just there for some easy "*halal*" sex, and many others were there for immigration papers. But when I made it clear I was a practicing Muslim woman with four children who I would not be willing to sacrifice for anyone, the vast majority fell by the wayside. Somehow, though, as hard as I tried to avoid Egyptians—by looking online instead of allowing the people in my neighborhood to suggest someone—I managed to meet a few Egyptian men who caught my attention. None were so captivating as Mahmoud, though.

A professor of English Studies at a university in Saudi Arabia, Mahmood was my intellectual and spiritual equal in every way. He and I would talk literature and philosophy for hours—his deep, rich voice resonating through the phone and into my belly. He was from Alexandria, too, so the possibility of meeting face-to-face on his upcoming trip home was a common discussion. He loved yoga, meditation, and philosophy, something I couldn't have imagined I'd find in a strict, conservative Muslim like him.

There was just one problem with Mahmood: though he was a father of four himself, he made it known to me, in no uncertain terms, that he wasn't the fathering type.

"I cannot live with children," he'd say. "I need peace and quiet at all hours if I am to be able to focus on my work." He actually suggested we live in adjacent apartments and simply visit one another when the fancy struck us.

"Yeah, I'm sorry, but that's not the sort of marriage I want to model for my kids," I replied. "They've already lived in a situation where their father isn't living with them full-time, and I don't want that for them. I think we'd better say '*Salaam*,' and wish one another the best."

Two weeks after I cut off communication with Mahmoud, he sent me a voice message. "I have been looking, Kaighla. I have. But I can't find someone I can relate to like we relate," he explained. "And I've been rethinking my feelings about the kids. Your kids seem well-behaved. Maybe I could handle it?"

I didn't respond to those messages, but I couldn't stop thinking about Mahmood.

Then one night, late, I got a simple text from him: "You awake, princess? I was thinking we should get married tomorrow."

I sat staring at my phone, in shock., for a solid three minutes.

I felt flattered by his continued attempts. I was stupid and wrong, so I agreed—against my better logic but true to my pattern—to meet him the next day at a café on the *corniche*, a short taxi ride from my apartment.

While we sat there next to the Mediterranean Sea, Mahmood held Izzy and cuddled him, seeming very natural. The gears were turning inside me, and I felt myself wanting him more and more.

"Listen, we don't have to get married in a *masjid*," he said. "I know that's what you've heard, but it's not the way of the *Salaf*—the first Muslims, the *true* Muslims. We only need two male witnesses, and you don't even need a *wali*, considering that you're divorced."

I sat and thought. That attractive, interesting, educated man was fervently begging me to marry him, and my defenses began to wear down, as they always did when a man didn't take "no" for an answer.

I agreed to marry him right there, right then.

He called a few friends to meet us at his apartment. They brought the official marriage papers and explained that if we wanted the marriage to be legally binding—something absolutely required in Egypt—we would have to, at some point, go through the arduous process Ameer and I had gone through three years earlier. For then, though, the signed papers sufficed to make us married Islamically, at least.

Having sealed the deal, as it were, we went to the jewelry district to choose my wedding set. We wandered for an hour or so, found one I liked, and waited for them to size it right there, on the spot. It was a beautiful set of 24k gold, the wedding band simple and the solitaire a pure crystal with intricate details around the band. It was far above and beyond the cheap, fake ring Ameer bought for me before giving me my $100 *mahr* all those years before.

Of course, the kids were shocked when they came home and from school and day-care to find a strange, new man sitting in their living room. I was advised again and again that it was wrong to introduce my kids to a man before marrying him.

"They're too young to understand. You'll just confuse them," they said. "Why introduce men into their lives before you decide on one? You are their Mama. Let them trust your judgment."

On the way home from the jewelry district, I called Ameer to tell him the news, knowing the kids would if I didn't first.

"*Masha'Allah*," he replied. "Congratulations to you both. And I am married again, too. So, we have both found what we wanted," he added, like he was trying to one-up me.

And so into my building we walked, hand-in-hand, without my having told a single person we were planning to be married. Unashamed, I walked around the streets with him and my brood in tow.

Just a few days later, Mahmoud had to go back to Saudi Arabia.

"It takes a year for the marriage paperwork to go through in Saudi, lamb. By then, I will have finished my fellowship. Just wait for me. I will come back to visit in six months," he whispered to me, but seeing how it didn't move me, he tried the more pragmatic approach. "If I break my teaching contract, I won't get the pension promised me. It's well over $10,000, Kaighla. okay, *habibti?* It will be fine."

And so, he left. I was alone, again. Once more, I was without a man to watch out for us in a country designed, run, and controlled by and for men.

* * *

There is a segment of the Muslim community who is extremely strict about their perceptions of the right way to find a spouse, and they largely expect people in the 21st century to live as if it were still the seventh century. Just like the Qur'an teacher told me when I first converted, Muslims in that narrow sect are expected to rely on their friends and family to connect them with someone from their community, or through a chain of communication.

In that setting, it's pretty easy to find out a person's character by asking around. In such cases, it doesn't really require very much time to establish if someone is right for you. But for myself and so many female converts, that system is dangerous. For one thing, we are typically not connected to the Muslim community well enough to be properly matched with a possible suitor in the first place. It doesn't help that we are so often pressured from day one to find a husband in order to "solidify our Islam." Then, when we actually find a spouse we like, we're rushed into sealing the marriage contract as soon as possible to "protect us from *haraam*."

Because of this rush to tie the knot, many first-time marriages for female converts end fairly quickly. Marriage, at least for young Muslims in the West in the 21st century, can rightly be called "Dating, But More Official."

But even before I was Muslim, I rushed into relationships far too quickly, afraid that if I didn't offer them something—sexual or otherwise—as soon as possible, they'd lose interest. I thought I needed to "strike while the iron is hot," if you will.

Two weeks after he went back to Saudi Arabia, Mahmoud and I were talking on the phone and I mentioned some research I had come across that said asking someone a specific set of one hundred questions could prove if you were compatible for marriage. Two researchers studying the inception of love had developed the questions and actually fell in love with one another in the process! I thought it would be a good way to get to know each other better—since I had, now for the third time in my young life, married a man I hardly knew.

The first few questions Mahmoud and I answered together from the list were simple and fun, but they quickly began to get deeper. By about the twentieth question, we were clearly disagreeing on things. Then we came to a question about our feelings on infidelity, and he floored me.

"Oh, I absolutely intend to marry other women," he said, dripping with confidence.

"I could never be okay with you marrying other women, baby!" I laughed, thinking he definitely could not be serious, considering how much we had discussed my previous experience with polygyny.

"*Habibti*, no offense, but I don't actually care if you're okay

306

with it. It's my right by God and I intend to marry again," he replied coolly.

I couldn't believe what I was hearing, and I felt sick.

"What? I told you all about what happened between me and Ameer. How could you... you know I don't want that, okay? Mahmoud, please stop messing with me!"

"Kaighla, let me be perfectly clear with you," he said then. "Let's say that I'm walking down the street and I see a woman I'd like to marry. I will marry her. Or, maybe I could decide I want to marry one of my students—no matter what, nothing will stop me from marrying her, not even her resistance, and certainly not your feelings."

My mouth was dry as I tried hard to swallow.

"I will have the four best wives on earth, make no mistake," he continued, driving the knife deeper. "I will keep marrying and divorcing women until I have the best. But don't worry! You, my sweetheart, are the very best of the very best. You will always be my favorite, though I will endeavor not to let the others know, of course..." he trailed off.

He was entirely serious. This man who had worked so hard to coerce me into marrying him was absolutely dead-set on doing the same thing to as many women as it took to build his perfect harem.

Everything about the situation felt eerily familiar, like I was in the Twilight Zone, being given a second opportunity to avoid what had happened with Ameer. I felt a sense of focused clarity come over me.

Mahmoud was Ameer, version 2.0, and I knew it.

"If you are serious, I demand a divorce right now," I responded.

"Baby, stawwpppp, okay? Just stop. We just married each other. I am not looking for another wife now, and I promise I won't until I come back to Egypt, okay?" he tried to reassure me. "*I promise not to do the thing I want to do without consulting you first,*" he was saying, just like Ameer had promised not to "re-marry" Shahida without my permission.

"Mahmoud, I demand a divorce right now. I have already been down this road, and I am not about to be married to another man like Ameer," I said calmly.

He hung up the phone and ignored my calls for a week. Finally, when I had made it clear via email that I was absolutely serious, he declared me divorced.

"I don't want your *mahr* back. Keep it. And I will not provide you a single dollar during your *iddah* time, either, so… *ma'a salaama*, I guess," he said as he closed Skype. I did not hear from him again after that.

I'd been had, *again.*

"I am very sorry to hear that, Um Abdullah," Ameer said when I told him about the divorce. Sensing his opening, he went in for the kill. "You can either come here and stay with me while you wait for your *iddah* to finish, and then marry me again, or you can stay there and find a way to provide for the kids yourself. I will not send you another dime for them," he said. "Your choice."

* * *

A few days later, I sat in my office, crying over tea with Khadijah, laying it all out for her.

"That's a straight bloody terrible choice to have to make, babe," she said, trying to comfort me. "I'm really sorry to hear it, too."

I knew I couldn't stay in that situation much longer. I had grossly underestimated the cost of living in Alexandria. My bosses refused to give me a raise or increase my pay, and I had no connections to find another job in Egypt. And, truth be told, I was exhausted. My heart was raw from yet another heartbreak, and I struggled to get up in the morning, having fallen into a deep depression.

Of course, there was always the chance to go home that AJ had offered me, but I couldn't relate to my own culture at all anymore, and I dreaded the prospect of trying to build a life for us there. When she bought us the tickets to fly home, I convinced her to get me a return ticket. I didn't know what I'd do, but one thing was for sure: providing for myself and building a new life for me and the kids would be much less expensive in Alexandria than in America. I figured I would send them to Ameer in Canada to live for a year while I sorted myself out in Egypt. But the idea of being away from them—let alone with an ocean between us—hurt too much.

"I can't leave them," I cried. "She said I would do that, my friend who blocked me. She said I'd leave them for the chance to fuck someone!"

"You're not *leaving them*, first of all. You're putting them in the care of their father, who has always looked out for them," she reassured me. "And there's no fuckery happening. So... she's dumb."

"They're my babies! I have never spent more than a few nights away from them. I need them!" I cried.

"And what do they need?" she asked. "Huh? I am their auntie and their honorary step-father—thanks to the year I helped you raise them—and I am telling you they need you to take some time and get your shit together so you can be their big momma bear again, okay?"

I thought about it for a week and finally decided she was right.

"Okay, listen," I said to Ameer. "I will be flying to Toronto the first week of November, and I need you to meet me at the airport to carry the luggage and kids, as my sister's car is only big enough for me and my luggage."

I had only brought the barest necessities, opting to leave behind everything but clothes and a few mementos I'd carried with me over the years, but it was still a lot of luggage when you considered we were one full-grown female adult and four small children.

"Okay, good. Good," he replied, sounding happier than I was comfortable with.

"Ameer, let me be very clear: I will not marry you again. Not now, not ever," I said before we cut the line. Since Sasha had left him, he was about to be a single parent, and he couldn't believe I was sincere in my refusal to marry him again. But I meant it.

22

The Cleaving Asunder

Ontario, Canada

Winter 2015

"But why are you trying to get into Canada?" the woman behind the desk asked me for the third time.

Izzy was crying profusely in the carrier I was wearing him in, and the entire front of my *abaya* was covered in wet, cold milk that I'd leaked. "I have answered that question already, several times. Please, I need to feed my baby. Are we done here?" I asked.

"We will be finished in a moment, ma'am," she replied.

The other kids were barely standing up at that point. Twenty hours on various planes and then two hours in line at Canadian customs was too much for their little bodies.

"As I've told you several times: I am bringing my children to their father in Mississauga, then I am going to the States with my sister who is waiting outside this airport right now, probably freaking out because she has no way to know where we are or how to contact me! Then, I am going back to Egypt! I have a return ticket!"

"Give me a moment," she said before disappearing behind a wall. When she came back five minutes later, she had a man with her who introduced himself as the supervisor. I visibly tensed up, prepared to be bombarded with yet more questions.

"Please relax, Ms. White. I understand your story, and I believe you. I have come to give just one final word of advice before we let you through," he began. "You have no right to stay in Canada. You must leave within 90 days or you will be counted an illegal immigrant. I understand you have said you intend to return to Egypt, but I need you to understand that lots of people say this and then just stay. It's illegal and unwise, so I hope you won't do that."

Having made it through customs, I made my way to a payphone, hoping to reach my sister, when someone came up behind me and picked up Rumi who had been crying and pulling on my *abaya*.

"Hi, sweetheart!" AJ said, brushing Rumi's wet hair out of her face and drying her tears. She then took me in her arms and hugged me so tightly, for so long. It was perhaps the third time in our entire lives that she showed me such powerful affection, and it was exactly the balm I needed.

"Have you heard from Ameer?" she asked, hugging Saji and Dayo, and kissing Izzy's forehead as he slept on my shoulder. I'd taken him out of the carrier and nursed him briefly in the bathroom before heading to the payphone. "I have been trying to message him on Facebook, but I have no signal," she added.

"Well there's free Wifi here inside the airport, so maybe try now?" I replied, shifting a sleeping Izzy from one shoulder to the next, the other one drenched in his sweat and drool.

* * *

An hour later, we were sitting in Ameer's basement apartment, the kids blissed out while he enveloped them in his arms and lap.

When we first came in, he showed us around his tiny place with such pride, obviously trying to show me how well-off he was.

"*Masha'Allah,*" I repeated again and again. "This seems like a safe neighborhood for the kids."

Later that evening, Ameer asked me and AJ to talk with him in the kids' bedroom while they watched a movie in the living room.

"I asked you both in here because I think we need to talk before you go back with AJ," he said to me. "I know I wasn't what you needed in Egypt, but we're here now, both of us, with our kids. You see how nice this place is, how nice the area is. Think about the kids. Think about what's good for them," he said.

I could feel where he was going, and my body tensed up.

Sensing that I wasn't going to fall into his arms so easily, he turned to AJ. "Please, AJ. You know I love the kids, and I love Kaighla. *Wallahi*, I never loved a woman like I love her. Things were so hard in Egypt for all of us. Please, AJ, I know you care about her and the kids. Please. Talk some sense into her."

For a split second, I imagined her actually listening to him and trying to persuade me to stay. My imaginings were interrupted, though, when she burst out laughing.

"Ameer, hear me clearly: you're a very bad husband!" she shouted. "You're a great father, but a horrible husband. In fact, I begged Kaighla to leave you," she said.

Ameer sat in rapt amazement, shocked beyond reason that someone would speak in such a direct way to him, he who had been coddled and ass-kissed his whole life.

"I would kill Kaighla before I watched her marry you again, mmmk?" she said, closing the subject forever.

I never loved her more, before or after, than I did at that moment, on that cold evening in southern Ontario. She had come to the rescue, again—my brave little sister—and I was eternally grateful, because, truth be told, I wasn't even entirely sure I had the strength to resist his pleas.

* * *

Just before I left Egypt, I had met a man on one of the marriage sites—before I closed my accounts forever—who was living in Toronto. He invited me to enjoy some traditional Afghani fare at his favorite restaurant. I had no plans to stay in Canada, so it seemed like harmless fun—the sort of relaxed dating I hadn't participated in since before I met Dayo's father when I was just twenty years old. Waheed seemed sane and normal enough, so we agreed to meet up when I arrived in Toronto.

I didn't have a working phone in Canada, so I told my sister where I was going that night. She was staying in the apartment with the kids while Ameer tended to things in the mosque, so I gave her the man's name and number and told her I would be back by ten.

Waheed was, by all accounts, a perfect gentleman over dinner. We sat at the restaurant he'd chosen, enjoying the delicious fare as he regaled me with stories of his childhood in Kabul. Though he was a recent immigrant to Canada, somehow his English was nearly perfect, and I enjoyed the easy, non-harried conversation; it was a nice distraction from my otherwise worry-filled life.

Having finished our meal, we slowly walked back to Waheed's SUV. I asked if I could text my sister from his phone to let her know we were on the way. He happily handed me his phone and I sent her the message, waited for her reply, and then handed it back to him.

We sat inside his car talking for a few minutes as he absent-mindedly fiddled with his keys. Things felt comfortable and not at all serious. Then, suddenly—when I was in the middle of a sentence—he leaped across the middle console and grabbed me hard, slamming his lips into mine, holding my neck with one hand and roughly fondling my breast with his other hand.

My lips were bleeding and I tried hard to pull myself away from him, but he was twice my size and his grip was like iron. He tore my hijab off and began sucking hard on my neck, ignoring my pleas to stop. I finally managed to free myself from his arms.

"Please, Waheed. Please. I am begging you. Please, just take me back to the house. I promise I won't report you or tell anyone what happened!" I promised, but he seemed nervous. "You know what the community will say if I reported you. They would blame me for even getting into your car alone, ok? Please, just take me home."

That seemed to assuage his fears, and he finally drove me back to Ameer's apartment.

* * *

Before going in, I stood in the bitter, cold wind and re-wrapped my tousled hijab, taking in deep breaths of icy air to try to calm myself. It wasn't the first time I'd been physically assaulted like that, and it wouldn't be the last time a man did such a thing—even a Muslim man—but it just never gets easier to cope with.

I walked inside and downstairs to see AJ sitting on the couch in the living room, sleepily half-watching some nature documentary. The kids were passed out on the various couches and loveseats, and Ameer was sitting at the kitchen table typing something on his laptop with his reading glasses perched on his nose. It looked like he was preparing his *khutba* for the upcoming Friday services.

Hoping to dodge both of them, I went to take a shower. I needed to get Waheed's scent off me and to cleanse myself of the guilt I felt for even getting into the car with him in the first place.

My sister came into the bedroom as I was drying my hair off, and she sat on the bed opposite me. Her eyes suddenly focused in on my neck. It was black and blue, and completely covered in scratch and bite marks.

"Uhh... so... are you... gonna tell me what happened? Are those... I mean, did you *enjoy* receiving all those marks, or are they the signs of a struggle?" she asked, cautiously. "No judgment either way, just... wondering..."

I began explaining the whole thing to her, and as I got going, I couldn't stop the tears. "Why did I put myself in that position?" I cried. "I should have known better! I don't know what's wrong with me!"

"He *sexually assaulted* you. That's not your fault, okay? It's not your fault he chose to break all boundaries of religion and decency and attack you," she said.

316

I didn't believe her. Years of the sheikh's teachings about the sort of women who allowed themselves to get assaulted were ringing in my head.

* * *

Eventually, we both fell asleep, but I awoke at dawn to pray. I assumed Ameer would be at the mosque, but there was a thick layer of snow outside and I found him praying in the living room. I hurried to get behind him, knowing that despite how much I hated him, praying in congregation was more pleasing to God than praying alone.

After we finished praying, he sat down on one of the couches and rubbed his face in his hands. He looked old and exhausted, and part of me felt for him.

I sat down next to him, knowing I was crossing a line, but old habits die hard. "Ameer," I said calmly. "I can't leave without telling you how I feel," I said.

A look of hope darted across his face.

"I want you to know you've broken me. I trusted you and you broke me. You took my joy," I said.

He looked away from me then, focusing his attention on the wintry wonderland outside.

"I hate what you have made me into. I hate what you have taught me. I hate the way you have driven a wedge between me and God," I said.

He turned then and looked me hard in the eyes for the first time since our divorce six months before. My eyes were bloodshot from crying and from lack of sleep, and my lips were still raw and cracked from the force.

"Okay, Kaighla. I understand. *Khalas*, we're over. I get it," he said. "But are you okay? You don't look well."

"No," I said. Without another word, I took off my hijab to show him the marks on my neck and upper chest.

He flinched at first, knowing full well that I should not be showing him my skin like that anymore, divorced as we were.

"A Muslim man did this to me last night, Ameer. I went on a date with him. I put myself in his car. I made myself vulnerable. I allowed a man to take what he wanted from me, and he almost got even more!" I cried.

He sat in shock, unsure of how to react. I could almost detect a hint of pity in his eyes, but no remorse.

"This is how I value myself now, Ameer! Don't you feel anything? This is all because of what you've done to me! Don't you see that?! I'm worthless now!" I shouted.

"Please, keep your voice down and cover yourself, *authu billah*. I am not responsible for the choices you make," he said calmly, brushing away my words with his hand in the air.

The next morning, I kissed the kids in their sleep and promised to come get them again just as soon as I could, and AJ and I headed home to Illinois. I never used my return ticket.

* * *

When we arrived home in Illinois, I felt impossibly fragile, totally shattered, and deeply unsafe. My priorities were simple: survive and get my children back.

For weeks, I slept in AJ and her boyfriend's guest room. When she and her boyfriend needed me to leave, I was invited into the Landis home. I was so nurtured and loved by my best friend, Hannah, and her husband, Drew. I would sit at their dining room table writing for hours, angrily pounding out words to get the pain out. Sometimes, I felt so overwhelmed by the joy of being finally free of him, and of being finally back in my own country—back in my own land—that I would stand at her window, looking out at the snow, weeping for joy.

For another few weeks, I was passed around by friends all over the country. I slept on couches, on makeshift palettes on the floor, and in guest rooms. I spent New Year's, 2016, in St. Louis visiting my old roommate from Lincoln. I crashed on the couches of near-perfect strangers, and friends-of-friends.

Finally, I ended up in Tennessee. A friend and fellow convert—whose husband had also tricked her into marrying him when he was still married, and who was also abusive in his own ways—invited me to stay with her, assuring me he worked third shift, so I needn't worry about him being around.

All the while, I worried about my children. I knew they were safe and loved and being coddled by their father and the community at large, but it didn't stop me from worrying about them—especially that they were emotionally suffering without me. But what choice did I have? I was *literally homeless,* and our experience in Texas taught me how damaging that sort of situation was for them.

Eventually, with the help of some of my aforementioned good friends—and the man my friends in Tennessee would later introduce me to, and who would become my current husband—I was able to make it through and even to establish a somewhat stable life.

Less than a year after I left them with their father on that snowy morning in Ontario, I brought my children home to live with me in Tennessee. A year later, we moved home to Illinois.

23

The Reconstruction

Central Illinois

January 3rd, 2019

Snow is falling. I'm sitting at my desk in my office, in my warm home, in my hometown. My husband and children are sleeping while I write at night—the best time to write. The house is quiet and my heart is contented.

In the three years since I left Egypt, I've written, edited, and published two books, finally completed my Bachelor's degree, and been accepted into a graduate program at Johns Hopkins University—my first and only choice.

My children are well-adjusted and resilient. They're kind, compassionate, loving human beings who treat one another and others with respect and dignity. Like me, their default setting is love. They're extremely intelligent, always scoring in the highest percentage of their respective grade levels. My kids surprise me continually with how brave they are, and with how relatively unfazed they seem by everything they have experienced in their young lives.

Our family—me, my four children, and my husband, the same man my convert friend introduced me to in Tennessee—is together, we're safe, and we're so loved by our friends and family members. We're happier and healthier than we've ever been.

* * *

That's what you, the reader, want to hear, right?

Though all of it's true, it's only half of the story.

I wish I could provide you with that pretty, wrapped-up-with-a-bow ending that so many books like this offer. But in the years since my divorce from "Ameer," we have been anything but okay.

I've experienced deep waves of heartache and grief that seem to strike from nowhere, gripping me with a force that nearly knocks me off my feet. Both Dayo and I struggle with anxiety. I have developed a full-blown panic disorder, and I've been unable to sleep more than four hours a night for months at a time. My children and I have had medical issue after medical issue, and there seems to be no end in sight. My new marriage is plagued by the ghosts and wounds of my past trauma, as well as the fact that Ameer only provides a few hundred dollars per month to support our children, and we have no legal recourse because he is safely outside of the United States, and is not an American citizen. We struggle to make things work, financially and otherwise, day-by-day.

I am traumatized, I am scared, I am anxious, and I struggle to maintain my faith in God. In short: my situation is definitely not situated.

* * *

"Trauma and its concurrent shame, doubt, or guilt," wrote psychologist Ronnie Janoff-Bulman, "destroy important beliefs, especially belief in one's own safety or competence to act or live in the world and one's view of oneself as decent, strong, and autonomous."[2]

Like so many trauma victims, I struggle to make my own autonomous decisions; I constantly feel the need to have my choices validated by those I believe are smarter, older, and more experienced.

I also struggle to reject the common accusation that I was somehow responsible for my abuse. I find it extremely difficult to discern how much of what happened to me was my fault for having been so trusting and ignorant. Sometimes, I feel guilty for staying so long, and other times I feel guilty for being too weak to stay longer.

I am ashamed that I am not as courageous or as strong as I want to be. I'm embarrassed that I wasn't able to meet the standards of my own internal feminism: I wasn't able to stand on my own two feet, without a man's help, to reclaim my autonomy and be the proud, independent woman AJ told me I could be.

Way back in the summer of 2007, when I was living in Kolkata, India, I was only twenty-one years old, and I had just married

---

[2] Vickroy, L. (2015). Introduction: Ways of Reading Trauma in Literary Narratives. In *Reading Trauma Narratives: The Contemporary Novel and the Psychology of Oppression,* pp. 6. Retrieved from http://www.jstor.org. ezproxy.snhu.edu/stable/j.ctt1729vnp.4

Dayo's father. I was idealistic and flying high on the coaster of love. My friend, Jane, sat me down on a bench in an alleyway as the two of us enjoyed some chicken hakka from a street vendor. Having known me for a mere few weeks, she was still the closest person to me during one of the most formative, happy experiences of my life, and she possessed a wisdom far beyond her years.

"It seems to me, honey, that your life has consistently been characterized by your making horribly unwise, hasty decisions in a moment of truly sincere desperation, and then being goaded for years afterward by the consequences, and so running into another horrible relationship or circumstance you later need someone to save you from, continuing the cycle," she said, gently touching my arm and trying to be as kind as possible.

Dear Lord was she right.

I see very clearly how much I have made myself and my children suffer by rushing into marriage, again and again, hoping that somehow, this time, my True Love would save me from the horrible consequences of my last desperate choice.

The truth hurts like a bitch, but at least she's reliable.

I am not comfortable with providing you, the reader, with a happily-ever-after ending, because though I have now married a very good—albeit very flawed—man, and though my children and I are loved and cared for by him and our family in ways I could never have dreamed we would be, that's not the end of the story.

If there's anything I've learned from my young life, it's that nothing is permanent, change is the inevitable, and death is a certainty. Trauma taught me to never relax too comfortably into happiness. Just as ease follows hardship, I've learned that hardship inevitably follows ease.

* * *

The past year has been the year of re-hauling, of re-examining, and of tearing down in order to rebuild. This is not a story of mending. Our lives, our hearts, our souls could not be mended; they were damaged beyond repair. No, this is a story of *reconstruction*. I found myself questioning everything I thought I knew about myself and God. Nothing seemed sure anymore as I tenaciously tore down, brick-by-brick, the shoddy foundation of faith the sheikh built for me. It took me twenty-two years to build a strong relationship with God, and the sheikh only two years to destroy it. The rebuilding of my faith is a work in progress.

I wondered often in the past year who God even is. How could I discern the authentic picture of God presented in the Qur'an from the Alpha Male God that Ameer taught me to fear rather than to love? This confusion made it hard, and sometimes impossible, to pray.

Then, after being harassed and jeered and threatened nearly every day for two years, I finally removed hijab in early 2018. In a town full of mostly white, mostly Republican, mostly Trump-supporting bigots, I became too afraid to even leave the house, and that level of fear only strengthened my new stalwart companions—anxiety and panic.

Shockingly, I lost more friends when I stopped covering my hair than when I openly admitted to them that I hadn't prayed in months. The obsession some Muslims have with policing one another, and with outer displays and façades of faith—rather than deeper, lasting, truer proof, evidenced in one's character—is truly startling and disconcerting.

I was plagued by doubts. *Does God love me? Does He want me even when my husband is disappointed in me? Does He find me valuable, and does He care at all for what has happened to me? Am I meant for this path at all until and unless I assimilate to Arab/Desi culture, as so many Muslims have told me for the past ten years?*

These questions, and more, haunted me until I came across, quite by accident, a book called *Speaking in God's Name*, written by Dr. Khaled Abou El Fadl—the distinguished professor of Islamic Law at the University of California in Los Angeles, and one of the world's leading authorities on Islamic Law, as well as a prominent, award-winning scholar in the field of human rights. I'd been recommended another of his books, but when I read the description for *Speaking in God's Name*, I knew it was the book I needed to read. I say I found the book 'by accident,' but it was no accident—God was calling to me again, gently caressing my heart to bring it back to life.

To sum it up, this landmark book serves as a much-needed review of the "ethics at the heart of the Islamic legal system," and it suggests that "these laws have been misinterpreted by certain sources in an attempt to control women."

It was in this book that I read, for the first time in my life as a Muslim, that, *of course*, a woman's salvation doesn't depend on pleasing her husband; *of course*, we shouldn't blindly accept those teachings which make our guts turn and force us to pause; *of course*, we should use the good common sense and intuition God gave us to investigate those teachings which rub us the wrong way.

From that book and from conversations I had with the author and his wife (who is also a convert), I learned about how traditions from some Arab and Desi cultures—as well as some traditions from Judeo-Christian European cultures—have come in and poisoned the pure, beautiful waters of Islam, even worming their way into what we have come to believe are authentic, reliable, pure Muslim sources.

I came to learn across the past year that it was a false, bastardized, misogynistic version of Islam that justified what "Ameer" did to me, but it was the one myself and 90% of the other converts I'd met had been indoctrinated with when we entered the fold.

Only the real thing—the beautiful, merciful, life-giving message of Islam—could save me.

I found hope, renewal, and joy in God, through Islam, thanks to the work of this dauntless scholar—a man feared, loathed, and targeted by hypocrites and corrupt "Muslim" governments and religious leaders around the world—all because he is willing to speak truth to power.

The more I learned about the rich depth and breadth of Islamic wisdom that has been collected over the centuries, the more sickened I felt by the narrow, extremist, twisted version of Islam that "Ameer," and the Salafi community at large, had brainwashed me into accepting as "the only way."

I felt an energy growing in me to get the word out that *there is another way.* I told anyone and everyone who would listen how sorry I was for propagating that version of Islam for so long. I distanced myself from all but the most understanding, compassionate, emotionally intelligent Muslims—several of whom are part of the Salafi sect, actually, as well as other fundamentalist groups—and I've never looked back.

I began to pray again, in earnest—both *du'a* and the ritual *Salah.* I began to turn toward God again in my pain, rather than turning away from Him. I began seeing Him again as my loving, merciful Creator—so very different than the angry, beard-stroking sheikh behind His desk I thought He was during my marriage to "Ameer."

Slowly but surely, through prayer, patience, and self-compassion, I have found God again through finding myself again, just like the Prophet said: "One who knows himself, knows his Lord."

Epilogue

Narrated Anas ibn Malik:

"Prophet Muhammad had a camel driver called Anjasha, and he had a nice voice (he used to goad the camels to go faster by singing songs to them). The Prophet said to him, 'Slowly, O Anjasha! Do not break the glass vessels!' And Qatada said, '(By "vessels") he meant the weak women.'"
—*Sahih Bukhari, Book 73, Hadith 230*

This *hadith* is the basis for many Islamic lectures and books, extolling men on the virtues of being kind to their wives. There's another well-known *hadith* wherein Prophet Muhammad was reported to have advised men not to try too hard to change their wives because women are "made from the rib of Adam, and if you bend them too far, they'll break."

"She's delicate," these teachings seem to say, "so you have to treat her with care so she doesn't shatter."

Somehow, *shockingly*, misogynistic Muslim scholars have been able to take these beautiful admonitions and twist them. Rather than seeing the clear meaning—i.e. don't abuse your wife or treat her like shit or try to make her your little doll, cuz things won't go well—they choose to focus on the bit about women being "weak" and "breakable," deciding this makes women inferior to men.

If you believe women are naturally fragile, delicate creatures who must be coddled and protected by the men around them, it's not hard to make the next logical step: a woman needs to make herself nice, submissive, courteous, blindly obedient, and grateful for the protection afforded her.

For six years, my ex-husband, the sheikh, crushed me—like I was a "glass vessel" or a "bent rib"—and he did so systematically and purposefully. But it's not because I was a woman, and it's not because I wasn't being protected—as you'll recall, several men *did* try to protect me, but I would have none of it. It's not just because I was a new convert either. Even women with a strong support system aren't safe from these sort of men. There's an epidemic of sheikhs marrying multiple women at once in secret, and it's spreading across North America, affecting thousands of women, both convert and heritage Muslims.[3]

Like so many Muslim women, I was brainwashed into giving up my right and responsibility to protect myself. I willingly laid down my arms and threw myself headlong at the danger coming my way because I believed—like sailors at sea tempted by Siren songs into their own deaths—that "Sheikh Ameer" was sent my way by God, and that by breaking me to his will, he was just doing what God wanted him to do.

* * *

I first sat down to write this book in November of 2017, during

---

[3] https://www.cbc.ca/news/canada/polygamy-canadian-muslim-community-1.4971971

National Novel Writing Month.[4] I woke every morning before my kids and aimed to write just 2,000 words a day. The words came slowly at first, but by the time the month ended, I had far exceeded the 50,000-word expectation.

After that month, I cut my writing time to just Thursday mornings because I couldn't handle the emotional exhaustion of reliving my trauma every day. I'd write all morning at my favorite local coffee shop, and then go home and lock myself in my room, leaving my husband to manage the kids and the house while I tried to process all I'd re-lived that morning.

My best friend, Hannah, is a birth doula, and she always gives me the same advice she gives her laboring clients: *just trust the process.* More than a few times this year, I felt sure my heart and my faith were all but dead. I am so glad I trusted her and the process, and that I pushed through the terror that overwhelmed me often while writing and editing this book.

It is not an exaggeration to say that writing this book almost killed me. It's no coincidence that my year of breaking down and rebuilding, my year of anxiety and panic, and the year in which I wrote this book happened at the same time. But I had to push through because I know that the best way for me to heal is through story-telling, and I am not alone in this sentiment. Trauma survivors, on the whole, *need* to tell our stories, as often as we can, until we are finally able to "remember simultaneously the affect and cognition associated with the trauma through access to language."[5]

I needed to write this book, first and foremost, to heal, but also

---

[4] Check out https://www.nanowrimo.org/

[5] van der Kolk, B. A. and Ducey, C. P. (1989), The psychological processing of traumatic experience: Rorschach patterns in PTSD. *The Journal of Traumatic Stress*, 2: pp. 271. Retrieved from https://doi.org/10.1002/jts.2490020303

because I refuse to be defined by this part of my story anymore. I don't want to spend the rest of my life being introduced to people as "the American Muslim convert who survived a horribly abusive marriage in rural Egypt." I am so much more than what happened to me there, and I want to move forward. From here on out, I don't have to tell this story ever again, directing curious people to this book, instead.

Aside from telling my perspective of the most formative, traumatic experience of my life thus far—wherein I came to the end of myself and somehow survived, albeit incredibly and in some ways irreparably broken—I needed to write this story so that I could forgive "Shahida" and "Mama Bushra," two very real women who did very real things to hurt me during our time together.

"Shahida" truly was the first person to witness the sheikh's evil—thus why I gave her the pseudonym "Shahida," meaning "the woman who witnesses." "Mama Bushra" was a victim of her upbringing and circumstances, and of the unnatural limits imposed on her by the patriarchal society wherein she was born.

I need the reader to know (and feel) that these women were normal women in extraordinary circumstances. All the horrid things they did to me had been done out of desperation and hopelessness. They both, in their own ways, exercised what little power they had in the only way they could (and indeed the only way most people who are oppressed can): they oppressed me— someone even more powerless than they were.

I forgive them, and I truly wish them all the best.

Even "Ameer" was a victim of his circumstances, and I understand, the more time passes, the complex dynamics that worked together to twist and maim his heart to the point that he *truly believed* the garbage he taught me about God and women.

But it is not my responsibility to inculcate compassion for "Sheikh Ameer"—my abuser. "Shahida" and I (and our children) are the true victims in this story. In fact, in many ways, Shahida is suffering much more than I have. After all, I am *free,* whereas she will never be free of Ameer until one of them dies, and there is no hope she could find another husband, somehow, if he did die before her.

At the time of this writing, "Sheikh Ameer" is a political refugee in Canada, thanks to his extensive involvement in the Muslim Brotherhood. Upon leaving Egypt in 2015 just after our divorce, he was told that if he ever came back, he'd be *disappeared*—a veritable death sentence. "Shahida" and her children will never see him again until and unless they pick up their lives and move to southern Ontario—and are then confronted with the truth that he has been secretly married to yet another naïve convert this entire time.

I pray that "Shahida" and her children find healing somehow.

* * *

The sheikh's favorite accusation to throw at me has always been that by telling my story, I am ruining his name, destroying his image, and wrecking his reputation, as well as casting suspicion on Muslim leaders everywhere. He is incensed that I don't just disappear into oblivion and let him get on with his pattern. He has tried time and time again to silence me, even once calling my husband and asking him to control his wife. We are not intimidated.

What the sheikh fails to understand is that maintaining a lasting, beautiful reputation requires that one do the hard work of maintaining a beautiful character, and that's something no one can destroy by telling the story of how you treated them. The truth always, *always* wins in the end.

While I used intentionally vague locations and gave almost everyone false names and *kunyas* in order to protect them, my choice to use a made-up name and *kunya* for the sheikh had nothing to do with protecting him; I have no interest in protecting him. This was a choice I struggled with, feeling deeply compelled to come out publicly with the horrid things he did to us, in hopes he'd lose his position of power and respect in the community and be less able to attract new victims—as he assures me, even to this day, that he has no plan to change his ways.

Calling the sheikh out by name would only send him into hiding, though, or else it would create an opportunity for him to claim victimhood, thereby increasing the chances that some sweet girl would feel sorry for him and give him a chance.

I have also chosen to hide the sheikh's true identity because I have seen what happens when honest, broken women get the courage to speak their truth.

In 2018, women around the world stood up and refused to have their voices silenced any longer. It was the year of #MeToo and #TimesUp and that environment urged me to finally begin using my own voice to tell my story. The Muslim community wasn't spared, and several well-loved sheikhs and teachers—many of the men who formed the backbone of my initial faith foundation—were publicly called out for their sexual and spiritual abuse.

Not everyone was happy to see the mighty fall. In fact, I had to part ways with several dear friends over this fall-out, including my old, dear friend, "Sofia," who saved me in Cairo. Though she and her husband witnessed the most atrocious things "Ameer" did to me, people like "Sofia" couldn't imagine that he was one of the thousands of other men like him, rather than an unfortunate but rare bad egg. She joined the masses in rallying by the side of her fallen leaders, refusing to believe the women who accused them, regardless of how much evidence was brought forth in many cases.

It wasn't just "Ameer" who tried to silence me; more than once in the past few years, I've had Muslims try to advise me, warn me, and sometimes downright threaten me about what would happen if I published this book. And it's no surprise. Perhaps more than any other genre of literature, trauma narratives serve to "pinpoint the misuses of power that create the trauma-based ... mentalities of survivors... [and]... bring to the surface social evasions of the psychological consequences of objectifying individuals."[6]

The reality is that there are many in the larger Muslim community—and in many faith communities—who simply don't want abuse victims to come forward because our honesty makes them feel vulnerable. After all, if it happened to us, what would stop it from happening to their daughters, sisters, and nieces? And how much of it did they see, enable, and even encourage?

By pressuring abuse victims to be quiet about our abuse—and by doing so using faulty, crooked interpretations of our religious texts—not only are Muslims ignoring the very real, very tangible consequences abuse victims have to cope with for years afterward, but they are inadvertently making matters worse for the thousands of new converts—most of whom are female—who join the Muslim community every day.

---

[6] Vickroy, pp. 179-180.

The more we work to sugar-coat life in the Muslim community—which is to say the human community—the more we keep potential converts in the dark about what they could face if they're not careful, and the more we create opportunities for people like Sheikh "Ameer" to take advantage of their lack of knowledge.

I have always believed it was my responsibility to serve the Truth, whether it feels good or not; in this book, for example, I have expressed many not-so-flattering truths about myself. In the end, I believe God expects me to do my damndest to enlighten the next naïve convert to the red flags that most assuredly will be waving at her if she meets the sheikh—or, more crucially, one of the thousands of wolves like him, roaming the earth, disguised in sheikh's clothing.

The truth is that my story is mild, and it's not uncommon.[7] As one reviewer and fellow convert said:

> *"I expected to be shocked. As I devoured Kaighla's memoir page by page, I kept waiting for the moment where I would gasp and clutch my chest in surprise at the Sheikh's actions. That moment never came. Why? Because I've heard it all before. We all have."*[8]

Women like "Sara," and so many others, have suffered even more traumatizing abuse than I have, and many of them have ended up either completely insane and in need of permanent psychiatric care, or else have left Islam completely and have

---

[7] For more information on how widespread this sort of abuse is, check out In Shaykh's Clothing—Overcoming Spiritual Abuse

[8] Review of *Things That Shatter*, by K.T. Lynn. http://ktlynn.com/2019/04/02/review-things-that-shatter/

turned into the sort of bitter ex-Muslims who write the sort of books I referred to in the preface.

My primary responsibility is to tell my truth and to do so ethically, and that's what I have attempted to do here. I hope that by showing my pain in an authentic way, it will encourage others to feel more comfortable telling their stories, even if they only tell their closest friends and confidants. I believe that healing only happens when we—both individually and collectively—face ourselves, shattered as we are, and begin to fill in the cracks with the abundant, liquid gold of compassion, humility, empathy, and dignity that God has given us.

Acknowledgements

Before this book was even remotely ready for your eyes, it passed through the hands and hearts of several people.

First and foremost, I have to thank my editor, Rebecca Garner. In her, I was so blessed to have found both an incredibly talented editor and a true sister on the spiritual journey. I cannot imagine this work having been what it is today without her exquisite, attentive work that refined and polished my humble story. As a fellow western convert, Rebecca was able to appreciate both the cultural and religious aspects of this story, and I am eternally grateful for her sensitive heart and careful pen. Should you have found any errors, I assure you they are my own fault, as I changed quite a bit of the book after her final edits.

I also had an incredible team of beta readers. Several have chosen to remain anonymous, but I'd like to specifically thank Anne Myers, Dr. Ronald Sion, Christine DuPuis, Stacy Knuth, Jane Nakayama, Candace Cooper, Azraa Khan, Zainab Bint Younus, and Nicole Bashbsheh for their feedback, encouragement, constructive criticism, and sincere tears and laughter.

The Beta Reader VIP award is shared by both Leah Darland-Hanoosh and Grace Song for going above and beyond the call of duty and pushing me, ever so gently, to walk through the wall of pain and pull back the final veil that protected me from both the ultimate grief, and the ultimate authenticity this story needed. Their honest, insightful, compassionate, and sometimes-sweary comments kept me both entertained and in-tune with the story that needed to be told.

Photo credit for the author photo on the back cover goes to the enchanting and talented Bethany Burt, of BURTCo., and credit for my "About the Author" photo goes to my sister, Emily, of Henderson Photographs.

Theresa Corbin—my co-author for *The New Muslim's Field Guide*—was truly the first person alive to recognize and encourage my writing talent, and I am eternally grateful for the hard-knock wisdom she's shared with me across the five years of our friendship. She's taught me the importance of setting boundaries, and of honoring my spirit, and of telling people to fuck right off when circumstances necessitated.

I need to thank the Landises and Georges, and all the other good people at Mad Goat Coffee, in Danville, Illinois, for the service, hospitality, and support they gave me during the writing and editing of this book. I set myself up there every single Thursday for more than a year, and everyone knew I wasn't there for relaxing or taking in the sights: this was serious, focused, kid-free, book-writing-and-editing time. I'd like to specifically thank baristas Jordan and Shelbie for remembering my regular order: a London Fog in a large mug, a chocolate-chip muffin—heated up!—and always, always, *always*, a tall glass of ice-water.

Though we are no longer in contact, I have to thank "Sofia" (she knows who she is) for the love, warmth, hospitality, and energy she invested in me and my children across the four years we lived in Egypt. She was my closest friend—my only real friend—during the most pivotal years of my life, and I am eternally grateful to her and her husband. Regardless of what happened between us, I wish her, her husband, and their beautiful baby boy all the best in this life and the next, *ameen*.

My best friend, Hannah Landis, is my muse, my confidant, my challenger, my mirror, and the Blessed Bringer of the Coffee. She loved me and welcomed me into her heart and life at a time when we both were so very hungry for a kind, non-judgmental shoulder to cry on. She is, without a doubt, my soul-mate, and this work would have died long ago without her unwavering support.

My dear husband came into this marriage a sweet, naïve bird with not the slightest clue what an insane ride this would be. He has had to cope with the aftermath of all the sheikh did to me, and he has tried to teach me to love myself and him without fear and without bitterness. He knows me fully now and is, shockingly, still my biggest fan. Without his belief in my ability to make it through, and his support—including the countless hours he held me as I tried to decompress from a day of writing—I'd never have been able to finish this book. He didn't understand why it mattered so much to me, viewing my writing as a sort of super-serious hobby, but he still did the hard work of providing for us while I invested every bit of energy I could spare into crafting this work. He worked third shift, sometimes sixty hours a week, so that I could complete my Bachelor's degree while writing not one but two books, and for that, I am forever grateful.

I owe my mother and siblings a sincere apology for everything I put them through over the years, and for the absolutely unfair and unkind expectations I laid on them since the day I converted to Islam. They still loved me through it all, and they waited for me to come around. We may be dysfunctional, but I'll be damned if we're not the most fiercely protective set of people you've ever met. No matter how confused and uncomfortable they've been as I evolved over the years, they've stood up for us—and all Muslims—in a society and time wherein to be an ally to the downtrodden is a very dangerous thing to do.

If there was ever a hero in my life, it's not a man, but my sister, Ariel (AJ). She saved my life on more than one occasion, and without her firm but loving assurance that I had lost my mind and heart, and just needed to lean into her and my other family members and friends to find myself again, I'd probably still be married to the sheikh, and still being broken by him—or worse. She has been my ride-or-die companion for the last twenty-seven years, and I hope she can tolerate me a bit longer.

My little sister, Emily, was just fourteen years old when I came home from Egypt, and we barely knew one another. Since then, we have become very close. She came to stay with us for the final month of my work on this book, in fact, and her presence was a welcome relief. We laughed, we watched too much Netflix, we danced like fools, and we cried together. She has been listening to my stories and commiserating since she was far too young to be dealing with such atrocities, so to her I say, "I'm sorry, and you're welcome for the wisdom. Now please: go be smarter than I was."

My mother, Kurste, chose not to abort me, against all odds, when she was pregnant at sixteen. Furthermore, she somehow managed to finish high school, work multiple jobs at once, and complete her Associate's degree—all while raising me and Ariel alone without any help from our fathers. She didn't have a mother herself, so she had no idea what she was doing in raising me—her "experiment kid," she likes to say. She tried her best to raise me as a confident, whole, self-sustaining adult, and it's not her fault I have failed in that endeavor on so many fronts throughout the years. She helped form in me a dedication to justice and to truthfulness, and she taught me to behave in an ethical fashion in all things, at all times, come what may. I'm so grateful we agreed to bury the hatchet last year and re-establish a relationship. I am who I am today because she loves me.

I'd be remiss if I didn't also thank my father, Doug, for abandoning and rejecting me over and over throughout my childhood and adult life, and my step-father, Jim, for molesting me and then abandoning us all, thereby creating the massive, burning hole in my psyche that drove me to seek acceptance and love in the worst of places, no matter what it cost me. I didn't find what I was looking for—sadly, nothing can replace a father's love—but I did find my true worth, something no man can give me.

Finally, I'd like to thank "Ameer" for the love we shared. Being in an abusive marriage is tricky because it is never all bad; if it were, we'd get out much sooner. I haven't forgotten the beautiful moments. I'd also like to thank him for the three beautiful children he assisted me in creating and raising for a few years.

I am so grateful to "Ameer" for the horrific suffering he made me endure in Egypt. That hell refined me. It purified me. It burned away the chaff. It eliminated the dross. I am who I am today because of Egypt, and I wouldn't trade the wisdom I gained there for anything at all. Egypt became my rock-bottom experience, so that—forever after—when I am facing some obstacle or hardship, I have a gauge: is it as bad as Egypt was? No? Then it's gonna be ok. We survived Egypt, so we can survive anything.

So long as there is a breath in my body, I will never stop trying to live my fullest, Kaighla-est, Muslim-est life, and I will never be silent. I will invest my pain and rage into raising our children to be as inquisitive and rebellious in the face of oppression as I was. I am inculcating in them all the qualities he tried to kill in me. If I have anything to do with it, my daughters will be brave, and wise, and compassionate women who know their worth and who won't put up with the things I did. My sons will be kind, and honest, and reliable men who honor their wives and who fear God above all else.

May God give the sheikh what he deserves.

About the Author

Kaighla White writes under her *kunya*, Kaighla Um Dayo—the mother of Dayo. She is a two-time Daybreak Press Book Award-winning writer, editor, and writing consultant. She lives in central Illinois with her husband and children, where she is completing her Master of Liberal Arts degree remotely at Johns Hopkins University.

You can connect with me on:
- https://www.thingsthatshatter.com
- https://www.facebook.com/kaighlaumdayo
- https://www.instagram.com/kaighlaumdayo

Also by Kaighla Um Dayo

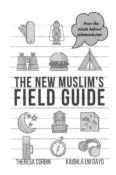

The New Muslim's Field Guide
Not another "Welcome to Islam!" book, this winner of the 2019 Daybreak Press Book Award for best Islamic non-fiction, *The New Muslim's Field Guide* is a practical, often humorous, honest guide to living life as a Muslim, written in conversational English by two American female converts—Kaighla Um Dayo and Theresa Corbin, of islamwich.com.